MODERN CONFLICTS AND CHANGING CHARACTER OF WARFARE

Implications for India

MODERN CONFLICTS AND CHANGING CHARACTER OF WARFARE

Implications for India

Editors

Major General Sanjeev Chowdhry (Retd)

Colonel Deepak Kumar

Ms Komal Chaudhary

Mr Vinayak Sharma

Ms Richa Sharma

(Estd. 1870)

United Service Institution of India

Army War College

PENTAGON PRESS LLP

First published in 2025 by

PENTAGON PRESS LLP
206, Peacock Lane, Shahpur Jat
New Delhi-110049, India
Contact: 011-26490600

Printed at Aegean Offset Printers, Noida

ISBN 978-81-993527-8-0

Disclaimer: The views expressed in this book are those of the authors and do not necessarily reflect those of the United Service Institute of India, New Delhi and Army War College, Mhow.

www.pentagonpress.in

Contents

Foreword

In the 21st Century, the nature of warfare has undergone a profound transformation. Multi-domain warfare and grey-zone conflicts are the new normal catalysed by niche and disruptive technologies. The lines between war and peace, state and non-state actors, and military and civilian targets have blurred, posing complex challenges for national security.

Recent global and regional conflicts have reinforced these shifts. The protracted Russia-Ukraine War has demonstrated the brutal persistence of conventional warfare, yet deeply infused with drones, information operations, and international economic sanctions. The devastating Gaza conflict has highlighted the catastrophic consequences of urban warfare, civilian targeting, and asymmetric strategies that weaponise both narratives and humanitarian crises. Closer home, Operation Sindoor reaffirmed for India the necessity of strategic clarity, operational synergy, and preparedness across multi-domain battlefields. Each of these episodes illustrates that modern conflict is no longer confined to borders or battlefronts—it is a contest across the physical, informational, and cognitive domains. In fact, long-range vectors have rendered security in strategic depth null and void.

This volume, **Modern Conflicts and the Changing Character of Warfare: Implications for India**, offers a timely and critical exploration of how evolving conflict paradigms are reshaping strategic thought and operational preparedness. From grey-zone confrontations and proxy wars to the increasing role of private military contractors and artificial intelligence-enabled weapons, this compilation captures the complexity of modern warfare and its relevance to India's security environment.

As India navigates a volatile strategic neighbourhood and rising global ambitions, it must rethink its doctrines, restructure its forces, and reinforce civil-military synergies. This book is not just a scholarly contribution—it is a strategic call to policymakers, military leaders, and analysts to prepare for the wars of tomorrow, today.

This publication represents the second edition of an annual collaborative endeavour between the United Service Institution of India (USI) and Army War College (AWC), an initiative that has already begun to establish itself as a cornerstone of India's evolving strategic thought. By bringing together USI's tradition of intellectual rigour with AWC's operational depth and training excellence, this collaboration offers both scholarly reflection and practical relevance. Its benefits extend beyond the professional military education ecosystem—strengthening policy discourse, enhancing jointness across services, and contributing to India's long-term defence preparedness. In a world increasingly defined by uncertainty and contestation, this sustained partnership between two premier institutions enriches strategic scholarship, sharpens operational foresight, and reinforces India's ability to anticipate and respond to future challenges with clarity and confidence.

I commend the authors for their in-depth analysis and the editorial teams of the USI and AWC for their meticulous effort and strategic foresight.

Major General BK Sharma, AVSM, SM (Retd)**
Director General, United Service Institution of India

Message

The contemporary world is undergoing a profound and unprecedented churn in geopolitical dynamics. Traditional power structures are shifting and the normative frameworks that have long governed international conduct are under visible strain. The protracted Russia-Ukraine conflict, devastating eruption of the Israel-Hamas War in Gaza, the recent escalation between Israel and Iran, and the assertive yet cautious posture of the United States in West Asia have all challenged long-held assumptions about deterrence, intelligence superiority, and the nature of state responses. These events illustrate how both state and non-state actors are reshaping the character of warfare across physical, informational, and cognitive domains. The seas, airspace, cyberspace, and human perception itself have emerged as contested battlegrounds. These developments carry profound strategic implications for India, necessitating agile responses and anticipatory thinking.

For India, these developments are not distant disturbances; they have direct and profound implications for national security. The execution of Operation Sindoor in the Indo-Pak context reinforces the criticality of strategic clarity, operational synergy, and multi-domain preparedness. It is a timely reminder that readiness in today's battlespace extends beyond traditional kinetic capabilities—it must be anchored in adaptability, innovation and foresight.

It is in this backdrop that the second edition of the United Service Institution of India (USI)–Army War College (AWC) publication becomes particularly significant. Its twin sub-themes—'***Contested World Order and its Strategic Security Implications***' and '***Lessons from the***

Ukraine and Gaza Conflicts: Implications for India'—are timely and deeply relevant. They provide a structured lens through which to examine the fault lines of the emerging security architecture and to assess the strategic recalibrations necessary for India.

This edition is not merely an academic discourse; it is a strategic tool. It encourages military thinkers, policymakers, and scholar-warriors to look beyond the immediate and engage with the deeper currents shaping the global order. From grey-zone warfare and civil-military fusion to technological asymmetries and information dominance, the nature of conflict is evolving rapidly, and India must be prepared not just to respond, but to lead with clarity and confidence.

The lessons emerging from current global flashpoints compel us to move from reactive thinking to anticipatory strategy. India's doctrines, capabilities, and institutions must reflect a comprehensive understanding of both conventional and hybrid threats. Resilience, strategic autonomy, and cognitive superiority will define India's edge in the years to come.

I commend the authors and the editorial teams of the AWC and USI for their continued commitment to intellectual excellence and strategic foresight. This collaborative publication, now in its second edition, symbolises the growing synergy between two premier institutions dedicated to advancing India's military professionalism and strategic scholarship.

May this edition serve as a catalyst for rigorous debate, informed policy formulation, and future-ready thinking. In a world increasingly defined by uncertainty and contestation, such endeavours play a vital role in shaping India's national security discourse.

Happy Reading!

Lieutenant General Harjeet Singh Sahi,
UYSM, AVSM, YSM, SM
Commandant Army War College

The Publication at a Glance

We are proud to present this second edition of the collaborative effort between the United Service Institution of India (USI) and Army War College (AWC). This edition brings together incisive analyses and thought-provoking articles on '***Modern Conflicts and Changing Character of Warfare: Implications for India***'. Modern conflicts have expanded beyond traditional battlefields into cyber, space, and cognitive domains, as seen in Operation Sindoor, Ukraine, West Asia, and Israel. Drones, cyber operations, logistics, and information warfare now shape outcomes, while Artificial Intelligence (AI) emerges as both a force multiplier and a source of ethical risk. For India, preparing for the future requires theatreisation, integration of AI and cyber capabilities, resilient logistics, adaptive leadership, and a whole-of-nation approach that balances technological innovation with human judgment.

The lead article, *Multi-Domain Warfare: Lessons from Operation Sindoor, Ukraine, and West Asia*, explores how modern conflicts integrate land, air, sea, cyber, space, and cognitive domains. The author calls for Indian Armed Forces to recalibrate their doctrines, accelerate theatreisation, and prepare for collusive and grey-zone threats. In the next article, *Multi-Domain Operations: Enhancing Cyber Operations Capability within the Armed Forces*, the author argues for upgrading the Defence Cyber Agency into a full-fledged Cyber Command, stressing offensive capability and legal clarity.

The third article, *Cognitive Domain Warfare: Lessons for India*, explains how adversaries manipulate narratives to weaken morale before conflict. It calls for a national strategy to counter hostile influence operations. The following article *Evolution of Operational Art and Strategy: Application in Modern Conflict*, outlines the evolution of operational art from classical foundations to modern warfare, shaped by industrialisation, global conflicts, and Cold War doctrines. It explores hybrid, multi-domain, cyber, space, and AI-driven operations, illustrated through recent case studies.

The fifth article, *Warfare Reimagined: Integrating Artificial Intelligence into Indian Armed Forces and Defence Industry*, underscores the dual imperatives of educating military leadership in AI and reforming the defence innovation ecosystem. The next contribution, *An Analysis of the Russia-Ukraine War and Lessons for India*, synthesises geo-strategic, economic, and military aspects, drawing lessons for Indian resilience and preparedness.

The article, The Changing Character of Warfare and its Implications for India, traces the transition from traditional battle formations to AI-enabled and cyber-powered conflicts. It argues that India must bridge technological gaps, strengthen indigenous defence production, and embrace a multi-domain operational approach. In the eighth article *Future Warfare: Will Technology Ultimately Replace the Soldier?*, the author analyses advances in robotics, drones, and autonomous systems. The article cautions that machines can never replace the ethical judgment and adaptability of human soldiers, making balanced man-machine integration essential.

In the next article, *Artificial Intelligence: Disrupting the Character of Warfare*, the author assesses the unchecked growth of AI and its unpredictable consequences. The analysis highlights the urgent need for ethical safeguards and deeper research to counter risks of instability. In the article that follows, *Leveraging Artificial Intelligence for Securing Cyberspace*, it examines how AI can bolster cyber defences against sophisticated threats in an era of digital and military networks. It calls for AI-enabled solutions to detect, deter, and neutralise cyberattacks. In the eleventh article, *Drone Warfare: Tactical Shift in Land Warfare*, the author explains how drones—ranging from commercial adaptations to AI-enabled swarms—are transforming battlefield intelligence and lethality. The author also stresses the need for robust countermeasures like electronic warfare and directed energy weapons.

Two articles on logistics follow: *Logistics Lessons from the Ukraine Conflict and its Impact on Indian Military Logistics,* and *Israel-Hamas War: Military Logistics Lessons for India*. Both demonstrate that logistics is not merely a support function but the very heart of strategy, emphasising resilience, decentralisation, and technology-driven supply systems. In the next article, *Joint Operations and Interoperability: Insights from Ukraine*, the author shows how Ukraine achieved synergy by combining legacy platforms with modern technology, offering lessons for India's theaterisation.

The concluding article, *A Nuanced Look at Indian Strategic Leadership*, re-examines decision-making in crises such as Kargil, Galwan, and Operation Sindoor and highlights India's adaptive leadership and evolving strategic culture.

Together, the articles in this joint publication illuminate the contours of modern conflict and India's choices ahead. They reaffirm a central insight: success in future wars will not be determined by conventional superiority alone, but by the ability to act with speed, clarity, and coherence across all domains of war and peace.

List of Contributors

Major General BK Sharma, AVSM, SM** (Retd), an Infantry veteran and the Director General of the United Service Institution of India, possesses extensive operational expertise in strategic affairs and multi-domain warfare. Decorated with three military awards by the President of India and a national award for nation-building, he is an alumnus of the Defence Services Staff College, Higher Command, and the National Defence College. He has represented India as a United Nations Military Observer in Central America and served as the country's Defence Attaché in Central Asia. His areas of specialisation include strategic net assessment, scenario building, strategic gaming, and red teaming. He is a prolific writer on geopoitics and a regular participant in global conferences and high-level Track 1.5 dialogues.

Lieutenant General (Dr) RS Panwar, AVSM, SM, VSM (Retd) holds a doctorate in Computer Science from Indian Institute of Technology, Bombay. A graduate of the National Defence College, he has tenanted important assignments including General Commanding Officer 101 Area, Commandant Military College of Telecommunication Engineering, Commander 81 Sub Area, and Commander Electronic Warfare Brigade. His current work focuses on technology-driven future warfare as relevant to the Indian Armed Forces. He is also an active participant in Track II diplomacy initiatives at the international level in responsible use of military artificial intelligence.

Major General AK Chaturvedi, AVSM, VSM (Retd) had a distinguished 38-year career in the Corps of Engineers before retiring in 2001. Popularly referred to as an intellectual soldier, he is an alumnus of College of Military Engineering, Pune; College of Defence Management, Secunderabad; and National Defence College, New Delhi. Post-retirement, he is pursuing a PhD on India's Energy Security and is actively involved in writing and lecturing on national security issues.

Major General (Dr) SB Asthana SM, VSM (Retd) is a globally acknowledged strategic and security analyst, PhD from Jawaharlal Nehru University, who has authored over 450 publications. A veteran General, former Director General Infantry of the Indian Army, who held key appointments in the army, United Nations (UN) and the United Service Institution of India. A seasoned television commentator with over 4500 international shows, he frequently delivers talks in various Strategic, Military forums, UN organisations, think tanks and universities globally. He also holds significant appointments in various national, international, and UN organisations. Awarded twice by President of India, twice by the UN and also by former Prime Minister of Moldova for 'International Diplomacy and Conflict Resolutions'.

Major General Sanjeev Chowdhry (Retd) is a veteran with over 37 years of commissioned service in the Regiment of Artillery. A graduate of the Defence Services Staff College and College of Defence Management, the General officer has served in all types of terrain and environment while on command, staff, and instructional duties. He specialises in the subject of Net Assessment and is presently the Director, Centre for Publications at the United Service Institution of India.

Mr Vinayak Sharma currently works as a Research Assistant at the United Service Institution of India and is an alumnus of Bharatiya Vidya Bhavan and Hansraj College. He is dedicated to the realms of international relations, diplomacy, and strategic thinking. With a profound interest in global affairs, geopolitics, and culture, he has been a consistent contributor to numerous publications since 2015, notably the USI Journal. He also holds a Master's degree in Defence and Strategic Studies.

Mr Neelotpal Mishra is a Senior Research Fellow at the United Service Institution of India. He is an alumnus of the Royal Military College of Science and the University of Oxford, United Kingdom. His areas of expertise include information warfare, cyber warfare, and emerging technologies. He has a keen interest in military history and strategic affairs and has undertaken consultancy assignments for various government organisations.

Colonel Umang Kumar Mittal, an alumnus of National Defence Academy and Indian Military Academy, was commissioned into the Regiment of Artillery. A graduate of Defence Services Staff College and the Higher Air Command Course, he commanded a field regiment in East Sikkim and the Western front. His staff appointments include General Staff Officer-1 (Operations) in a Strike Corps and General Staff Officer-2 in an artillery brigade. He is a recipient of the General Officer Commanding-in-Chief and Chief of the Army Staff Commendation Cards. He has served as an instructor in Senior Command Wing and is currently posted as Colonel General Staff (Artillery) at the Faculty of Studies and Leadership, Army War College.

Colonel Mohit Kuntal, SM an alumnus of the Indian Military Academy, was commissioned into the Corps of Engineers. A graduate of the Defence Services Staff College and the Higher Command Course, he commanded an Engineer Regiment in Eastern Ladakh. His staff appointments include General Staff Officer-1 (Operations) in a Mountain Division in Sikkim and General Staff Officer-2 (Intelligence) in an Engineer Brigade on the Western Front. He is currently posted as Colonel General Staff (Engineers) at the Faculty of Studies and Leadership, Army War College.

Colonel Neeraj Mann, an alumnus of the National Defence Academy and Indian Military Academy, was commissioned into the Corps of Electronics and Mechanical Engineers (EME). He specialises in Aviation Technology and is a graduate of the Defence Services Staff Course and the Higher Command Course. He commanded an EME Battalion on the Northern Borders during Operation Snow Leopard. His staff appointments include Assistant Quartermaster General of an Infantry Division in Arunachal Pradesh and General Staff Officer-1 (Training) at the Military College of EME. He is currently posted as Colonel General Staff (EME) at the Faculty of Studies and Leadership, Army War College.

Colonel Harpreet Singh, an alumnus of the National Defence Academy and Indian Military Academy was commissioned into the Corps of Signals in Dec 2000. A graduate of the the Defence Services Staff College,and Higher Command Course, he commanded a Mountain Division Signal Regiment in Western Ladakh. His staff appointments include General Staff Officer-1 in an Infantry Brigade and Colonel Signals-1 at the Directorate General of Signals. He has also served as Company Commander and Instructor Class 'A' at the Indian Military Academy and the Military College of Telecommunication Engineering. He is currently posted as Colonel General Staff (Signals) at the Faculty of Studies and Leadership, Army War College.

Colonel Abhishek Chauhan, VSM, an alumnus of the Indian Military Academy, was commissioned into the 1st Battalion, 3rd GORKA RIFLES in Dec 2003 and later commanded the 4th Battalion in East Sikkim. A graduate of the Defence Services Staff College and the Higher Command Course, he has extensive experience in counter-insurgency operations in Assam and Jammu and Kashmir, as well as multiple high-altitude tenures, including the Siachen Glacier. His staff appointments include Instructor at the Officers Training Academy, Gaya, and Colonel General Staff (Operations) in a Mountain Strike Corps. He is currently posted as Colonel General Staff (Infantry) at the Faculty of Studies and Leadership, Army War College.

Colonel Deepak Kumar, an alumnus of the Indian Military Academy, was commissioned into the Army Ordnance Corps in Dec 2000. He holds a specialisation in Inventory and Ammunition Management and is a graduate of the Defence Services Staff College and the Higher Defence Management Course. He has commanded the Central Ordnance Depot, Mumbai, and an Infantry Divisional Ordnance Unit in high altitude along the Northern Borders during Operation SNOW LEOPARD. His staff appointments include Staff Supply Officer (Transport and Victualling) at Headquarters Andaman and Nicobar Command and G4 Logistics at Headquarters 301 Infantry Brigade. He is currently serving as Colonel General Staff (Ordnance) at the Faculty of Studies and Leadership, Army War College.

Colonel Rajesh Kumar Ranjan, an alumnus of the National Defence Academy and the Indian Military Academy, was commissioned into 514 Air Defence Regiment (Self Propelled) in 2002 and later commanded the same as part of an Armoured Division on the Western Front. He is a graduate of the Defence Services Staff College and the College of Air Warfare and has served as Instructor Class 'B' at the Army Air Defence College, Gopalpur-on-Sea, and as General Staff Officer-1 (Operations) during counter-insurgency operations in Manipur. His other staff appointments include Colonel General Staff (Equipment Management) in the Eastern Theatre and Colonel (Organisation) at Headquarters Integrated Defence Staff. He is presently serving as Colonel General Staff (Army Air Defence) at the Faculty of Studies and Leadership, Army War College.

Colonel Neeraj Kotwal, SM, an alumnus of the National Defence Academy and the Indian Military Academy, and is a graduate of the Defence Services Staff College and the Higher Command Course. He has commanded a second-line Army Service Corps Battalion in a Strike Corps along the Western Front and a Forward Logistics Depot on the Northern Borders. His key staff appointments include Assistant Quarter Master General of an Infantry Division, and he has also served with the Border Roads Organisation in Bhutan. He is presently serving as Colonel General Staff (Army Service Corps) at the Faculty of Studies and Leadership, Army War College.

Colonel Piyush, an alumnus of the Indian Military Academy, was commissioned into 8 RAJPUTANA RIFLES in Dec 2003. He later commanded 25 RAJPUTANA RIFLES and has extensive operational experience in counter-insurgency operations in Jammu and Kashmir as well as high-altitude tenures, including the Siachen Glacier. A graduate of the Defence Services Staff College and the Higher Command Course, he has served as an instructor at the National Defence Academy and the Rajputana Rifles Regimental Centre. He has also represented India as a United Nations Military Observer in Abyei. He is presently serving as Head of Department and Directing Staff at the Faculty of studies and Leadership, Army War College.

Multi-Domain Warfare: Lessons from Operation Sindoor, Ukraine, and West Asia

Major General BK Sharma, AVSM, SM (Retd)**

"It is the mind that wins wars, not just the sword"

—Field Marshal Sam Manekshaw, MC

Abstract

This article explores the evolution and strategic implications of multi-domain warfare through three defining case studies: India's Operation Sindoor (2025), the Russia–Ukraine War, and hybrid conflicts across West Asia. Each exemplifies how contemporary warfare has transcended traditional domains, integrating kinetic and non-kinetic actions across land, air, sea, cyber, space, and the cognitive realm. Operation Sindoor marked a doctrinal inflection point in India's counter-terrorism strategy, collapsing the distinction between state and non-state actors and challenging the nuclear deterrence threshold. The Russia–Ukraine and West Asia theatres further illuminate the effectiveness of proxies, drone swarms, cyber sabotage, urban combat, and information warfare in shaping conflict outcomes. The article argues for a fundamental recalibration of India's security doctrine, strategic posture, and institutional frameworks to address grey-zone and collusive threats. It calls for accelerated theaterisation, integrated command structures, artificial intelligence-enabled capabilities, cyber resilience, and a whole-of-nation approach to civil defence. It also advocates leveraging strategic diplomacy and narrative shaping to reinforce deterrence and operational legitimacy. Ultimately, India's future military success hinges not merely on conventional superiority but on its ability to act with speed, coherence, and clarity across visible and invisible domains of modern conflict.

Introduction

Operation Sindoor, launched by India on 07 May 2025, following the brutal terrorist attack in Pahalgam, marked more than a robust military response—it signified a doctrinal inflection point in India's counterterrorism strategy.[1] What set it apart was not merely the scale or precision of the strikes, but a decisive shift in strategic thinking. India executed calibrated kinetic operations targeting terrorist hideouts and Pakistani military infrastructure, while simultaneously deploying non-kinetic measures, including the suspension of Indus Waters Treaty provisions. This integrated approach redefined India's response threshold and, for the first time, rejected the artificial separation between state and non-state actors, effectively calling Pakistan's nuclear bluff.

Operation Sindoor must be viewed in the wider context of ongoing geopolitical conflicts—particularly the Russia–Ukraine war and hybrid confrontations across West Asia—which collectively underscore the emergence of Multi-Domain Warfare (MDW). This evolving paradigm blends conventional and unconventional tactics, integrates kinetic and non-kinetic capabilities, and spans across land, air, sea, cyberspace, outer space, and the cognitive domain.[2] It reflects the convergence of state and non-state actors operating in grey-zones with strategic ambiguity, necessitating urgent adaptations in doctrine, strategy, and force posture.

India's confrontation with Pakistan after 22 Apr 2025, culminating in Operation Sindoor, collapsed the traditional boundaries between sub-conventional and conventional deterrence. State-sponsored terror was no longer treated as a proxy irritant—it was elevated to an act of war. In parallel, the Ukrainian and West Asian theatres offered powerful lessons in hybrid conflict, where the decisive advantage lay in integration, innovation, and disruption.

In the Eurasian theatre, Ukraine's Operation Spiderweb, launched on 01 Jun 2025, exemplified the future of hybrid warfare. After months of clandestine preparation, Ukraine deployed Artificial Intelligence (AI)-enabled drone swarms to strike five Russian airbases—some thousands of kilometres deep inside Russian territory, including Irkutsk. These drones, smuggled in parts through civilian routes and reassembled covertly within Russia, were activated through local mobile networks and flew below radar coverage, destroying 41 aircraft. It was a masterclass in distributed lethality, deception, and techno-operational innovation.[3]

Soon after, Israel launched Operation Rising Lion on 13 Jun 2025. This targeted elimination campaign, dismantled senior Iranian military leadership, and disabled key nuclear infrastructure at Natanz and Isfahan—without any ground troops. It relied instead on pre-positioned autonomous drones, deep human intelligence from Mossad operatives, and precision strikes. The operation reaffirmed the power of stealth, deception, and AI-driven lethality in the age of strategic deniability.[4]

The situation escalated rapidly with Operation Midnight Hammer, a joint United States (US)-Israel air campaign that deployed B-2 stealth bombers and cruise missiles to strike hardened Iranian nuclear sites, including the heavily fortified Fordow facility. Iran responded with a salvo of over 200 missiles targeting Israeli cities, critical infrastructure, and even the Al-Udeid base in Qatar, a logistics base for US operations. This marked the first direct state-on-state strike of such magnitude in West Asia since Israel's historic attacks on Iraq's Osirak (1981) and Syria's Deir ez-Zor (2007) reactors.[5]

These developments signal that future warfare will not unfold in linear, phased formats. A drone swarm, a cyber blackout, a deepfake-fuelled riot, and a financial market shock may occur not as sequential events, but as synchronised, multi-domain disruptions. The traditional military lexicon—warning periods, D-Day, H-Hour, and mobilisation timelines—is increasingly anachronistic.

Taken together, Operation Sindoor and parallel conflicts across Ukraine and West Asia offer a compelling primer on the character of 21st Century warfare. They underscore the imperative for India to rapidly reimagine its doctrinal frameworks, embrace techno-operational fusion, and build resilient multi-domain capabilities to confront a new era of collusive, hybrid, and unpredictable threats.

Key Takeaways from Operation Sindoor

A Doctrinal Watershed. Operation Sindoor, launched on 07 May 2025, marked India's most assertive use of military force since the Balakot airstrikes of 2019. In a calibrated and coordinated offensive, India conducted multi-domain precision strikes against nine terrorist camps deep inside Pakistani territory. These were followed by escalatory strikes on eight critical airfields—including the strategically significant Nur Khan Airbase—in direct retaliation to Pakistani drone and missile incursions. Under mounting military and diplomatic pressure, Pakistan proposed a ceasefire on 10 May effectively halting further escalation. In his address to the nation, Prime Minister Narendra Modi redefined India's red lines, signalling a new threshold of tolerance against cross-border terrorism.

Strategic Paradigm Shift. Operation Sindoor was not merely tactical—it was rooted in a clear political directive for a proportionate, time-bound response targeting terrorist infrastructure, including in Pakistan's heartland of Punjab Province. Crucially, India challenged two long-standing Pakistani assumptions: first, that nuclear deterrence would prevent Indian retaliation; and second, that terrorism occupies a separate rung in the conflict escalation ladder. By treating state-sponsored terrorism as tantamount to an act of war, India placed the burden of escalation management squarely on Pakistan. New Delhi also signalled that it no longer bears the burden of proof to establish Pakistan's complicity—a profound shift toward intent-based legitimacy in counter terror operations.[6]

Pre-emptive Precision Strikes. India's strikes were both calibrated and discriminating. Nine terrorist infrastructure nodes were neutralised without targeting civilian areas or regular military installations. This demonstrated India's ability to conduct high-precision, stand-off warfare while maintaining moral and strategic credibility. The absence of granular proof did not undermine international acceptance of India's actions—highlighting a growing shift in global counter-terror norms that value credible intent and proportionality over evidentiary thresholds. However, the operation also exposed the compressed decision-making windows in a nuclearised environment, underlining the need for institutionalised rapid-attribution frameworks and flexible diplomatic signalling to manage escalation dominance.[7]

Dynamic Responsive Escalation Doctrine. Operation Sindoor showcased the evolution of India's military doctrine into a dynamic response escalation framework—integrating air, land, sea, cyber, space, and information capabilities. The Indian Armed Forces deployed an array of platforms: fighter aircraft, BrahMos and Système de Croisière Autonome à Longue Portée (Long-Range Autonomous Cruise Missile System) cruise missiles, Highly Agile Modular Munition Extended Range bombs, Harpy and Sky Striker loitering munitions, Akash surface-to-air missiles, D-4 missiles linked with the S-400 air defence system, and a suite of electronic warfare assets. The Integrated Air Command and Control System, enabled by AI and developed by Defence Research and Development Organisation (DRDO) and Bharat Electronics Limited's Centre for Artificial Intelligence and Robotics, provided real-time detection, tracking, and engagement of threats, blending human intelligence with cutting-edge technology.

From Retaliation to Strategic Coercion. Strikes on high-value targets such as Nur Khan and Bholari airbases revealed a doctrinal pivot from tactical retaliation to strategic coercion. The ambiguity introduced by drone and missile usage across multiple domains complicated adversary assessments, increasing the fog of war and risk of miscalculation. The experience underscored India's urgent need to invest in counter-unmanned aerial vehicle systems, real-time drone attribution capabilities, and robust rules of engagement to navigate sustained grey-zone confrontations.[8,9]

Collusive Multi-Domain Warfare Threat

The conflict underscored the collusive threat posed by Pakistan and China. Beijing's support was visible, ranging from satellite intelligence via the BeiDou constellation to supply of Electronic Warfare (EW) and cyberwarfare capabilities. China remains Pakistan's largest defence supplier, contributing over 80 per cent of its hardware including combat drones, radar systems, and advanced missiles. Pakistan leveraged this digital ecosystem for electromagnetic dominance in a network-centric battlespace.

Operation Sindoor calls for serious introspection to bridge these gaps through indigenous Intelligence, Surveillance, and Reconnaissance (ISR) development and tighter integration of civil-military space assets. Looking ahead, China may equip Pakistan with antiship ballistic missiles, the Yaogan satellite system for ISR, KJ-500 Airborne Early Warning and Control aircraft, HQ-19 missile defence systems (akin to Terminal High Altitude Area Defence), and advanced microwave weapons such as the FK-400. The naval balance is also shifting with Pakistan's induction of Chinese Hangoor-class submarines and Type 054A frigates. Beyond arming Pakistan, China is using it as a live testing ground for its military platforms—enhancing both strategic leverage against India and its global profile as a defence exporter. A more aggressive Chinese posture, with increased forward deployment and arms transfers, cannot be ruled out.[10]

Circumventing the Terrorism Trap

The Pahalgam attack revealed vulnerabilities in India's threat anticipation architecture. Strengthening internal security—through AI-based analytics, multi-layered border monitoring, and cross-agency intelligence fusion—is indispensable. At the sector and sub-sector levels, better coordination and predictive tools are critical to enforce a zero-tolerance counter-terrorism posture. Pre-emptive disruption of high-visibility terror acts must remain the cornerstone of India's strategic deterrence ecosystem.[11]

Diplomacy and International Optics

The ceasefire optics were clouded by the Trump administration claiming credit for brokering the deal. Further complicating the diplomatic narrative were Pakistan's immediate ceasefire violations and Washington's hyphenated commentary equating Indian restraint with Pakistani aggression. Unwarranted references to Jammu and Kashmir and calls for mediation, especially in a post-terror strike scenario, revealed persistent gaps in Western understanding of the India–Pakistan dynamic.[12]

Strategic Communication: Narrative Dominance

One of the lesser discussed but critical strengths of Operation Sindoor was India's coherent strategic communication. Daily professional briefings countered Pakistan's disinformation blitz, which included doctored images and false narratives. While democratic openness poses structural challenges to narrative unity, India's media handling—focused, data-backed, and authoritative—helped shape international perception. However, the conflict revealed a need for institutionalised, real-time counter-messaging frameworks capable of pre-empting and neutralising adversarial propaganda in a rapidly evolving infosphere.[13]

Whole-of-Government and Nation Approach

Operation Sindoor was emblematic of a maturing Indian defence ecosystem. The synergy between armed forces, DRDO, public-private industry, and national leadership reflected the ideals of *Atmanirbhar Bharat* (Self-reliant India) in action. Civil-military coordination was smooth, and inter-ministerial cooperation ensured operational fluidity. India demonstrated unprecedented preparedness across domains—from strategic planning and kinetic execution to civil defence and media engagement. The operation stood as a testament to a whole-of-government and whole-of-nation approach—a critical prerequisite in an era of MDW.[14,15]

Russia–Ukraine War and West Asia: Laboratories of Multi-Domain Warfare

The ongoing Russia–Ukraine War and the protracted conflicts across West Asia have emerged as defining laboratories for the evolution of MDW. These theatres showcase how modern warfare seamlessly blends conventional, sub-conventional, and non-kinetic tools across the military, digital, and cognitive domains.[16,17]

Proxy and Subterranean Warfare

Both conflicts exemplify the increasing reliance on proxy and surrogate forces to wage strategic campaigns without triggering formal escalation. Iran has deepened its strategic depth through armed proxies such as Hezbollah, the Houthis, and Iraqi Shia militias, creating a layered, region-wide influence architecture. Russia, meanwhile, has employed private military contractors like the Wagner Group, along with North Korean troops and other irregulars, to stretch Ukrainian defences while maintaining plausible deniability.

This indirect approach complicates attribution, slows international response, and preserves the illusion of limited war. The battles of Mariupol, Bakhmut, Mosul, and Gaza underscore the complexity of dense urban warfare, often conducted in subterranean environments—tunnels, bunkers, and underground logistics systems—which blur the frontline and amplify the challenge of precision targeting and civilian protection.[18]

Drones, Cyber, and Information Warfare

The prolific use of unmanned aerial systems has redefined force projection for both state and non-state actors. From Houthi drone swarms in the Gulf to Ukraine's AI-enabled kamikaze drones and ISR platforms, drones now offer inexpensive yet impactful means to strike deep, monitor movements, and gather tactical intelligence. Systems like high mobility artillery rocket system, precision glide bombs, and AI-enhanced artillery have further expanded the scope and accuracy of long-range fires, reshaping battlefield dynamics.[19]

In parallel, cyberspace has become a central domain of conflict. Russian cyber-attacks on Ukraine's critical infrastructure—targeting power grids, telecom networks, and command systems—demonstrate the strategic value of cyber warfare. Similarly, Iranian and Israeli cyber duels have become a recurring feature of the West Asian conflict spectrum.

Israel's precision strikes on low-tech communication systems—such as pagers and walkie-talkies used by Hamas and Hezbollah—illustrate a sophisticated application of EW to disable command-and-control among Iran's regional proxies. Once considered secure due to their simplicity and resilience in EW-contested environments, these tools became liabilities when exploited through advanced jamming and geolocation technologies.

Escalation Management and Nuclear Signalling

Both theatres offer insights into escalation control under nuclear overhangs. Russia's use of nuclear signalling—via rhetoric, posture adjustments, and ambiguous deployments—has deterred direct North Atlantic Treaty Organization intervention while allowing Moscow to manage escalation on its terms. Simultaneously, Iran's hybrid strategy—activating proxy networks in measured doses while avoiding direct retaliation—shows a calibrated application of sub-threshold warfare to avoid inviting full-scale war.

The risks, however, are mounting. Accidental or deliberate attacks on nuclear facilities, the deployment of tactical nuclear weapons in third-party countries, and the spectre of false flag nuclear incidents have introduced new layers of atomic instability, raising serious concerns about strategic deterrence and crisis management in hybrid war zones.[20]

Civil–Military Synergy and Innovation Ecosystems

The success of Ukraine and Israel in sustaining operational tempo owes much to their civil–military innovation ecosystems. Ukraine's war effort has been bolstered by a nationwide mobilisation of civilian tech talent—startups, coders, drone enthusiasts, and volunteers—who have developed critical ISR tools, logistics software, and autonomous strike platforms in real time.

Similarly, Israel's integration of private-sector capabilities into national defence architecture—through dual-use technologies, rapid prototyping, and innovation hubs—has enhanced its operational agility and resilience. Civil defence mobilisation, reserve force readiness, and robust intelligence networks further contribute to a national warfighting posture.

The key lesson is clear: embedding civilian industry, technological infrastructure, and societal resilience into defence operations dramatically enhances a state's ability to wage and withstand prolonged, multi-domain conflict.[21]

Implications for India's National Security

The evolving nature of warfare, shaped by Operation Sindoor, the Russia–Ukraine war, and hybrid conflicts in West Asia, has fundamentally altered the way India must approach its national security. MDW now stretches beyond conventional domains to include cyberspace, outer space, and the cognitive realm. India must adapt holistically across all these dimensions to protect its interests and maintain strategic stability in an increasingly volatile world.

Cognitive Domain and Societal Resilience

One of the most urgent vulnerabilities lies in the civilian and cognitive domain. The space of ideas, emotions, and digital perceptions has become an operational battlefield. In this theatre, adversaries like Pakistan and China are likely to strike by leveraging misinformation, deepfakes, and simulated failures to erode public morale, sow division, and cripple institutional credibility. India's societal diversity and democratic openness make it especially susceptible to such asymmetric tools. While the country has made progress in strengthening conventional deterrence, it remains underprepared to defend against these insidious attacks. What is needed is a comprehensive national programme to build societal resilience—anchored in public awareness, digital hygiene, and community-level preparedness. The concept of a National Civil Defence Grid could offer a robust framework, integrating AI for threat detection, drone-jamming technology, encrypted communications, and real-time alert systems developed in partnership with both public and private actors.

Nuclear Security and Strategic Deterrence

The changing security environment demands a serious reappraisal of India's nuclear posture and infrastructure security. With Pakistan dispersing and hardening its nuclear assets, India must ensure not only the survivability of its own deterrent but also its readiness to handle scenarios involving radiological contamination or nuclear sabotage by terrorist groups. These risks require investments in rapid attribution capabilities, radiological response teams, and nuclear forensics. The time has come to move beyond a declaratory posture and toward a nuclear doctrine that is assertive, flexible, and tailored to respond to a range of evolving threats—including those that blur the lines between state and non-state actions.

Doctrinal Recalibration and Theatre Commands

India's strategic doctrine must be recalibrated to reflect the realities of collusive, grey-zone, and multi-domain conflict. The threshold for response, as demonstrated in Operation Sindoor, is shifting—and this new reality must be institutionalised through a dynamic escalation framework. A revised doctrine should prioritise effect-based operations and decision superiority in a contested, AI-enabled battlespace. This recalibration necessitates the urgent acceleration of theatre command implementation. The integration of land, maritime, air, cyber, and space forces under unified commands must move beyond organisational reform to become a functional enabler of joint operations. Additionally, the National Security Council Secretariat must be transformed into a round-the-clock strategic nerve centre, conducting real-time red-teaming, war-gaming, and escalation simulations to support policy and operational decision-making.

Technological Modernisation and Interoperability

A technology-led defence posture is indispensable to secure India's strategic advantage in the coming decades. Indigenous development under the *Atmanirbhar Bharat* initiative must expand to cover AI-powered decision systems, swarm drones, next-generation munitions, and advanced surveillance and reconnaissance platforms, particularly in the space domain. However, India's defence ecosystem is still burdened by interoperability challenges arising from its mixed inventory of Russian, Western, and indigenous platforms. This technical disconnect needs to be addressed through unified data protocols, modular system architecture, and common interface standards to enable seamless integration across platforms. Moreover, India must rapidly scale its inventory of expendable drones, precision-guided weapons, and EW capabilities to sustain operations in a high-intensity conflict environment.

Cyber and Strategic Communication Warfare

In modern conflict, control of the information domain is as important as control of physical territory. India must develop a national capability for strategic communication that synchronises civil and military messaging, builds narrative dominance, and counters adversary propaganda in real time. Establishing a Strategic Communication Command with dedicated cyber and media cells will be crucial in this regard. Alongside narrative control, the development of offensive cyber capabilities must become a strategic priority. India needs the tools to disrupt enemy mobilisation, degrade critical infrastructure, and interfere with hostile command-and-control systems. Simultaneously, the resilience of Indian cyberspace must be enhanced through stronger encryption, secure cloud architecture, supply chain security, and critical infrastructure protection measures.

Internal Security and Predictive Intelligence

India's internal security architecture must evolve from a reactive to a predictive model. The recent Pahalgam terror attack demonstrated the high costs of delayed or diffused intelligence. National and state-level counter-terrorism centres must be established to fuse human intelligence with signal, satellite, and open-source inputs, creating a seamless threat-detection network. Surveillance of vulnerable regions such as Jammu and Kashmir and the Northeast should be upgraded through AI-powered smart fencing, real-time sensor networks, and autonomous drones. Internal security forces must also be equipped with advanced tools for tunnel detection, robotics, and integrated ISR to effectively counter emerging threats in urban and subterranean environments.

Civil-Military Fusion and Innovation

The future of warfare demands a whole-of-nation approach. India must foster deeper collaboration between its armed forces, academic institutions, research organisations, and the private sector. Programmes like Innovations for Defence Excellence and defence industrial corridors must be empowered to incubate and fast-track dual-use technologies that can meet battlefield requirements. Innovation must be focused not only on cutting-edge platforms but also on supporting logistics, battlefield medicine, situational awareness, and command resilience. At the same time, civilian preparedness must be prioritised, especially in border and conflict-prone areas. Community training in civil defence, emergency response, and psychological support will enhance the resilience of the national fabric during protracted crises.

Diplomacy as a Force Multiplier

Strategic diplomacy must be a parallel instrument to military preparedness. Operation Sindoor demonstrated the importance of managing perceptions and alliances during crises. India must deepen its diplomatic leverage by utilising multilateral platforms like the Group of Twenty-One; Brazil, Russia, India, China, South Africa Plus; the Quadrilateral Security Dialogue; and the Shanghai Cooperation Organisation to isolate state sponsors of terrorism and promote itself as a responsible and mature nuclear power. Strategic autonomy remains central to India's foreign policy. However, it must be exercised with agility—balancing deeper security cooperation with partners like the US, Japan, and France, while preserving flexibility in relations with Russia, Iran, the Gulf states, and Association of Southeast Asian Nations. Agreements like Communications Compatibility and Security Agreement, Basic Exchange and Cooperation Agreement (for geospatial intelligence), and Logistics Exchange Memorandum of Agreement must transition from diplomatic frameworks to operational instruments, enabling real-time intelligence sharing, coordinated cyber operations, and joint logistics missions.

Strategic Review and Decision Matrix

India must now undertake a comprehensive strategic review that goes beyond threat assessments. It must re-examine the intent, capabilities, and behavioural patterns of its adversaries and allies, revisit legacy assumptions, and question the analytical frameworks that drive its policy. Mental maps that were drawn in the past century may no longer be relevant. Strategic planning must address not only known threats but also decision dilemmas—how far is India prepared to escalate, at what cost, and with what exit strategy? What end states are acceptable at various levels of conflict, and how do we shape the escalation ladder to stay ahead of adversaries? India's next war may not begin with missiles or tanks. It may emerge through fragmented crises—cyber blackouts, market shocks, targeted assassinations, or disinformation campaigns. These threats, dispersed across invisible frontiers, demand a united, agile, and forward-looking response that integrates national will, technological power, and strategic clarity.

Conclusion

The lessons from Operation Sindoor, the Russia–Ukraine war, and hybrid conflicts in West Asia underscore a pivotal truth: future conflicts will be fought as much in the cognitive and technological domains as on physical battlefields. For India, the imperative lies in translating tactical agility into strategic deterrence. This demands doctrinal boldness, technological self-reliance, real-time intelligence fusion, and proactive narrative shaping. As the regional and global security landscape becomes increasingly volatile, India's ability to deter, dominate, and de-escalate across various domains will define its stature as a credible and future-ready power.

Endnotes

[1] "From Surgical Strikes to Operation SINDOOR: tracking 11 years of internal security measures", *DD News*, 01 Jun 2025, accessed 10 Sep 2025 https://ddnews.gov.in/en/from-surgical-strikes-to-operation-sindoor-tracking-11-years-of-internal-security-measures/

[2] Jared Donnelly and Jon Farley, "Defining the 'Domain' in Multi-Domain", *JAPCC*, Jun 2019, accessed 10 Sep 2025 https://www.japcc.org/essays/defining-the-domain-in-multi-domain/

[3] John T Psaropoulos, "Ukraine's 'Spiderweb' drone assault forces Russia to shelter, move aircraft", *Al Jazeera*, 18 Jun 2025, accessed 10 Sep 2025 https://www.aljazeera.com/news/2025/6/18/ukraines-spiderweb-drone-assault-forces-russia-to-shelter-move-aircraft

[4] Zineb Riboua, "How Israel's Operation Rising Lion Dismantled Iran from Within: A Case Study in the Art of Deception", Reports, *Hudson Institute*, 13 Jun 2025, accessed 10 Sep 2025 https://www.hudson.org/defense-strategy/how-israels-operation-rising-lion-dismantled-iran-within-case-study-art-deception

[5] Howard Altman, Tyler Rogoway, and Joseph Trevithick, "B-2 Strikes On Iran: What We Know About Operation Midnight Hammer", *TWZ*, 22 Jun 2025, accessed 10 Sep 2025 https://www.twz.com/air/b-2-strikes-on-iran-what-we-know-about-operation-midnight-hammer

[6] VR Chaudhari, "Operation Sindoor signals a real paradigm shift", *The Print,* 03 Jun 2025, accessed 10 Sep 2025 https://theprint.in/theprint-otc/operation-sindoor-signals-a-real-paradigm-shift-says-ex-iaf-chief-we-hit-where-it-hurts-the-most/2644480/

[7] Press Information Bureau, "Operation Sindoor: Indian Armed Forces Carried out Precision Strike at Terrorist Camps", *PIB*, 07 May 2025, accessed 10 Sep 2025 https://www.pib.gov.in/PressReleasePage.aspx?PRID=2127370

[8] BK Sharma, "Operation Sindoor: A harbinger of India's dynamic escalation response doctrine", *The Week*, 31 May 2025, accessed 10 Sep 2025 https://www.theweek.in/news/defence/2025/05/31/operation-sindoor-a-harbinger-of-indias-dynamic-escalation-response-doctrine.html

[9] Harsh V Pant and Vinay Kaura, "Post Op Sindoor, A Battle For Narrative Dominance", *Observer Research Foundation*, 21 May 2025, accessed 10 Sep 2025 https://www.orfonline.org/english/research/post-op-sindoor-a-battle-for-narrative-dominance

[10] Sharma, "Operation Sindoor: A harbinger of India's dynamic escalation response doctrine"

[11] Consulate General of India, Istanbul, Turkey, "Summary of Operation/ SINDOOR", *CGI Turkey*, 10 May 2025, accessed 10 Sep 2025 https://www.cgiistanbul.gov.in/section/news/summary-of-operation-sindoor/

[12] Amit Baruah, Nidhi Razdan and Angshuman Choudhury, "Has the fallout from Operation Sindoor isolated India?" *Frontline*, 16 Jun 2025, accessed 10 Sep 2025 https://frontline.thehindu.com/world-affairs/operation-sindoor-india-pakistan-diplomacy-geopolitics/article69700900.ece

[13] Shashi Asthana, "Operation Sindoor: Application of Operational Art and Strategic Messaging", *Modern Diplomacy*, 15 Jul 2025, accessed 10 Sep 2025 https://moderndiplomacy.eu/2025/07/15/operation-sindoor-application-of-operational-art-and-strategic-messaging/

[14] Press Information Bureau, "Operation SINDOOR: Forging One Force, The Synergy of India's Armed Forces", *PIB India*, 18 May 2025, accessed 10 Sep 2025 https://www.pib.gov.in/PressReleasePage.aspx?PRID=2129453

[15] Press Information Bureau, "Operation SINDOOR: India's Strategic Clarity and Calculated Force", *PIB India*, 12 May 2025, accessed 10 Sep 2025 https:/ /www.pib.gov.in/PressNoteDetails.aspx?NoteId=154448&ModuleId=3

[16] Matthew Slusher, "Lessons from the Ukraine Conflict: Modern Warfare in the Age of Autonomy, Information, and Resilience", *Center for Strategic and International Studies*, 02 May 2025, accessed 10 Sep 2025 https://www.csis.org/analysis/lessons-ukraine-conflict-modern-warfare-age-autonomy-information-and-resilience

[17] CSIS, "Human Domain Lessons from Russia-Ukraine", *Center for Strategic and International Studies*, 06 Mar 2025, accessed 10 Sep 2025 https://www.csis.org/analysis/human-domain-lessons-russia-ukraine-conflict-focus

[18] Punit Shyam Gore, "The Emerging Relevance Of Subterranean Warfare", *Bharat Shakti*, 08 Mar 2024, accessed 10 Sep 2025 https://bharatshakti.in/the-emerging-relevance-of-subterranean-warfare/

[19] Zachary Kallenborn, "InfoSwarms: Drone Swarms and Information Warfare", Parameters 52, no. 2 (2022): 87-102, *Army War College*, accessed 10 Sep 2025 https://press.armywarcollege.edu/parameters/vol52/iss2/13/

[20] Michael Krepon, VP Malik, PR Chari, BM Kapur, Rajesh Rajagopalan and Gurmeet Kanwal, "Escalation Control In a Nuclear Environment", Report of the Seminar organised by *IPCS* and *Stimson Centre*, 22 Nov 2024, accessed 10 Sep 2025 https://www.ipcs.org/comm_select.php?articleNo=1566

[21] Kathleen McInnis, "No Strategy Without Society: Rethinking NATO's Coordination Mechanisms", *Center for Strategic and International Studies,* 24 Jun 2025, accessed 10 Sep 2025 https://www.csis.org/analysis/no-strategy-without-society-rethinking-natos-coordination-mechanisms

Multi-Domain Operations: Enhancing Cyber Operations Capability within the Armed Forces

Lieutenant General (Dr) RS Panwar, AVSM, SM, VSM (Retd)

Abstract

The article examines the significance of cyberspace as a distinct warfighting domain within multi-domain operations. The analysis explores the role of offensive cyber operations in achieving strategic objectives and evaluates international legal frameworks applicable to cyberspace conflicts. It provides an overview of the capabilities of global cyber powers and highlights India's standing amongst these powers. It argues that conducting such operations against military targets in a justified war is acceptable under international law, and that the armed forces are perhaps best suited to conduct these operations. Notably, it underscores the imperative for India to enhance its offensive cyber capabilities by upgrading structures like the Defence Cyber Agency to a full-fledged Cyber Command and transforming human resource and training policies to enable the development of this highly specialised capability.

Introduction

The character of warfare is undergoing a transformational change in the 21st Century. This change is often characterised by depicting the modern battlespace as a five-dimensional construct, comprising the land, sea, air, space, and cyberspace domains[1], and operations across these five domains are referred to as Multi-Domain Operations (MDO). Here, it is the newer domains of space and cyberspace which reflect the changing character of warfare. Most militaries today consider the cyber domain as a warfighting domain in its own right.

This article has been reproduced from the USI Strategic Year Book 2025.

The notion of warfighting in cyberspace, however, is not as comprehensible as in the traditional kinetic domains of land, sea, and air. Unlike these physical domains, the cyber domain is virtual and ill-defined, and cyber weapons as well as their effects are largely nebulous and intangible. Importantly, because of the non-attributability and non-contact attributes of cyberattacks, in addition to states' cyber criminals and other non-state actors being able to act across national boundaries with near impunity, pose a threat to national security.

The armed forces of any state are the traditional defenders of the state against external threats which violate national sovereignty through the use of force. Militaries, however, are attuned to fighting wars in the physical domains against combatants of an adversary state. Indeed, international law governing warfare between states is grounded in the notion of *Jus Ad Bellum* (Justified War) and framed in the context of international and non-international armed conflicts, wherein, combatants target combatants. Over the last two decades, experts at the United Nations (UN) and other international forums have been struggling to arrive at a consensus on how the laws of war apply in cyberspace, given its unique characteristics, with limited success so far.

Against the above backdrop, this article attempts to analyse the nuances of warfighting in cyberspace, with focus on offensive cyber operations. It relates this role to the traditional charter of the armed forces, which is to defend the sovereignty of a state against external threats and identify cyber operations as an important component of MDO. It assesses the effectiveness of cyber operations in creating strategic effects towards achieving politico-military objectives. The work discusses the current understanding at the global level on how international law applies in cyberspace for operations conducted across the spectrum of conflict. It provides the rationale on why the Indian Armed Forces are best suited to be allocated the mandate for offensive cyber operations vis-à-vis other agencies and suggests measures for enhancing their current capability to effectively fulfil this mandate.

Cyber Operations: A Potent Component of Multi-Domain Operations

- **Nations at War: The Diplomacy, Information, Military, and Economic Paradigm**. All warfare waged by a state is a whole-of-nation endeavour, carried out by leveraging comprehensive national power in all its forms in order to achieve its political objectives. The Diplomatic, Information, Military, and Economic (DIME) paradigm captures the main elements of comprehensive national power.[2] Conflicts in cyberspace are covered under the 'Information' component. Of the four elements, 'Military' represents the kinetic element, with the other three being non-kinetic in nature. In current conflict scenarios, the potency and effectiveness of Non-Kinetic Warfare (NKW) have increased considerably, leading military strategists to coin new terms to reflect this evolutionary trend in warfare, such as 'Hybrid Warfare' (United States [US])[3], 'Unrestricted Warfare' (China)[4] and 'New Generation Warfare' (Russia)[5], all of which represent a combination of all kinetic and not-kinetic means of warfare.

- **Grey-Zone Warfare (GZW)**. While hybrid warfare spans the entire spectrum of conflict, GZW may be said to encompass all the means adopted by states in the operational space between peace and all-out conflict to achieve politico-military objectives. In general, non-kinotic operations have greater relevance in the grey-zone, while kinetic operations are more effective during all-out conflicts. This is especially true for cyber operations.

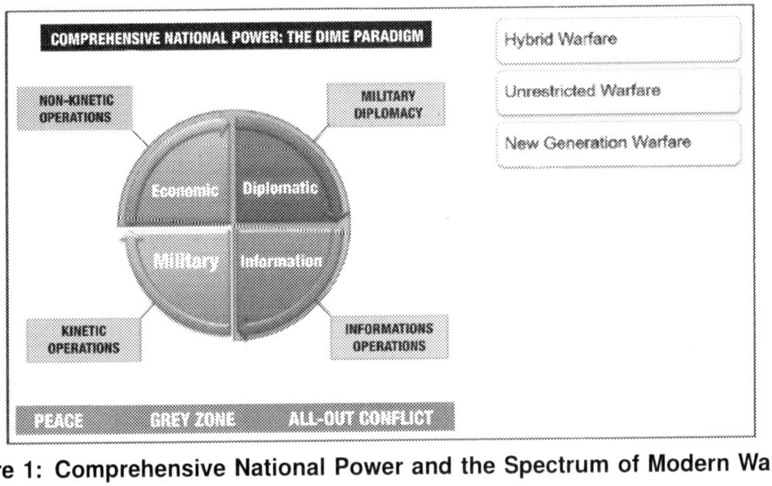

Figure 1: Comprehensive National Power and the Spectrum of Modern Warfare

- **Multi-Domain Operations**. While the DIME paradigm, NKW, and GZW are concepts applicable at the level of a nation state, MDO is purely a military construct. In the five-dimensional battlespace construct referred in Figure 2, if the fifth dimension is restricted to cyberspace alone, then there appears to be no field of play for two other components of military NKW, namely, Electronic Warfare (EW) and psychological/cognitive operations. Cyberspace as a term here, therefore, should be understood as encompassing the 'Electro-Magnetic' (EM) and 'Cognitive' domains as well.

It is important to differentiate amongst the three primary components of military NKW: the weapon in the case of EW is EM energy which targets electronics in machines; in cyber operations, it is a piece of malicious code targeted against data and software; and in cognitive operations, the weapon is the message designed to create effects in human minds.[6]

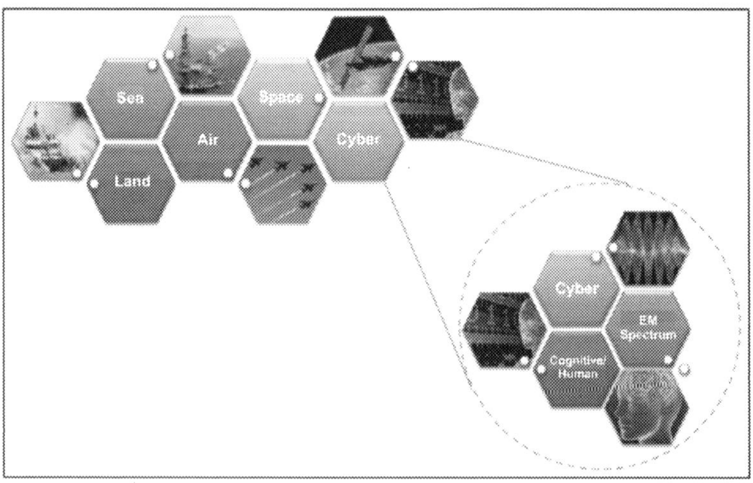

Figure 2: Muti-Domain Operations and Cognitive-Cyber Spectrum

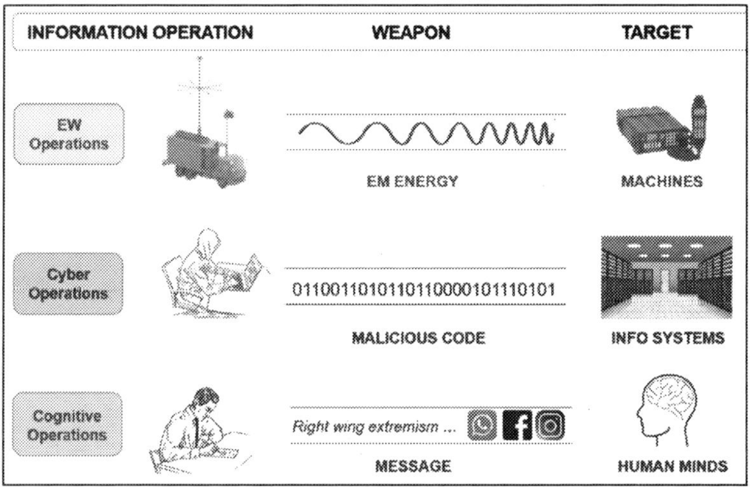

Figure 3: Dimensions of Information Operations: EW, Cyber and Cognitive Domains

Cyber Armageddon: Hype or Reality?

❑ **National Cyberspace and Critical Information Infrastructure**. National cyberspace (or national information infrastructure) may be grouped into two components: Critical Information Infrastructure (CII) and Non-CII (NCII). CII have broadly been identified by the Government of India as intranets which fall into six categories: government (including defence), transport, telecommunications, power and energy, banking and finance, and strategic and public enterprises.[7] Each intranet which makes up these distinct cyberspaces is separately plugged into the logical expanse of global cyberspace (essentially the internet). Importantly, each such blob needs to be individually protected from attacks launched from anywhere in global cyberspace.

❑ **Strategic Cyberattacks**. Broadly speaking, cyberattacks may be classified under five heads, namely, cyber-crime, cyber-hacktivism, cyber espionage (strategic or industrial), cyber terrorism, and cyber war. Cyber war here refers to destructive or disruptive cybereffects carried out by a state in adversary territory, either through state-owned cyber capabilities, such as a cyber command, or sponsored through non-state actors to achieve strategic effects. Unlike cyber espionage, these are not passive and, hence, may be termed as offensive cyber operations. A state's CII are the natural target of all offensive cyber operations.

- **Effectiveness of Offensive Operations**. In 2010, the Stuxnet attack, carried out purportedly by the US in conjunction with Israel, destroyed 20 per cent of Iran's nuclear centrifuges, causing substantial damage to its nuclear program[8]—the first case of a cyberattack with strategic effects. In 2015, the Russian attack on Ukraine's electrical grid disrupted electrical supply to a quarter million citizens for several hours[9]—the first known instance of an attack on critical infrastructure. The 2017 NotPetya malware attack, attributed to Russia, which was directed initially against Ukraine but spilled over across the entire globe, is estimated to have caused damages amounting to USD 10 bn dollars[10]—considered to be the most devastating cyberattack till date. The 2021 ransomware attack on the US Colonial Pipeline, which carries 45 per cent of all fuel to the US East Coast, resulted in its shutdown for almost a week, and the President declared a state of emergency in 17 US states.[11] The Russian attack on Viasat's satellite network, in conjunction with the launch of the Ukraine operations, impacted tens of thousands of customers located in Ukraine and Europe[12]—a good example of a cyberattack as part of MDO. These examples show that it is feasible to create strategic effects purely through actions in cyberspace.

- **Cyberattacks on India's Critical Infrastructure**. Notable cyberattacks on India's critical infrastructure include the attack on Mumbai's electric grid in Oct 2020[13], the targeting of Ladakh's electrical grid in early 2022[14], and the ransomware attack on Oil India Limited, also in 2022.[15] The first two are believed to have originated in China.

- **Cyber Operations in the Ukraine Conflict**. In the Russia-Ukraine conflict, during the build-up phase, Russia targeted industries, government, and Information Technology (IT) organisations by deploying malicious code, such as WhisperGate and HermeticWiper.[16] After breakout of hostilities, the attack on Ukraine's Viasat network disrupted 30,000 modem connections in Ukraine, severely disrupting Ukraine's military communications. SpaceX's Starlink network was also briefly disrupted in Mar 2022[17], and has since been constantly targeted by Russia. In response, Ukraine, in an unconventional move, raised an ad-hoc IT Army comprising of several lakh volunteers.[18] The US Cyber Command, the United Kingdom (UK)'s Government Communication Headquarters (GCHQ), friendly North Atlantic Treaty Organization countries such as Estonia, Poland and the Netherlands, as well as western private sector entities such as Microsoft provided substantial support in defending Ukraine's cyber assets.[19] However, once operations commenced, cyberattacks paled in comparison to the much more destructive kinetic operations.[20]

Offensive Cyber Operations Vis-à-vis International Law

Can a responsible state justifiably conduct offensive cyber operations against another state under international law? The answer to this question lies in the notion of *jus ad bellum*. Article 2(4) of the UN Charter prohibits the threat or use of force against the territorial integrity of any state. Article 51 recognises a state's inherent right to self-defence if an armed attack, sometimes referred to as an act of war, occurs. Cyber operations meeting the threshold of an armed attack would permit victim states to respond with proportionate measures, including the use of force. As per the prevailing view, cyber operations may cross the threshold of an armed conflict if they are comparable in effects to those resulting from traditional kinetic attacks.[21]

Two other thresholds, both below the threshold of armed conflict, are relevant when discussing the legal implications of cyberattacks: violation of the principle of non-intervention and violating the sovereignty of a state. The principle of non-intervention prohibits coercive actions by a state in the core functions of another state, such as elections, public administration, or economic stability. Internationally acceptable retaliatory actions for violating this threshold are limited to retorsion measures, which are unfriendly but lawful actions, such as restricting diplomatic relations, economic sanctions, or suspending cooperation agreements. The lowest threshold refers to cyber operations which may breach the sovereignty of a state without violating the principle of non-intervention, for instance, by carrying out unauthorised intrusions into another state's cyber infrastructure. Retorsion measures might be justified on crossing this threshold as well, though opinion amongst states here is divided.

To summarise, cyberattacks which cross the threshold of armed conflict would justify a response both in the kinetic and cyber domains. Conversely, if kinetic actions trigger a response under Article 51, offensive cyber actions would again be justified. Cyberattacks which create effects below this threshold would attract retorsion measures, including responses in cyberspace. Non-attributability of cyberattacks as a complicating factor is also to be dealt with, on lines similar to state-sponsored terrorist attacks.

Offensive cyberattacks (disruptive and destructive physical effects) and cyber espionage are, respectively, the attack and exploit functions within cyber operations. Notably, while espionage violates the sovereignty of the targeted state, it is widely treated as an acceptable activity.

Offensive Cyber Operations: Nuances across the Spectrum of Conflict

It has been brought out above that beyond the threshold of armed conflict, offensive cyber operations by a state would be justified under Article 51 of the UN Charter, independently or in conjunction with kinetic operations, in furtherance of an MDO strategy. Cyberattacks carried out just short of the outbreak of all-out hostilities may also be clubbed under this category.

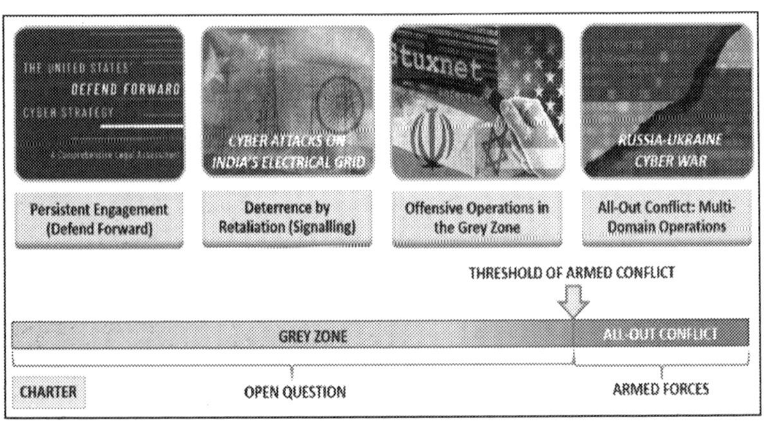

Figure 4: Spectrum of Cyber Conflict: from Grey-zone to All-Out War

In the grey-zone below this threshold, however, there are other motivations for a state to resort to offensive cyber operations. It could attempt to pre-emptively destroy or degrade the cyberattack infrastructure of adversaries. The persistent engagement/defend forward strategy of the US Department of Defence (DoD) is perhaps driven by this objective.[22] Deterrence-by-retaliation is another cyber strategy, which implies deterring adversary cyberattacks by way of declaring an offensive-defence strategy and/or resorting to limited effect cyberattacks for the purpose of signalling. The attacks on the electric grids of Mumbai and Ladakh, purportedly by China, were perhaps an operationalisation of this strategy. Finally, a state might resort to cyberattacks for achieving strategic effects even in the grey-zone under certain circumstances, a classic example of this being the Stuxnet attack. The manner in which such disruptive cyber operations in the grey-zone should be treated under international law is still largely an open question. Some characterise these state of affairs in cyberspace as akin to the wild west.

Global Powers: Overview of Cyber Capabilities

An overview of the cyberspace capabilities of major world militaries is given out in the succeeding paragraphs.[23]

- **United States**. The cyber governance architecture was adopted by tho US achieves synergy amongst the US Cyber Command, the National Security Agency (NSA), and the Cybersecurity and Infrastructure Security Agency (CISA), under its Department of Homeland Security. The Cyber Command is tasked with tackling external strategic threats, while the CISA focuses on cyber threats from the perspective of internal security. 13 cyber mission teams of the Cyber Command are meant specifically for the protection of CII. Further, the authority for the conduct of offensive operations in cyberspace appears to be vested solely with the DoD.

- **United Kingdom**. The UK established the National Cyber Security Centre (NCSC) in 2016 under the GCHQ, an intelligence agency in support of the government and armed forces, which focuses on cybercrime. It also raised a National Cyber Force in 2020 with a strength of 1,000, to be boosted to 3,000 by 2030. It is a partnership between the armed forces and the GCHQ, with its primary charter being offensive cyber warfare directed against external threats in cyberspace.

❑ **China**. The raising of the People's Liberation Army (PLA)'s Strategic Support Force (SSF) by China in 2016 signified the operationalising of its Integrated Network EW and 'Three Warfares' strategies. This transformative reorganisation resulted in the integration of not only cyberattack and exploit functions but also of cyber, electronic, and cognitive operations capabilities. In 2024, the PLASSF was again restructured into three forces, namely, the Cyberspace Force, the Aerospace Force, and the Information Support Force, the rationale for which is still being analysed by experts.

❑ **Russia**. Russia's Glavnoye Razvedyvatel'noye Upravleniye (GRU), or the Main Intelligence Directorate of the Russian military, together with the Sluzhba Vneshney Razvedki (SVR or the Foreign Intelligence Service) and the Federal'naya Sluzhba Bezopasnosti (FSB or the Federal Security Service), has arguably demonstrated the most devastating effects in cyberspace. It has also been well established that the GRU was behind the cyberattack on Ukraine's electricity grid in 2015, the devastating 2017 NotPetya cyberattack, and the interference in the US Presidential elections in 2016, amongst others.

On close analysis of the above cyber governance architectures, it emerges that over time, there has been an inexorable shift in the offensive cyber mandate from the intelligence agencies to the armed forces.

India's Standing as a Cyber Power

❑ **Cyber Governance**. In India, the following establishments are tasked with defence of the national cyberspace.

- The National CII Protection Centre (NCIIPC), under the Prime Minister's Office, is the national nodal agency for CII protection. Its charter includes identification of CII, protection strategies, and issuance of cyber advisories. However, the responsibility for protecting any component of CII lies with the agency running it.[24]

• The Indian Computer Emergency Response Team (CERT-In), under the Ministry of Electronics and Information Technology, issues advisories and responds to cyber incidents. CERT-In and NCIIPC may be viewed as focusing on the NCII and CII, respectively.

• The Defence Cyber Agency (DCyA) was established in 2019 for providing cyber operations support to the Indian Armed Forces.

• The Cyber and Information Security Division of the Ministry of Home Affairs deals with matters relating to cyber security and cybercrime from an internal security perspective.

• The NCSC, functioning under the National Security Council Secretariat, coordinates with different agencies at the national level on cyber security matters.

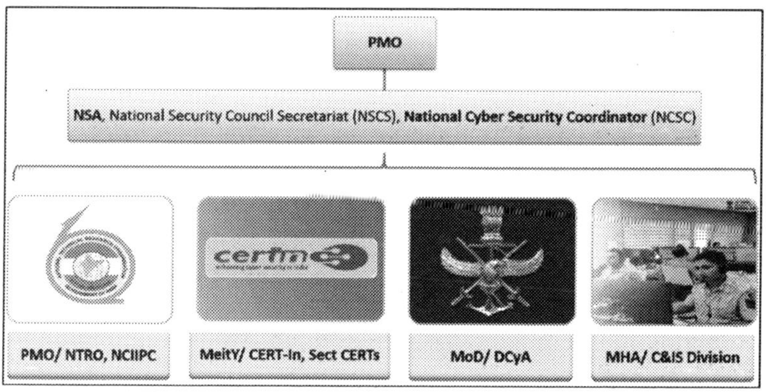

Figure 5: India's National Cybersecurity Governance Structure

❑ **Belfer Cyber Power Index**. As per the reputed Belfer Cyber Power Index 2022, China ranks at second position in comprehensive cyber power amongst 30 aspiring cyber powers in the world, while India's ranking is 26. In offensive cyber capability, China is at number 3 and India is at number 22. This indicates a wide differential in offensive cyber capabilities between China and India, to the latter's disadvantage.[25]

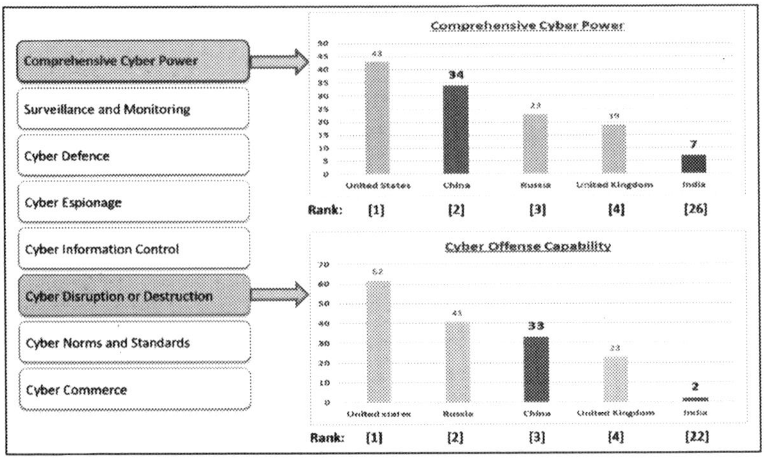

Figure 6: Global Rankings in Comprehensive Cyber Power and Offensive Cyber Capibilities

Offensive Cyber Operations: Role of Armed Forces

Broadly speaking, cyber capabilities in various states were initially developed by civilian intelligence organisations (NSA in the US, SVR/FSB in Russia, GCHQ in the UK, and the National Technical Research Organisation in India). This is because the extent of the capabilities was limited to covert gathering of cyber intelligence. As cyber operations mature to the point of creating cyber-physical effects of significant magnitude, the mandate for offensive cyber operations seems to be shifting inexorably from civilian intelligence to military organisations. Though a rational transformation, in India, there is very little movement in this direction.

In India, offensive cyber operations are still viewed as largely a covert activity, to be carried out under a mantle of plausible deniability, and, thus, more suited for intelligence rather than military agencies. It is under this assumption that India's offensive cyber capabilities in the military context are rarely discussed openly. Perhaps another reason is that India lacks the confidence in its ability to disrupt/degrade military targets through cyberattacks.

However, a previous section argues that carrying out cyberattacks against targets of military value as part of *jus ad bellum* would be acceptable under international law. This is quite logical, given that the employment of much more destructive kinetic weapons is justified under such circumstances. Indeed, overt declaration of cyber capabilities and the intent to use them strengthens cyber deterrence.

In the traditional domains of land, sea, and air, the Indian Armed Forces are mandated to protect the country's national sovereignty. However, this mandate does not extend to the cyberspace domain. The armed forces charter in cyberspace is restricted to protecting defence cyberspace (not national cyberspace), together with a limited mandate for conducting offensive cyber operations.

In the author's view, the responsibility for handling the full spectrum of strategic cyber conflicts must be given to the armed forces, in line with their role in the physical domains of conflict. More importantly, conducting offensive cyber capabilities against adversary states must be the exclusive domain of the armed forces.

That said, at the national level, there is a need to ponder over the ethics of carrying out disruptive cyber-physical attacks against India's adversaries in the grey-zone, even covertly, as these might be in violation of international law. Even if such operations are undertaken as a national imperative, they are best left to covert agencies. However, this does not preclude the armed forces from conducting either cyber intelligence or other covert intrusive actions in cyberspace in the grey-zone in preparation for cyber operations which may be undertaken subsequently as part of justified military operations.

Enhancing Offensive Cyber Capability

The following major conclusions may be drawn from the above analysis: offensive actions in cyberspace can facilitate the achieving of politico-military objectives, either independently or as part of MDO; conduct of offensive cyber activities is permissible under international law in *jus ad bellum*; there is a significant differential in offensive cyber capabilities between India and China in favour of the latter; and the armed forces are arguably the most suited agency for conducting offensive operations in cyberspace, in synergy with its operations in the kinetic domains. Therefore, the armed forces must strive to enhance their offensive cyber capabilities as an urgent imperative.[26]

❑ **Desired Capability**. During the build-up and conflict stages, the armed forces should have integral capability to target the adversary's critical infrastructure to degrade his combat potential. In addition, they should be able to gather military cyber intelligence throughout the spectrum of conflict. Finally, at the national level, the armed forces must deter/prevent adversaries from achieving strategic outcomes in and through the national cyberspace. Each of these capabilities requires a highly specialised cyber force of adequate strength.

❑ **Current Status**. The DCyA is presently the primary armed forces establishment for the conduct of full spectrum cyber operations, together with establishments integral to respective services. Each Service imparts some form of training for conducting cyber operations. For instance, in the Indian Army, the Military College of Telecommunication Engineering trains officers from the Corps of Signals and other arms officers on cyber security and network defence. Civilian expertise is also being tapped by some cyber establishments. In the author's view, these capabilities need to be considerably enhanced. Towards this end, some recommendations are given out below:

- **Upgrade Defence Cyber Agency to Cyber Command**. The DCyA should be upgraded to a full-fledged Cyber Command on priority, manned by over 5,000 cyber experts. Since accretions may not be feasible, this should be achieved through re-structuring.

- **Create Offensive Cyber Cadre/Profiles**. The cyber specialists who are posted to the Cyber Command must be captive for the most part. This entails a transformative change in the training and Human Resource (HR) policies for achieving the desired levels of specialisation. These policies must be framed around cyber profiles for officers and a special cadre/ trade for other ranks.

- **Training**. The existing centres of excellence for cyber training need to be upgraded and resourced adequately to impart the desired levels of specialised training.

Conclusion

Warfighting in the non-kinetic domains has increased in potency and intensity over the previous two decades. The fact that cyber operations can achieve strategic effects in the information as well as physical domains has been amply demonstrated in recent years. The prevalent view that offensive cyber operations are internationally unacceptable and, therefore, need to be carried out covertly under the shield of non-attributability is somewhat misplaced. The conduct of such operations against targets of military value as part of MDO in *jus ad bellum* is perfectly acceptable under international law, and the armed forces are logically the most appropriate agency for conducting these operations.

India's adversaries, in particular China, have invested significant resources into developing offensive cyber capabilities. As per current assessments, Chinese cyber capabilities are far superior to those of India. It is imperative, therefore, for the Indian Armed Forces to significantly enhance their capabilities. Upgrading the DCyA to a full-fledged Cyber Command, bringing about transformative changes in its training and HR policies, and upgrading/establishing training infrastructure are some of the steps which need to be implemented on high priority.

Endnotes

1 "Cyberspace Operations", *US DOD Joint Publication* 3-12 (R), 08 Jun 2018, pp 1 2, accessed 14 Jan 2025 https://irp.fas.org/doddir/dod/jp3_12.pdf

2 US Joint Chiefs of Staff, "Strategy", *US Joint Doctrine Note* 1-18, 25 Apr 2018, accessed 14 Jan 2025 https://www.jcs.mil/Portals/36/Documents/Doctrine/jdn_jg/jdn1_18.pdf

3 Frank Hoffman, "Conflict in the 21st Century: The Rise of Hybrid Wars", Arlington, Virginia: *Potomac Institute for Policy Studies*, US, 2007, accessed 05 Jan 2024 https://www.potomacinstitute.org/images/stories/publications/potomac_hybridwar_0108.pdf

4 Qiao Liang and Wang Xiangsui, "Unrestricted Warfare", Beijing: *PLA Literature and Arts Publishing House*, Feb 1999, accessed 14 Jan 2025 https://www.c4i.org/unrestricted.pdf

5 James Derleth, "Russian New Generation Warfare: Deterring and Winning the Tactical Fight", *US Army Military Review*, Sep-Oct 2020, accessed 14 Jan 2025 https://www.armyupress.army.mil/Portals/7/military-review/Archives/English/SO-20/Derleth-New-Generation-War-1.pdf

[6] RS Panwar, "Impact of Technology Enabled Cognitive Operations in Hybrid Warfare", Occasional Paper, *United Service Institution of India*, No. 3, 2024, p 3, accessed 14 Jan 2025 https://www.usiofindia.org/pdf/20240912144421.pdf

[7] Leah Sadoian, "NCIIPC Explained: Safeguarding India's Critical Infrastructure", *UpGuard*, accessed 14 Jan 2025 https://www.upguard.com/blog/nciipc-explained

[8] David Kushner, "The Real Story of Stuxnet", *IEEE Spectrum*, 26 Feb 2013 (updated 24 May 2024), accessed 14 Jan 2025 https://spectrum.ieee.org/the-real-story-of-stuxnet

[9] "Compromise of a power grid in eastern Ukraine", *Council on Foreign Relations*, Dec 2015, accessed 14 Jan 2025 https://www.cfr.org/cyber-operations/compromise-power-grid-eastern-ukraine

[10] Sean Steinberg et al, "NotPetya: A Columbia University Case Study", *School of International and Public Affairs, Case Consortium*, Columbia University, 2021, p 6, accessed 14 Jan 2025 https://www.sipa.columbia.edu/sites/default/files/2022-11/NotPetya%20Final.pdf

[11] G Gonzalez, B Lefebvre, E Geller, "Jugular of the US fuel pipeline system shuts down after cyberattack", *Politico*, 09 May 2021, accessed 18 Jan 2025 https://www.politico.com/news/2021/05/08/colonial-pipeline-cyber-attack-485984

[12] "Case Study–Viasat", *Cyberpeace Institute*, Jun 2022, accessed 18 Jan 2025 https://cyberconflicts.cyber peaceinstitute.org/law-and-policy/cases/viasat

[13] Vidya, "Maharashtra cyber cell submits report on Mumbai power outage, confirms malware attack hit power grid", *India Today*, 01 Mar 2021, accessed 18 Jan 2025 https://www.indiatoday.in/india/story/maharashtra-cyber-cell-mumbai-power-outrage-1774522-2021-03-01

[14] "Continued Targeting of Indian Power Grid Assets by Chinese State-Sponsored Activity Group", *Insikt Group*, 06 Apr 2022, accessed 18 Jan 2025, https://www.recordedfuture.com/research/continued-targeting-of-indian-power-grid-assets

[15] Press Trust of India, "Oil India suffers cyber-attack, receives Rs 57 crore ransom demand", *Business Standard*, 14 Apr 2022, accessed 18 Jan 2025 https://www.business-standard.com/article/companies/oil-india-suffers-cyber-attack-receives-rs-57-crore-ransom-demand-122041301002_1.html

[16] "Update: Destructive Malware Targeting Organizations in Ukraine", *US CISA*, 28 Apr 2022, accessed 18 Jan 2025 https://www.cisa.gov/news-events/cybersecurity-advisories/aa22-057a

[17] Elizabeth Howell, "Elon Musk says Russia is ramping up cyberattacks on SpaceX's Starlink systems in Ukraine", *Space.com*, 14 Oct 2022, accessed 18 Jan 2025 https://www.space.com/starlink-russian-cyberattacks-ramp-up-efforts-elon-musk

[18] S Soesanto, "The IT Army of Ukraine: Structure, Tasking and Ecosystem", *ETHzurich*, Jun 2022, accessed 19 Jan 2025 https://www.research-collection.ethz.ch/handle/20.500.11850/552293

[19] Nick Beecroft, "Evaluating the International Support to Ukrainian Cyber Defense", *Carnegie Endowment for International Peace*, 03 Nov 2022, accessed 18 Jan 2025 https://carnegieendowment.org/research/2022/11/evaluating-the-international-support-to-ukrainian-cyber-defense?lang=en

[20] GB Mueller, et al, "Cyber Operations during the Russo-Ukrainian War", *CSIS*, 13 Jul 2023, accessed 18 Jan 2025 https://www.csis.org/analysis/cyber-operations-during-russo-ukrainian-war#h2-russian-cyber-operations

[21] MN Schmitt, "Grey Zones in the International Law of Cyberspace", *The Yale Journal of International Law Online*, Vol 42:2, 18 Oct 2017, pp 7, 13, 15, 21, accessed 18 Jan 2025 https://ssrn.com/abstract=3180687

[22] "CYBER 101 - Defend Forward and Persistent Engagement", *US Cyber Command*, 25 Oct 2022, accessed 18 Jan 2025 https://www.cybercom.mil/Media/News/Article/3198878/cyber-101-defend-forward-and-persistent-engagement/

[23] RS Panwar, "Cyberspace Governance in India: Transform or Perish Part II: India's Existing Architecture and Global Practices", 26 May 2020, accessed 18 Jan 2025 https://futurewars.rspanwar.net/cyberspace-governance-in-india-transform-or-perish-part-ii/

[24] *Information Technology (NCIIPC and Manner of Performing Functions & Duties) Rules 2013*, GOI Gazette Notification GSR 19(E), 16 Jan 2014, accessed 14 Jan 2025, https://www.meity.gov.in/writereaddata/files/NCIIPC-Rules-notification.pdf.

[25] Voo, J., Hemani, I. and Cassidy D., *National Cyber Power Index 2022*, Sep 2022, accessed 18 Jan 2025, https://www.belfercenter.org/sites/default/files/pantheon_files/files/publication/ CyberProject_National%20Cyber%20Power%20Index%202022_v3_220922.pdf.

[26] RS Panwar, "Towards an Effective and Viable Information Warfare Structure for the Indian Armed Forces", *Journal of the United Service Institution of India*, Vol. CXLVIII, No. 612, Apr-Jun 2018, accessed 18 Jan 2025, https://www.usiofindia.org/publication-journal/towards-an-effective-and-viable-information-warfare-structure-for-the-indian-armed-forces.html.

Cognitive Domain Warfare: Lessons for India

Major General AK Chaturvedi, AVSM, VSM (Retd)

Abstract

This article discusses how cognitive warfare, though practiced since time immemorial, has only recently been formally identified as a distinct domain of conflict. Cognitive warfare is meant to build narratives that influence the heart and mind of the adversary to such an extent that, even before conflict begins, the adversary either feels defeated or doubts their own capability. Although, narrative build up is based on certain fault lines, which already either exist, are created ab-initio, or are based on suppression of facts. Information warfare is an integral part of cognitive warfare campaign. This article also explores the role of digital tools like artificial intelligence and social media, which are central to the execution of this modern warfare tactic. India has been subjected to this kind of warfare for a long time; initially by British colonisers and post-independence, it is a deliberate strategy of China, and in recent times, by the United States. Pakistan has also joined in recent times to do influence operations. India needs to realise the seriousness of impact of this form of warfare and formulate a 'National Strategy' to deal with it.

Introduction

Cognitive warfare is a set of activities that aim to influence attitudes and behaviours of the target group/people to gain an advantage over an adversary. These activities are done in conjunction with other instruments of power. It is unleashed through all or some of the activities, such as psychological operations, legal influence, communication technologies, fake news stories, and perception manipulation. Essentially, cognitive warfare entails generating and perpetuating a false narrative to spread a false information, which is made to look as real as possible by communicating the same information through multiple sources and over a period of time.

This article has been reproduced from the USI Strategic Year Book 2025.

Objectives of cognitive warfare could be one or more than one of the following:

- Exploit individual/group/societal vulnerabilities.
- Systemically weaken an adversary by degrading his rationality.[1]
- Cause mistrust in open information sources.
- Make people lose faith in democratic processes.
- Modify perceptions of people fully or partially.
- Influence elections/stirring up popular unrest in target country through service interruptions and information theft.

Means of achieving these objectives could be subversion of minds through whispering campaign/exploit 'Trust Fault Lines' to trigger civil disturbances. Digital tools are the main source of waging cognitive war and target is human mind. Thus, it is a 'Psycho-social-technical Warfare'. Cognitive warfare is increasingly becoming a new domain of warfare, wherein, cyber tools are used to alter adversary's cognitive process, exploit mental biases to cause thought distortions both at the individual, collective, and decision-making levels. Needless to add that in years ahead, it will become a critical realm of the warfare. There is a popular belief that the regime change in Bangladesh was done through a carefully crafted narrative that Sheikh Hasina Wazed was an autocrat. The existing societal fault lines and economic insecurities in Bangladesh were exploited for the purpose.

The scope and scale of the cognitive war can stretch from tactical level to the strategic level. Three examples in this connection would suffice:

- During the ongoing Russo-Ukrainian War, both sides are using a combination of communication technologies to plant fake news stories, and, thus, attempting to manipulate perceptions. No wonder if either of the side is to be believed, the war should have ended in their respective favour long back.
- The United States (US) used the bogey of the erstwhile Saddam Hussain regime in Iraq gaining access to nuclear weapons to prepare an enabling environment for lodging an offensive to destroy his regime.

- Use of cognitive warfare at a strategic level is distortion of the Indian history by Britishers with a view to make successive generations of Indians to suffer from an inferiority complex, from which many Indians have still not been able to come out.

The idea of cognitive warfare is not new. Chanakya advocated that, "If opposed by an alliance of nations, a king should secretly 'Sow Dissensions' within the alliance of adversaries, until one or more of the parties in the alliance becomes weak".[2] Obviously, it would have entailed generating a false narrative and perpetuating it over a period of time. Sun Tzu in China suggested " 'Breaking the enemy resistance without fighting' by targeting the cognitive processes of the human mind".[3] In recent times, China has achieved a degree of finesse in cognitive warfare and as such, uses it as a means to achieve victory by influencing public opinion, unleashing of psychological operations, and legal influence as a part of her 'Three Warfares' strategy.[4] The US, and particularly North Atlantic Treaty Organization, is also working in this domain quite extensively. They are generating data and analysing the same with a view to shape the strategy for future.[5] It is interesting to note that both the US and China consider cognitive warfare as information warfare. Russians also call it the same but equate it to a strategic threat akin to the nuclear threat.[6]

One of the important aspect of cognitive warfare is its invisibility in the beginning. By the time its impact is felt, it is too late to do damage control.

Cognitive warfare is already being used by a number of state and non-state players trying for regime change in target countries. The perpetrators are invariably highly focused, well-versed in human psychology, and understand evolving geopolitics and power of digital interventions. Thus, there is a need to have cognitive ability to discern the design of perpetrators to respond effectively.

Cognitive warfare can also be compared to cognitive dominance, which may result into seizure of territory or control over the economy of a state. On the other hand, it is possible to achieve dominance through cognitive operations, if psychology of the target groups/societies and their social and mental vulnerabilities are well known.[7] Use of Artificial Intelligence (AI) is an effective tool for such a digital colonisation.

Thus, there is a need to have an organisation dedicated to work on counter strategy. Technology needs to be leveraged as a force multiplier to alter the cognition of human targets. This organisation needs to develop tools to discern and neutralise the potential threats besides continuously working to generate awareness among the uninitiated. Effective use of social media and digital tool are important means available at the disposal of the defender.

Post regime change in Bangladesh, the world has suddenly taken note of the power of cognitive warfare. There is a need to cut the clutter on the subject. Among many others, neuro-ethicist James Giordano[8] has described the brain as the site for the battlefields of the 21st Century and studied the weaponisation of neurosciences. General David Lee Goldfein[9], a retired US Air Force general, has stated that we have moved on to wars of attrition to wars of cognition. Lieutenant General Vincent Stewart[10] of the US Defence Intelligence Agency sees modern warfare as a cognitive battleground, and General Gilles Desclaux[11], a retired Air Force General of the French Army, considers the command and control chain as a cognitive triangle of 'Knowledge Dominance', 'Cyber Confidence' and 'Decision Superiority', which facilitates achievement of operational objectives. Thus, cognitive war affects the capacity/ capability of adversary without firing a bullet.

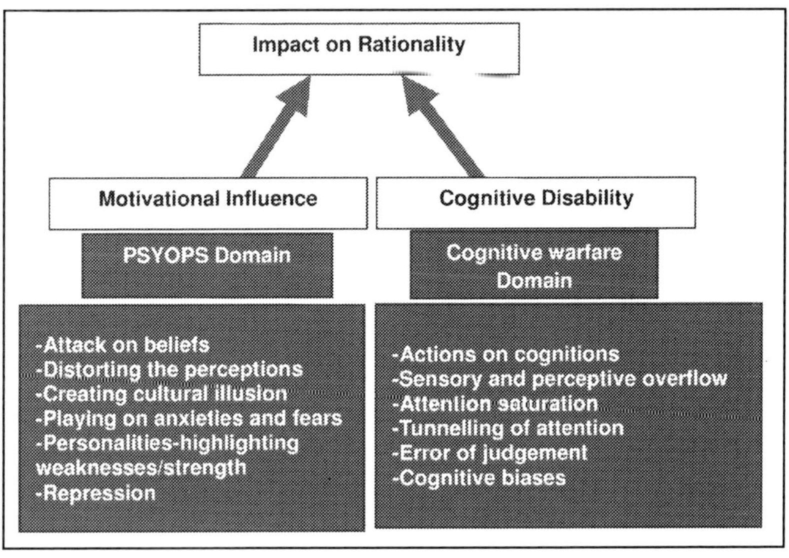

Figure 1: Ways and means to influence rationality of a person/group/society[12]

The effect of cognitive warfare accentuated by combining Psychological Operations and measures to impact cognition and this synthesis helps in impacting the rational thinking of the subject, which can be well understood by following model:

Preparing for Cognitive Warfare

In view of the above for offensive cognitive warfare, a detailed study of the patterns adopted by the adversaries and generation of data to establish patterns to work out necessary strategies is required, and the first step in that direction is to build a believable narrative and share the same with people whose life and mind the strategy is meant to influence and if a counter-strategy is to be built, the system should be able to anticipate such designs and be prepared to build a counter narrative. As explained in Figure 1, the cognitive dimension is also based on a knowledge of psychosociology and culture of specific populations or groups and rationality of various players. Cognitions also relate to cybernetics, soft power, morality, and use of religion.

Extension of Human Memory for Enlarging the Scope of Cognitive War through Artificial Intelligence

Capacity of human mind is getting extended through use of AI and other related developments. It may not be lethal in physical terms but can definitely impact the outcome of an engagement with 'Advantage Initiator'. This evolution has substantially helped in merging the physical, digital, and mental personas with a view to integrate strength of each of systems to enhance response capability. However, challenges faced by a responder entail; cognitive security of individuals; establishing and maintaining cognitive superiority; developing and certifying the performance of intelligent systems or AI systems intended to augment human labour improve the collective intelligence of human-autonomy teaming, along with improving complex and shared decision-making. Therefore, to develop capacity to respond to such challenges, training and a dedicated organisation would be needed to do continuous analysis of situation in a manner that even the smallest of oddity is not missed.

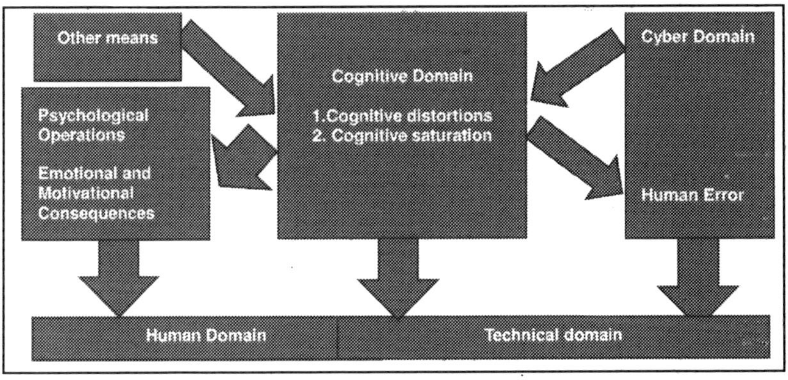

Figure 2: Interplay of human and technical domains

Tools for Cognitive Warfare

Over the last 20 years or so, the design of digital tools has taken into account the differences and characteristics of users and their integration of human users within the system. The intention is to control response of humans. The attacker's use of digital tools is meant to affect enemy's cognitive processes to cause cognitive distortions and cognitive saturation. Some of the consequences of such an action are as follows:

- Sowing seeds of doubt or consolidating existing uncertainties among the target group.
- Inducing human errors directly to affect the cyber network or the information it carries.
- Cognitive capabilities of target individuals are chronically altered.

This kind of warfare will assume new dimensions as we develop wearable technologies and connected objects, and in particular, the likely potential of the internalisation of these new tools with the appearance of the augmented soldier.

India: Influence Warfare by Forces Inimical to Bharat

India has been fighting cognitive warfare on many fronts, which include undeclared war waged by western Deep State (consisting of a clandestine network of members of the federal government of the US, especially the Federal Bureau of Investigation and Central Intelligence

Agency, working in conjunction with high-level financial and industrial entities, including non-governmental organisations like Open Society Foundations of George Soros, Rockefeller Foundation, and Ford Foundation, to exercise power alongside or within the elected US government) and nearer home unleashed by her two nuclear adversaries. In this connection, role of the western media has been quite dubious on themes like minority rights, democracy, and freedom of religion.[13]

Western Attempts. The attempts of the West to portray India as an intolerant country is reflected in a number of writings. Four of such reports/events are quoted here:

- In the Human Development Report titled 'Breaking the Gridlock: Reimagining Cooperation in a Polarised World' for 2023-24,[14] India is ranked 134 whereas countries like Saudi Arabia (40), the United Arab Emirates (17), Russia (56), Iran (78) and Bangladesh (129) are ahead of India.

- US Commission on International Religious Freedom-2024 says that India is experiencing a deteriorating and concerning trajectory for religious freedom. The report recommends that the US Department of State should designate India of particular concern. The report has been rejected by India.[15]

- World Press Freedom Index-Journalism under political pressure by Reporters without Borders has placed India at 159 out of 180 countries listed in the index, below Pakistan at 152 and Somalia at 145.[16]

- Response of 'Five Eyes Countries' of the alleged extra judicial killing of Khalistan protagonist Hardeep Singh Nijjar in Canada by blaming the Indian Government without producing even an iota of evidence. It is reflective of their effort to show that the government of India is intolerant of dissent and also creates doubt in the minds of minorities about the integrity of the country.

These reports/incidents show not only a bias but their deliberately engineered database with selective omissions is meant to project India in a bad light. Here, it also needs to be noted that these reports are meant to create confusion in the minds of the Indian public, especially those in India who suffer from a persecution syndrome.

Indicators of Chinese Cognitive war. In Aug 2021, the New Delhi based think tank Law and Society Alliance released a report titled 'Mapping Chinese Footprints and Influence Operations in India', highlighting how the Chinese Communist Party cultivates, funds, and sponsors institutions in India in fields like cinema, technology, fintech, and education, to shape public opinion suiting Beijing's interests.[17] A year later, in Aug 2022, a US-based think tank claimed that a Beijing-based AI company 'Speech Ocean' had collected voice samples from military-sensitive regions of India (like Jammu and Kashmir [J&K], and Punjab), probably with the view to use that data for their influence war.[18] Chinese state media outlets have also been operating social media accounts in multiple Indian languages. It has also come to light that they have been seeking active engagement with Indian journalists for certain pecuniary considerations. Modus operandi of Beijing has been to use AI to disseminate fake news and disinformation. This was underlined in a 2022 report by analytics firm Graphika, revealing a pro-Chinese operation running since 2019.[19] China is also adopting a strategy to woo India's neighbours and counter cultural affinity of Bharat with her neighbours. Also, Chinese cyber warfare operations against India intensified since the Galwan Valley clashes along the Indo-China border in May 2020.[20]

Pakistan's Influence Operations. Inter Services Public Relations (ISPR) serves as the central agency for conducting influence operations.[21] For these operations, ISPR recruits and trains young minds to engage in information warfare, especially against India. Thus, Pakistan has got an army of tech-savvy youth for the purpose.[22] This network, while disseminating praise for Pakistan's armed forces, conducted attacks against India (especially focused on alleged human rights abuses in J&K) through short news bulletins, screenshots of media articles, and photos. Graphika found that the network was coordinated by a Pakistan-based public relations firm with connections to the ISPR. In Oct 2022, a Sweden-based Nordic Research Monitoring Network report highlighted that Pakistan had set up a cyber army unit with Türkiye's help to shape public opinions and attack adversaries.[23] In this connection, it is highlighted that a unit of 6,000 Pakistani police officers was trained by Türkiye to counter Pakistan's negative perception using social media.[24] Several studies and reports have revealed that a vast network of Turkish influence operations across the world are developing. This holds special significance for India, as Türkiye actively supports Pakistan's Kashmir agenda on global platforms like the United Nations and the Organisation of Islamic Cooperation. Also, it needs to be noted that Ankara's strategic considerations and efforts in the information warfare domain are in sync with Pakistan.[25] Turkish media broadcasters TRT World and Anadolu Media work with Pakistani and Qatari counterparts, spreading disinformation about India, especially after the abrogation of Article 370, in the Gulf region and other Islamic countries.[26] According to reports from 2020, Türkiye had allocated funds for its intelligence agencies to radicalise Indian Muslims with the help of preachers recruited from surrendered Islamic State cadres.[27] For India, the size and diversity of the targeted population within the country magnifies the scale of the threat. To make matters worse, as high as 87 per cent of those sharing information from social media consider it true.[28] In Sep 2021, the Supreme Court of India expressed concern over the dissemination of inflammatory fake news by social media and web portals.[29] As such, in Dec 2022, India banned 104 YouTube channels and other social media platforms.[30] However, many platforms are still active. India needs to appreciate this diabolical plan and work out a counter strategy to call the bluff of forces inimical to India's growth because such inaccurate reports will have a cognitive effect on Bharat in the long-term.

Requirement of a National Information Strategy

As a part of a defensive strategy, India should aim to use non-military methods like intrigue, duplicity, and fraud before waging an armed conflict.[31] To enhance the effectiveness of the strategy, the technology needs to be leveraged. Two of the important elements which need to be developed in this connection are capability to observe the slightest deviation from normal and appraise its growth trajectory; secondly, enhance intelligence gathering and response capability to counter hybrid and integrated information war. It needs to be noted that it would call for a 'Whole-of-Government' approach during crisis contingencies. Some of the important initiatives India has/being taken are as follows:

- A new national cybersecurity policy (2024-26)[32], which is an update of the previous strategy promulgated in 2013.

- National Counter Ransomware Taskforce under the Ministry of Home Affairs was raised, which is taking a 'Whole-of-society' approach on the principles of 'Common but differentiated responsibility'.
- New cyber warfare units to counter online threats have been operationalised with mandate to strengthen the cybersecurity posture of the Indian Army.[33]
- Plans to amend the Information Technology rules 2021 to monitor and regulate user content of social media for being false or misleading by the Press Information Bureau.[34]

Conclusion

The cyber space is now all-encompassing and it affects the cognition domain. It is a fast-growing domain and their impact will cause a threat to national security. Thus, there is a need to build capacity to anticipate threats born of future technologies and start working on counter strategies, both defensive and proactive, so that a threat is nipped in the bud itself.

Endnotes

1 Bernard Claverie, François du Cluzel, "The Cognitive Warfare Concept", accessed 11 Doc 2024 https://www.act.nato.int/activities/cognitive-warfare/#:~:text=Cognitive%20Warfare%20 fooueses%20on %20attacking,non%2Dmilitary%20targets%20are%20involved

2 Kautilya, *Arthasastra,* 7.14.2: p 366, accessed 12 Dec 2024.

3 Sun Tzu, *Art of War*, Para 2 (Chapter-3), "Attack by Stratagem Page-10", Allandale Online Publishing 2 Park House (2000), accessed 14 Dec 2024.

4 Abhijit Singh, "China's "Three Warfares" and India", *Manohar Parikar Institute of Defence Studies and Analyses*, accessed 13 Dec 2024 https://idsa.in/system/files/jds_7_4_AbhijitSingh.pdf

5 Claverie, Cluzel, 'Cognitive Warfare'.

6 K Khan (2012), "Understanding information warfare and its relevance to Pakistan", *Strategic Studies*, 32(4), pp 138-159, accessed 15 Dec 2024.

7 Y Danyk, C Briggs (2023), "Modern Cognitive Operations and Hybrid Warfare", *Journal of Strategic Security*, 16(1), pp 35-50, accessed 16 Dec 2024.

8 James Giordano, PhD, MPhil, is the Chief of the Neuro-ethics Studies Program, Scholar-in-Residence, leads the Sub-Program in Military Medical

Ethics, and Co-director of the O'Neill-Pellegrino Program in Brain Science and Global Health Law and Policy at the Pellegrino Center for Clinical Bioethics; and is Professor in the Departments of Neurology and Biochemistry at Georgetown University Medical Center, Washington, DC, US.

[9] David Lee Goldfein, born 21 Dec 1959, is a retired US Air Force general who was the 21st Chief of Staff of the US Air Force.

[10] Lieutenant General Vincent Stewart was the Director of US DIA from 2015-19.

[11] General Gilles Desclaux is a retired Air Force General of French army, presently working on how cognitive technologies and AI could make the military decision cycle works better and faster.

[12] DS Hartley III, KO Jobson (2021), Cognitive Superiority: Information to Power, New-York (NY, USA): Springer.

[13] Prema Gandhi (Aug 2020), "Western Media Bias against India", *Vivekananda International Foundation*, accessed 20 Dec 2024 https://www.vifindia.org/article/2020/august/15/western-media-bias-against-india%20

[14] Human Development Report 2023, *UNDP*, accessed 21 Dec 2024 https://www.drishtiias.com/printpdf/human-development-report-2023-24#:~:text=According%20to%20the%202023%2D24,Nations%20Develo pment%20Programme%20(UNDP)

[15] "India rejects US panel's malicious religious freedom report, offers advise", *India Today*, accessed 16 Dec 2024 https://www.indiatoday.in/story

[16] The Hindu Data Team, "India's press freedom has rapidly declined in recent years: Data", 15 May 2024, accessed 23 Dec 2024 https://www.thehindu.com/data/india-press-freedom-has-rapidly-declined-in-recent-years-data/article68160411.ece

[17] Law and Society Alliance New Delhi, "Mapping Chinese Footprints and Influence Operation in India", 2021, accessed 21 Dec 2024.

[18] C Balding, A Sinha, and J Wu (2022), "Chinese Military Civil Fusion Firms: The Case of Speech Ocean Improving Activity Obfuscation, Pursuing State Interests, Engaging in Third Country Data Gathering", New Kite Data Labs, accessed 25 Dec 2024.

[19] Graphika (2023), "Deepfake, It till You Make It - Pro-Chinese Actors Promote AI-Generated Video Footage of Fictitious People in Online Influence Operation", accessed 16 Dec 2024 https://public-assets.graphika.com/reports/graphika-report-deepfake-it-till-you-make-it.pdf

[20] M Kaushik, "200% rise in cyberattacks from China in a month; India tops hit list post Galwan face-off", *Business Today*, Jun 2020, accessed 21 Dec 2024 https://www.businesstoday.in/technology/news/story/200-percent-rise-in-

cyberattacks-from-china-in-a-month-india-tops-hit-list-post-galwan-face-off-262195-2020-06-24

[21] D Malhotra, "Inter-Services Public Relations (ISPR) Assessment of the Pakistan Military's Discreet Propaganda Factory Post-1990", *Journal of Defence Studies*, 2020, 14(4), pp 37-57, accessed 16 Dec 2024.

[22] Ibid.

[23] A Bozkurt, "Turkey helped Pakistan set up a secret cyber army for influence operation against US, India", *Nordic Monitor,* Oct 2022, accessed 20 Dec 2024 https://nordicmonitor.com/2022/10/turkey-helped-pakistan-set-up-a-secret-cyber-army-for-influence-operation-against-us-india/

[24] Ibid.

[25] M Quamar, "The geopolitics of OIC activism on Kashmir", *Financial Express*, Jul 2021, accessed 16 Dec 2024 https://www.financialexpress.com/business/defence-the-geopolitics-of-oic-activism-on-kashmir-2288676/

[26] S Bhatt, "Pakistani propaganda on Kashmir has a new launchpad – Erdogan's Turkey", *The Print*, Jun 2022, accessed 18 Dec 2024 https://theprint.in/opinion/pakistani-propaganda-on-kashmir-has-.a-new-launchpad-erdogans-turkey/1003485/

[27] European Parliament, "Turkish funding for anti-India extremism", *European Parliament archives*, Jan 2021, accessed 19 Dec 2024 https://www.europarl.europa.eu/doceo/document/E-9-2021-000549_EN.htm

[28] "Despite Misinformation Concern 54% Indians derive factual information from social media, reveals OUP study", *Live Mint*, Jun 2022, accessed 12 Dec 2024 https://www.livemint.com/news/india/despite-misinformation-concern-54-indians-derive-factual-information-from-social-media-reveals-oup-study-11656420664780.html

[29] "Supreme Court expresses grave concern over fake news on social media and YouTube", *Times of India*, Sep 2021, accessed 13 Dec 2024 https://timesofindia.indiatimes.com/india/supreme-court-expresses-grave-concern-over-.web-portals-spreading-fake-news/articleshow/85858300.cms

[30] Abhik Sengupta, "Govt blocks 104 YouTube channels, several social media accounts for threatening national security", *India Today*, Dec 2022, accessed 16 Dec 2024 https://www.indiatoday.in/technology/news/story/govt-blocks-104-youtube-channels-social-media-accounts-threatening-national-security-fake-news-2312595-2022-12-23

[31] SA Philip, "Gen Naravane's Chanakya neeti for future wars will require India to spend money smartly", *The Print*, Mar 2020, accessed 18 Dec 2024 https://theprint.in/opinion/brahmastra/gen-naravanes-chanakya-neeti-for-future-wars-will-require-india-to-spend-money-judiciously/376449/

[32] "Digital and Cyber Security Strategy", accessed 16 Dec 2024 https://treasury.gov.au/sites/default/files/2024-07/digital-and-cyber-security-strategy-2024-2026.pdf

[33] "Indian Army raising new units to counter China, Pak in cyber warfare: Report", *ANI*, Apr 2023, accessed 18 Dec 2024 https://www.hindustantimes.com/india-news/indian-army-raising-new-units-to-counter-china-pakistan-in-cyber-warfare-reports-101682581848934.html

[34] S Singh, "The Battle Beyond the Frontlines: Social Media Driven Information Warfare in the India-Pakistan Context", *CENJOWS*, Jul 2023, accessed 21 Dec 2024 https://cenjows.in/the-battle-beyond-the-frontlines-social-media-driven-information-warfare-in-the-india-pakistan-context/

Bibliography

A Cole, H Le Guyader (2020), *Cognitive : a 6th Domain of Operations*, Norfolk (VA, USA): Innovation Hub, NATO ACT Edition

B Claverie (2021), *Des théories pour la cognition: Différences et Complémentarité des Paradigmes*, Paris (France): L'Harmattan

Bernard Claverie, François du Cluzel, 'The Cognitive Warfare Concept', https://innovationhub-act.org/wp-content/uploads/2023/12/CW-article-Claverie-du-Cluzel-final_0.pdf

Divyanshu Jindal, *The War on Conscience: India in the Age of Cognitive Warfare*, published by India Foundation as a Monograph-01 in Sep 2023

DS Hartley III, KO Jobson (2021), *Cognitive Superiority: Information to Power,* New-York (NY, USA): Springer

J Remanjon (2021), 'Le cerveau sera-t-il l'ultime champ de bataille', *Revue de la Défense Nationale*

K Kelly (2011), *What technology wants*, New York (NY, USA): Penguin Books. ISBN: 978-0143120179

K Underwood (2017), 'Cognitive Warfare Will Be Deciding Factor in Battle: Lt. Gen. Stewart's remarks at DoDIIS17', *Signal, The cyber edge* https://www.afcea.org/content/cognitive-warfare- will-be-deciding-factor battle. https://youtu.be/Nm-IVjRjLD4

L Devilliers (2021), *Désinformation: les Armes de l'Intelligence Artificielle*, Pour La Science, 523, pp 26-33

MC Roco, WS Bainbridge (2003), *Converging Technologies for Improving Human Performance: Nanotechnology, Biotechnology, Information Technology and Cognitive Science*, New-York (NY, USA): Springer-Verlag

T Wall (2010), 'US Psychological Warfare and Civilian Targeting', *Peace Review* 22, 3: pp 288–294

Evolution of Operational Art and Strategy: Application in Modern Conflicts

Major General (Dr) SB Asthana, SM, VSM (Retd)

"In contemporary conflicts, where tactical actions can carry strategic weight and perception often rivals firepower, operational art must embrace both the cognitive and physical dimensions"

Abstract

This article traces the evolution of operational art and strategy from classical foundations to their contemporary manifestations in modern conflicts. Beginning with Kautilya and Sun Tzu's insights on psychological dislocation and deception, it examines how Clausewitz, Jomini, and Soviet theorists shaped the intellectual and doctrinal framework of operational art. The study highlights the impact of industrialisation, World Wars, and the Cold War in transforming strategic thought, leading to concepts such as Blitzkrieg, Deep Operations, deterrence, and proxy wars. It further explores post–Cold War revolutions in military affairs, hybrid and multi-domain warfare, cyber and space operations, and the role of artificial intelligence. Through case studies of the Russia–Ukraine War, Israel–Hamas conflict, and India's campaigns, the article underscores the challenges of integrating military and non-military instruments, narrative warfare, and conflict termination. It concludes that future operational art must balance classical principles with innovation to ensure strategic advantage in a volatile multipolar world.

Introduction

Operational art and strategy form the connective tissue between military tactics and political objectives. Their evolution reflects centuries of doctrinal refinement, from Kautilya's *Arthashastra* (The science of wealth) and Sun Tzu's Art of War to modern doctrines of

This article has been reproduced from the USI Strategic Year Book 2025.

hybrid, cyber, and multi-domain warfare. In today's dynamic security environment, characterised by durable disorder, hybrid threats, and blurred boundaries between peace and war, operational art has become more relevant than ever.

Warfare has continuously evolved in scope, intensity, and character with technological advancements, political shifts, and doctrinal innovation. The industrial revolution revolutionised combat with enhanced firepower, mobility, and communication, leading to the emergence of operational art as a distinct level of war between tactics and strategy. In the 20th and 21st Centuries, besides technological advances, new domains such as cyber and space, and the rise of hybrid threats have further expanded its complexity. Operational art now represents the vital link between tactical actions and strategic outcomes, providing the framework for translating military power into decisive political results.

The concepts of operational art and strategy, once confined to linear battles and state-centric wars, have expanded in scope to encompass hybrid warfare, cyber operations, and information dominance. While Clausewitz's dictum of war as a continuation of politics remains valid, the methods of conducting war have undergone radical transformation. This article examines the evolution of operational art and strategy from their classical roots to their contemporary manifestations, emphasising the dynamics of modern conflicts.

Historical Foundations of Operational Thought

Kautilya and Sun Tzu.

- Kautilya[1] had emphasised psychological dislocation and collapse of the adversary through strategic design rather than brute force, foreshadowing modern ideas of perception management and cognitive warfare, which can be claimed as historic beginning of operational thoughts.
- Similarly, Sun Tzu[2] famously asserted that the highest excellence lies in breaking the enemy's resistance without fighting, highlighting deception, morale, and anticipation as decisive factors. Classical Foundations of Strategy.

- The western literature indicates that the intellectual foundation of operational art and strategy was laid by Antoine-Henri Jomini and Carl von Clausewitz. Jomini[3] advocated systematic principles of manoeuvre, interior lines, and decisive points. Clausewitz[4] conceptualised the 'Fog and Friction' of war and emphasised it to be viewed as an extension of politics by other means. Their contrasting perspectives shaped the intellectual bedrock of operational art. Their insights continue to influence doctrines worldwide.

Evolution through Industrial Age and Major Wars

Initial Contours of Operational Art. The late 19th and early 20th Centuries witnessed the industrialisation of warfare. The First World War revealed the limitations of attritionist approaches, where immense destruction produced stalemate. The strategic stalemate despite tactical innovations, created the demand for a new level of military thinking—operational art. Soviet theorists such as Alexander Svechin and Mikhail Tukhachevsky formalised the concept of the 'Operational level of war', bridging tactics and strategy, articulated Deep Battle,[5] which connected tactical actions to strategic effects across depth and time. This became the essence of operational art.

Napoleonic Wars. The Napoleonic era marked the beginning of operational manoeuvre warfare, as large armies manoeuvred over vast spaces, integrating logistics and strategy in unprecedented ways. Napoleon's ability to align operational manoeuvre with political goals added to the foundation of modern operational art.

World War II. Blitzkrieg and Deep Operations. In World War II, the Germans introduced Blitzkrieg, integrating tanks, air power, and mechanised infantry to achieve rapid breakthroughs. They epitomised speed, mass, and deception, exploiting vulnerabilities to shatter cohesion. Conversely, the Soviets developed Deep Operations, emphasising depth, overwhelming the enemy by echeloned and sustained offensive operations. The United States (US) conceptualised Air Land Battle, while India's 1971 Eastern campaign reflected the decisive application of manoeuvre warfare. All these approaches exemplified the maturation of operational art.

Contemporary Theories of War

Defining Operational Art Post World Wars. By the end of world wars the definition of Operational art being the skillful linkage of means, ways, and ends was well conceived. It involves identifying the adversary's centre of gravity, orchestrating firepower and manoeuvre, and structuring campaigns through decisive points, sequencing, and shaping the battlefield. It emphasises not only physical outcomes but also psychological effects—seeking to unhinge the enemy's decision-making and will to resist.

Attritionist Approach. Attrition seeks to degrade adversary capacity through superior firepower and sustained destruction and endurance. While effective in certain conditions (e.g., Kargil 1999), it is costly in lives and resources. Its relevance diminishes in an era of battlefield transparency, precision munitions, and drones—evident in Russia's struggles in Ukraine.

Manoeuvrist Approach. Manoeuvre warfare is focused on speed, shock, and dislocation to collapse cohesion and will, rather than simply destroying forces. seeks to collapse enemy cohesion psychologically and physically through rapid, unexpected actions. The Inchon landings and India's 1971 Eastern campaign illustrate its success. Modern doctrine blends attrition with manoeuvre.

Modern conflicts increasingly combine attrition (e.g., long-range fires, drone warfare) with manoeuvre (mobility, tempo, psychological shock), making hybrid applications the norm.

Transformations in Operational Art during Cold War and Beyond

Strategy under Nuclear Shadow. The advent of nuclear weapons[6] redefined strategic thought. Theories of deterrence, dissuasion and mutually assured destruction dominated strategic discourse, prevented great-power kinetic conflict. Conventional operational art, however, adapted to limited wars and proxy conflicts.

Guerrilla and Revolutionary Warfare. The Cold War also saw the proliferation of asymmetric strategies, such as Mao Zedong's 'People's War', and the Viet Cong's guerrilla campaigns. These conflicts demonstrated that political will and protracted insurgency could offset superior conventional operational art.

Revolution in Military Affairs (RMA). The 1991 Gulf War epitomised the RMA, marked by precision-guided munitions, stealth technology, and real-time command and control. The US demonstrated how technology-driven operational art could achieve 'Shock and Awe'.

Operations Other Than War. Humanitarian interventions, peacekeeping, and counterterrorism in Somalia, Bosnia, and Kosovo illustrated the broadening of strategy beyond traditional battlefields. Operational art now included political sensitivities, media management, and coalition dynamics.

21st Century Conflicts: Hybrid and Multi-Domain Warfare

The Global War on Terror. Post-9/11 conflicts in Afghanistan and Iraq showcased the challenges of applying traditional operational art to counterinsurgency.[7] The US Army's FM 3-24 doctrine emphasised population-centric approaches, but strategic fatigue highlighted the limits of prolonged interventions.

Hybrid Warfare. Conflicts in Georgia (2008), Ukraine (2014–present), and Syria revealed the rise of hybrid[8] warfare, blending conventional forces, irregulars, cyber operations, and disinformation campaigns. Russia's 'Gerasimov Doctrine' emphasised the fusion of kinetic and non-kinetic tools. Russia's Crimea campaign, China's 'Incremental Encroachment Strategy'[9] in the South China Sea, and Pakistan's proxy strategies against India exemplify this model.

Fourth-Generation and Unrestricted Warfare. The lone wolf insurgent/terror operations by terrorist groups/non state actors have added on to Fourth-Generation Warfare. The 'War amongst the people' concept shows how tactical events can have strategic impact. Modern conflicts emphasise indirect instruments—economic coercion, lawfare, media manipulation, and information dominance. Chinese 'Three Warfare Strategy' namely media, psychological and legal warfare and 'Strategy of Three Evils'[10] namely terrorism, separatism and religious extremism are significant to note. Chinese indicated no bounds and no rules in their 'Unrestricted Warfare'.

Multi-Domain Operations (MDO). Modern operational art now integrates land, air, sea, cyber, and space domains. The US, North Atlantic Treaty Organization, and China have developed doctrines for MDO,[11] where victory is achieved by dominance across interconnected domains.

Technology as a Force Multiplier

Cyber Warfare. Cyber operations have emerged as a critical strategic tool. Stuxnet[12] (2010) demonstrated how cyber weapons could achieve strategic objectives without kinetic conflict. Nations now view cyberspace as a decisive operational domain.

Artificial Intelligence and Autonomy. The integration of Artificial Intelligence (AI), drones, and autonomous systems is reshaping operational planning. Precision targeting, predictive analytics, and unmanned swarms enhance both offensive and defensive strategies.

Space as a Strategic Frontier. With the establishment of the US Space Force and China's anti-satellite capabilities, space warfare has become integral to modern operational art, influencing communications, navigation, and intelligence.

Current Strategic Theories

Network-Centric Warfare. Developed in the 1990s, network-centric warfare[13] emphasises information superiority and interconnected forces. By compressing decision cycles, it enhances operational tempo.

Gray-Zone Operations. China's strategy in the South China Sea and Russia's actions in Crimea reflect grey-zone tactics, where incremental gains are pursued below the threshold of conventional war, challenging traditional notions of strategy.

Resurgence of Proxy Wars/Shadow Wars. From Yemen to Ukraine, proxy conflicts highlight how states employ local actors, private military companies, mercenaries, legions and militias to achieve strategic depth without direct confrontation.

Operational Art in Modern Context

Components of Operational Art. Operational art involves synchronising military and non-military instruments to achieve strategic objectives with minimal cost and within time constraints. Key components in modern times include operational factors (time, space, force), functions (command, intelligence, logistics, fires, protection), and principles (Centre of Gravity, culmination points, sequencing).

Operational Objectives and Core Elements. Clausewitz emphasised three paths to defeat an adversary: destroying forces, occupying territory, or breaking will. Accordingly, operational objectives can firstly be force oriented involving destruction of reserves, tying down critical forces, secondly, Terrain related like seizing vital ground or communication hubs or infrastructure-focused crippling logistics, networks, or digital systems and thirdly, psychological- inducing paralysis in enemy leadership and morale. Supporting elements include fire and manoeuvre, intelligence, deception, reserves, and logistics, all synchronised to shape tempo and exploit opportunities.

Proliferation of Low-Intensity Conflicts. Since 1945, most conflicts have been low-intensity, often involving great-power participation directly or indirectly. Counterinsurgency, proxy wars, and hybrid threats dominated global scene till few recent wars.

Expansion of War Domains. From land, sea, and air, modern conflict now encompasses space, cyber, and the cognitive domain. Command, control, communications, computers, intelligence, surveillance, and reconnaissance networks, drones, and precision targeting redefine operational possibilities.

Durable Disorder[14] and Strategic Competition. Institutions are weakening, and non-state actors are weaponised by states. Economic, political, technological, and informational wars now coexist with kinetic operations.

The Cognitive and Information Dimension

- **Media and Narrative Warfare**. Modern conflicts are fought under global media glare. Narratives around Galwan, Gaza, or Ukraine shape legitimacy and will. Operational art integrates strategic communication with kinetic action.

- **Influence Operations and Perception Management**. China's Three Warfares, Russia's disinformation, and Pakistan's narrative-building highlight how perception warfare can be decisive.

Conflict Termination: Strategy beyond the Battlefield

Conflict Termination and Exit Strategies. As Liddell Hart[15] warned, the objective of war must be a better peace. Operational art must therefore envision conflict termination—defining achievable political aims, sequencing campaigns to avoid exhaustion, and integrating diplomatic and informational instruments to secure favourable outcomes. The US withdrawals from Vietnam and Afghanistan underline the risks of neglecting this phase.

Principles of Conflict Termination. Conflict termination is about shaping a favourable peace, not merely winning battles. Liddell Hart stressed that without envisioning the post-war order, victory may become pyrrhic.

Ingredients of Victory. Achievable political objectives, defined end-state, degradation of adversary potential, population disillusionment, and avoidance of prohibitive casualties are essential.

Exit Policies. As seen in US withdrawals from Vietnam and Afghanistan, exit strategies must be integral to operational art. Stabilisation, reconciliation, or status quo acceptance often replaces outright victory.

Application of Operational Art in few Modern Conflicts

Russia-Ukraine War (2022–present)

- The conflict illustrates both the failures and adaptations of operational art. Russia's initial offensive exhibited a turning move[16] to turn the defences of Donbass region but it got stalled due to logistical shortcomings, and miscalculating the potential of

Ukrainian resistance in fighting from built up areas, aided by modern western technology, intelligence, surveillance, and reconnaissance and top attack projectiles.

- However, in subsequent attrition warfare, after adopting a viable defence line, drone usage, missile campaigns underlining the fusion of old and new operational approaches, Russians could turn the tide in their favour capturing over 20 per cent of Ukrainian territory and keeping the momentum and tempo of operations till now. Of late, while Russians have a clarity in aim and strategy, the western adversaries are struggling with unclear aim, strategy with no idea of end state and exit strategy.

Israel–Hamas Conflict

- The Israel-Hamas-Iran War, sparked by Hamas's 2023 dastardly terror attack and escalating to 2025, reveals critical flaws in the parties' operational art and strategy. Israel's intelligence-driven, precision, multi-front strikes dismantled Hamas and Hezbollah's infrastructure but lacked a viable end state and post-conflict governance plan, risking Hamas's resurgence amid Gaza's humanitarian devastation, global criticism and isolation. This 'Mowing The Grass' approach, reliant on airpower and AI targeting with impractical political endgame of 'Greater Israel',[17] exposed a bias for short-term action over sustainable deterrence, exacerbating civilian casualties in dense urban terrain and inviting accusations of disproportionality and genocide.
- Hamas's guerrilla tactics, using hostages as human shields, embedding in civilian areas, and leveraging tunnels for surprise incursions, ensured limited tactical resilience but invited crushing Israeli retaliation, sacrificing lives without advancing Palestinian statehood, barely ensuring its ideological survival at immense human cost. Iran's proxy-centric 'Axis of Resistance' strategy, arming groups to encircle Israel, faltered as depleted proxies like the Houthis and Iraqi militias offered negligible support during direct 2025 clashes, failed to counter Israeli pre-emption, highlighting Tehran's loss of control and exposure of its nuclear ambitions to devastating strikes, ultimately eroding its regional deterrence without achieving existential goals against Israel.

❑ Overall, these misapplications of operational art—prioritising ideological vendettas over pragmatic exits—have transformed a localised conflict into a quagmire of mutual exhaustion.

Indian Experience in Application of Operational Art

The 1971 India–Pakistan War. India's Eastern campaign remains a classic case of operational brilliance. Superior synergy among political, military, and diplomatic instruments; focus on Dhaka as the centre of gravity; and synchronised army–navy–air force operations ensured rapid victory within 13 days. Strategic offensive on Eastern Front and strategic defence on Western Front ensured strategic balance generating adequate combat ratios.

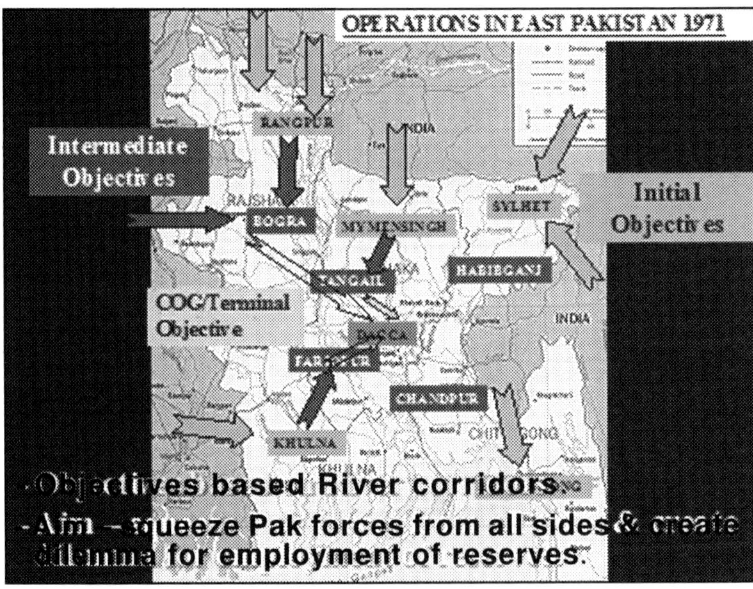

Map 1 (Source: Author)

Kargil War 1999. By contrast, Operation Vijay was attrition-oriented, relying on heavy artillery and high force ratios to dislodge entrenched Pakistani troops. The campaign succeeded but at great cost, highlighting limitations of attrition warfare, when manoeuvre is restricted by terrain and other geopolitical reasons.

Image 1: 155 mm FH-77B Field Howitzer in Kargil[18]

Operation Sindoor. Operation Sindoor[19] marked a watershed in India's strategic doctrine, launched after the Pakistan-sponsored Pahalgam terror attack of Apr 2025. It showcased India's shift from restraint to calibrated offensive action to integrated military precision strikes using all instruments of national power to include diplomatic, economic, military, technological and informational tools. By degrading terror infrastructure, suspending the Indus Water Treaty, and leveraging indigenous technologies like Akashteer and *Système de Croisière Autonome à Longue Portée* (French for 'Long-Range Autonomous Cruise Missile System'), India demonstrated comprehensive national power and *Atmanirbhar* (Self-reliant) capability. By carefully applying principles of operational art—clear end-state, centre of gravity identification, surprise, deception, escalation control and exit strategy—India executed multi-domain precision strikes while avoiding a full-scale war. The operation exposed gaps in information warfare, reaffirmed the role of drones, tri-service integration, while establishing a new deterrence doctrine: terrorism will be treated as an act of war

Image 2: Akasteer Surface to Air Missile[20]

Operational Art in India's Current Context

India's strategic environment—with collusive threats from nuclear-armed China and Pakistan—demands refined operational art. Key dimensions include:

- **Conflict Management and Deterrence**. Proactive concepts for limited war, preventive deployments against China's salami-slicing, and credible nuclear deterrence posture.
- **Force Projection and Regional Influence**. Protecting Indian Ocean sea lanes, regional peacekeeping, and power projection by the navy.
- **Counter-Terrorism and Insurgency**. Intelligence-driven, flexible operations (e.g., Operation Rakshak in Kashmir) highlight operational art beyond conventional war.
- **Technology and Modernisation**. Integration of drones, cyber, space assets, and AI-enabled systems into operational design.
- **Non-Kinetic and Influence Operations**. Cyber warfare, psychological operations, and media narratives increasingly shape outcomes.
- **Humanitarian and Disaster Relief**. Rapid deployments during the 2004 Tsunami and 2015 Nepal earthquake and many disasters subsequently showcase operational art in non-combat contexts.

Contemporary Challenges in Operational Art

Compressed Time and Space. Urbanisation and advanced surveillance have reduced operational depth and possibility of achieving surprise.

Multi-Domain Environment. Future campaigns require simultaneous dominance across land, air, sea, cyber, and space. Need for simultaneity and non-linearity of operations.

Durable Disorder. Non-state actors, proxy wars, and hybrid threats complicate operational design.

Information and Narrative Warfare. Media and perception often shape legitimacy as much as battlefield outcomes.

Technology Dependence. Reliance on AI and networks makes modern militaries vulnerable to cyber disruption.

Ethical and Legal Dimensions. Autonomous weapons and hybrid operations raise challenges under international law. Unacceptable civilian casualties and collateral damages in Gaza leading to condemnation of Israel is a case in point.

Civil-Military Integration. Modern strategy requires whole-of-nation approaches, incorporating diplomacy, economics, and information.

Escalation Risks. Multi-domain warfare increases the chances of inadvertent escalation, especially with nuclear powers.

The Future of Operational Art and Strategy

Multi-Domain Operations. Operational art will continue to evolve under the pressures of great-power competition and technological innovation. The challenge for strategists lies in balancing traditional military power with adaptive, innovative approaches that integrate new technologies while addressing political realities. Future conflicts are likely to feature some of the underlined characters. Future operations will demand simultaneous dominance across land, sea, air, cyber, and space. The US MDO 2028 concept envisions integrated deterrence and synchronised campaigns, combining nuclear, conventional, cyber, and space assets.

Artificial Intelligence and Autonomy. AI-enabled decision-making with reduced human intervention, autonomous drones, and predictive analytics will transform tempo and scale. The ethical implications of autonomous lethal systems pose challenges. Strategic competition in the cognitive domain, where narrative control may prove as decisive as battlefield outcomes.

Resilience and Adaptabllity. Future operational art will emphasise resilience in the face of cyber disruptions, hybrid threats, and narrative warfare. Strategists must anticipate escalation pathways and design flexible campaigns.

Conclusion

The evolution of operational art reflects an ongoing dialogue between classical wisdom and modern innovation. From Kautilya and Sun Tzu to Blitzkrieg, hybrid warfare, and multi-domain operations, the essence remains constant: aligning military means with political ends. In contemporary conflicts, where tactical actions can carry strategic weight and perception often rivals firepower, operational art must embrace both the cognitive and physical dimensions.

In the 21st Century, the decisive edge will belong to those who can synthesize traditional principles with emerging innovations, leveraging both kinetic and non-kinetic means to achieve national objectives.

In the Indian context, its application extends beyond conventional war to deterrence, counterinsurgency, technology-enabled operations, and humanitarian response. Success depends not only on superior combat power but also on psychological dislocation, narrative control, and innovative leadership. As India faces a volatile neighbourhood and rapid technological change, operational art will be central to shaping campaigns, deterring adversaries, and ensuring strategic advantage.

Endnotes

[1] Kautilya, *The Arthshatra*, Translated by LN Rangarajan, 1992, Gurgaon: Penguin Book, India.

[2] Sun Tzu, *The Art of War*, Translated by Lionel Giles, 1910, Project Gutenberg, United Kingdom: Luzac and Co.

[3] AH Jomini, "Summary of the Art of War", 1838, *US Army,* Translated by Craighill and Ftendell, 1862.

[4] C von Clausewitz, *On War*, 1832, Translated by JJ Graham JJ, (1874-1st edition), 1909, London reprinting.

[5] D M Glantz, *Soviet Military Operational Art: In Pursuit of Deep Battle*, First Edition, 1991, London: Taylor and Francis, London.

[6] L Freedman, *The Evolution of Nuclear Strategy*, 1981, London: Palgrave Macmillan.

[7] Petraeus, D. et al, (2006), FM 3-24 Counterinsurgency, U.S. Army/Marine Corps.

[8] D Petraeus et al, *FM 3-24 Counterinsurgency*, 2006, US Army/Marine Corps.

[9] SB Asthana, "Chinese active defence strategy translates to incremental encroachment strategy: what should India do?", *Economic Times*, 14 Aug 2022, accessed 10 May 2025 https://government.economictimes.indiatimes.com/news/governance/chinese-active-defence-strategy-translates-to-incremental-encroachment-strategy-what-should-india-do/93537035

[10] SB Asthana, "Decoding Chinese Strategy of Combating Three Evils", *Strategic Year Book, USI of India*, Vij Books: India, pp 75-83, 12 Jun 2019, accessed 10 Sep 2025 https://asthanawrites.org/2019/06/12/decoding-chinese-strategy-of-combating-three-evils/.

[11] TRADOC, "The U.S. Army in Multi-Domain Operations 2028", *US Army Training and Doctrine Command*, US Army, Washington DC, 2018, accessed 10 Sep 2025.

[12] JR Lindsay, "Stuxnet and the Limits of Cyber Warfare", *Security Studies*, 22(3), pp 365-404, 2013, accessed 10 Sep 2025 https://doi.org/10.1080/09636412.2013.816122.

[13] DS Alberts, JJ Garstka, and FP Stein, *Network Centric Warfare: Developing and Leveraging Information Superiority*, CCRP, 1999, Washington DC: National Defence University Press.

[14] Sean McFate, *The New Rules of War: Victory in the Age of Durable Disorder*, 2019, New York: Harper Collin and Blackstone Publishing.

[15] BH Liddell Hart, *Strategy*, 1967, New York: Praeger.

[16] SB Asthana, "Evaluating Strategies and Operational Art Applied by Parties to Russia-Ukraine War", *Kootneeti*, 19 Apr 2022, accessed 10 Sep 2025 https://thekootneeti.in/2022/04/19/evaluating-strategies-and-operational-art-applied-by-parties-to-russia-ukraine-war/.

[17] SB Asthana, "Strategies and Operational Art in one Year of Conflict: Israel vs Iran and Proxies", *Modern Diplomacy (EU)*, 08 Oct 2024, accessed 10 Sep 2025 https://moderndiplomacy.eu/2024/10/08/strategies-and-operational-art-in-one-year-of-conflict-israel-vs-iran-and-proxies/.

[18] Reddit. "Indian Army's Haubits FH77 Bofors Howitzer." *r/IndianDefense*, Reddit, April 18, 2025, accessed 10 Sep 2025, https://www.reddit.com/r/IndianDefense/comments/1ja9272/indian_armys_haubits_fh77_bofors_howitzer/.

[19] SB Asthana, "Operation Sindoor: The blending of operational art, kinetic force and strategic messaging", *Economic Times,* 15 Jul 2025, accessed 10 Sep 2025 https://government.economictimes.indiatimes.com/blog/operation-sindoor-indias-strategic-response-to-terrorism-and-hybrid-warfare/122476601.

[20] Shraddha Pandey, "Know all about Indian 'Iron Dome' Akashteer, the indigenous Air Defence System that stopped the wave of Pakistani missiles and drones sent to target Indian cities, May 9, 2025, accessed 10 Sep 2025, https://www.opindia.com/2025/05/akashteer-indigenous-air-defence-system-pakistan-to-target-indian-cities-with-missiles-and-drones/

Warfare Reimagined: Integrating Artificial Intelligence into India's Armed Forces and Defence Industry

Major General Sanjeev Chowdhry (Retd)
Mr Vinayak Sharma

Abstract

This article examines the transformative role of Artificial Intelligence (AI) in modern warfare and its strategic implications for the Indian Armed Forces. It traces AI's evolution from early theoretical concepts to its integration into military applications, including intelligence, surveillance and reconnaissance, autonomous systems, electronic warfare, and training simulations. The core focus is on two foundational pillars: military leadership development and defence innovation. It highlights the urgent need to embed AI education across all ranks to build technologically literate military leadership capable of leveraging AI-driven systems effectively. Simultaneously, it calls for structural reform in India's defence innovation ecosystem to support indigenous AI development through pre-prototype funding, simplified procurement, and private sector empowerment. Drawing lessons from ongoing conflicts in Ukraine, the Middle East, and the Red Sea, the article argues that India must align operational preparedness with industrial capability. Only through synergising leadership readiness and a reformed innovation landscape can India build a credible, future-ready AI-enabled defence force.

Introduction

By its very nature, a battle is an extremely chaotic environment, with more than half a hundred variables or components determining its outcome. These components come in the form of the soldiers, their training, the weapons employed, topography, larger strategic goals of the belligerents, tactics, and logistics, among others. The list is endless,

---

This article has been reproduced from the USI Strategic Year Book 2025.

and armies worldwide, from time immemorial, have sought to engineer an edge by constantly evolving the variables. From swords and spears to rifles and bayonets, to tanks and aircraft, to cyber and space domains, all have substantially altered the nature of warfare. To meet the demand for constant innovation, the military employs every technological advancement sooner rather than later. For example, the Wright Brothers' invention of the aircraft led to its first use during the Italo-Turkish War, when an Italian pilot made a one-hour reconnaissance flight over enemy positions in Libya.[1] In other cases, technological advancements are borne of nations' need to improve their military might. This has been the case with radar, the internet, and even the microwave. Thus, it is with Artificial Intelligence (AI).[2]

This was theorised initially by mathematician Alan Turing, the English mathematician and computer scientist, whose work in cracking the German encryption device Enigma was extensively used by the Nazis in encrypting wartime communication during World War 2, resulting in the laying the foundation for modern AI.[3] After the war, in 1950, Turing published *Computing Machinery and Intelligence*, which introduced the 'Turing Test', a theoretical means of determining if a machine could exhibit intelligent behaviour indistinguishable from a human.[4] His thesis has metamorphosed into the most substantial defence-related innovation since the atomic bomb. During the Cold War, the United States (US) began tinkering with using AI in warfare through the Defense Advanced Research Projects Agency. The Agency was created in response to the launch of the Soviet satellite Sputnik in 1957 to ensure that the US did not face another 'Strategic technical surprise'.[5] Thus, began the 'Space Race' and the application of AI to gain an edge in combat.

Fast-forward to the 21st Century, the seeds of the 60s have come to bear fruit. To the point that Unmanned Aerial Vehicles (UAVs) have become a significant component of the ongoing Russo-Ukrainian War, the latest iteration of the Israel-Hamas conflict, and the Red Sea Crisis. Be it Intelligence, Surveillance, and Reconnaissance (ISR) or elimination of targets (both large and small), the UAVs, through the use of AI data sets and the ability to process large amounts of data through machine learning, have provided a cheap alternative to a human soldier. Furthermore, the AI umbrella spans across technologies and platforms, this includes autonomous systems, swarm drones, among others. In the three conflicts mentioned above, these technologies have displayed the ability to alter the battlefield and the larger theatre of war substantially.[6,7]

Therefore, it behoves the Indian Armed Forces to learn from the abovementioned conflicts to maintain pace in a fast-changing world marked by an ever-evolving geopolitical climate. This article is written in an attempt to identify the usage of AI in improving in-field decision-making and combat readiness of the armed forces. Moreover, the advancements cannot be achieved by the tri-services acting alone. They require the backing of the defence manufacturing industry, which itself needs institutional support from the government and, more importantly, fundamental policy changes to realise its nascent potential.

How Artificial Intelligence Works

AI has become a notable conversation topic requiring a deeper understanding of its inner workings. It is often assumed that AI is an automated system. However, it is not so. AI, in its fully developed form, is a substantially evolved version of an automated system. It is rather an autonomous system. There is a stark difference between the two. An automated system is a computer program based on a clear 'If-then-else' rule. It is a deterministic code. If all external factors (or inputs) remain unchanged, then the output will always be the same (except if something fails). Conversely, when given a set of inputs, an autonomous system makes guesses about the best possible course of action. In such a system, the responses will vary and show a range of responses.

Human intelligence generally follows a sequence known as the perception–cognition–action information processing loop, in which individuals perceive something in the world around them, think about what to do, and then decide to act once they have weighed up the options. AI is programmed to do something similar, in that a computer senses the world around it through inputs and then processes the incoming information through optimisation and verification algorithms, with a choice of action made in a fashion similar to that of humans. Figure 1 illustrates how an autonomous system embedded with AI 'Thinks'.[8] If AI is the brain, autonomous systems are the body. The brain processes information and makes decisions, while the body acts upon those decisions.

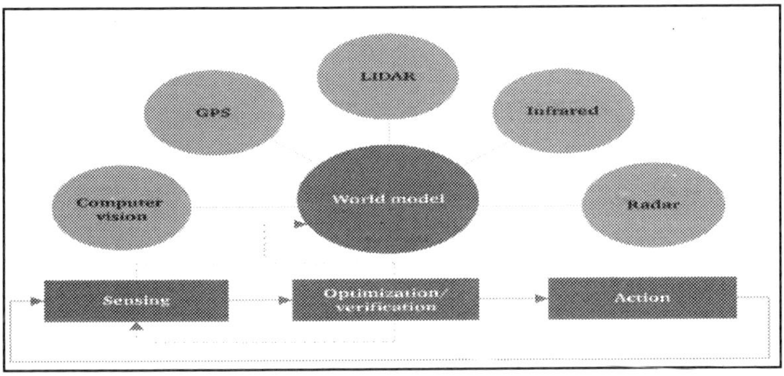

Figure 1: How an AI System Works[9]
Source: Chatam House

Therefore, an autonomous system embedded with AI passes the Turing Test. An automated system cannot pass the same as it does not exhibit human-level intelligence in performing the same tasks and, as a result, cannot offer a better/more efficient method of doing the same. For example, the production of cars in factories is done by an automated system, it is more efficient than humans; however, it cannot provide suggestions for improving the process. A self-driving car is an example of an autonomous system because it can suggest different routes when weighing the options and adjust to traffic conditions without outside interference.

Indian Armed Forces and Artificial Intelligence

AI can be used in many military operations on an operational level. It can function as a tool to improve the efficiency and effectiveness of operations at the tactical level, which, in turn, benefits the armed forces and the nation strategically. Some of the applications are explained below:

- **Intelligence, Surveillance, and Reconnaissance**. AI is transforming ISR capabilities across the Indian Army, Navy, and Air Force by enabling rapid analysis of satellite, drone, radar, and sonar data. It identifies threats like troop movements, hidden bases, and maritime risks with exceptional speed and accuracy. AI-powered facial recognition and behavioral analysis help track individuals and groups, aiding operations in sensitive regions, such as Kashmir and the Red Corridor. By distinguishing threats embedded among civilians, AI reduces collateral damage. With machine learning, it processes data exponentially faster than humans, supporting precision targeting, real-time decision-making, and enhancing the overall effectiveness of joint military operations.

- **Electronic Warfare and Cybersecurity**. AI plays a vital role in enhancing cybersecurity by detecting and mitigating cyber threats in real time, ensuring the protection of critical defence infrastructure. AI tools can identify anomalies in network traffic, predict potential breaches, and automate responses to cyberattacks, thereby, strengthening the armed forces cyber defence capabilities. Additionally, in the domain of electronic warfare, AI can effectively jam enemy communications, safeguard military networks, and counter adversarial AI systems, providing a decisive edge in modern conflict scenarios.

- **Predictive Analysis**. Predictive analysis, an AI tool, can assist commanders in decision support. Analysing battlefield data and predicting enemy actions based on the data collected over a period of time through reconnaissance can shorten the observe, orient, decide, act loop, the compression of which is highly sought-after in the armed forces, as it leads to accomplishing tasks faster, giving an edge at the strategic level and at the tactical level, saving lives.

- **Anti-Access/Area Denial (A2/AD)**. A2/AD is a military approach which is used to deny ingress to enemy forces in a theatre of war. A2/AD relies on using long-range capabilities like ballistic and cruise missiles, advanced air defences, and cyber capabilities to deter or disrupt enemy forces from entering an area. In essence, it serves as a method for creating a 'No-go' zone for the enemy, cutting costs and saving human lives by creating a deterrence for the adversary. AI substantially boosts A2/AD capabilities by improving detection, targeting, and decision-making processes. This enables weapons systems to autonomously target enemy positions autonomously, massively increasing speed and accuracy, and cutting down on the time needed for the same when compared to a human. For example, the Russians use S-400 and S-500 air defence systems (both AI-enhanced) to distinguish between decoys and real threats.[10]

- **Lethal Autonomous Weapon Systems (LAWS)**. LAWS denote an advanced military artillery with detector suites and pre-programmed algorithms combined to it. Similar systems help in detecting, opting, and tracking hostile targets painlessly. After cranking, the munitions can autonomously engage targets using its hostile fire discovery and positioning features.

- **Weapons Platforms**. AI-powered systems are reshaping warfare across all three services of the armed forces. In the Army, projects like Israel's Carmel aim to provide AI-enabled armoured vehicles that can identify threats, suggest tactics, and engage targets autonomously. For the Navy, AI supports unmanned underwater vehicles and predictive maintenance of warships. In the Air Force, AI assists in target recognition, mission planning, and autonomous drone operations. Together, these technologies enhance situational awareness, operational speed, and precision across land, sea, and air domains.

- **Training and Simulation**. AI-driven simulators are revolutionising training across the army, navy, and air force by offering realistic, high-fidelity combat scenarios. These simulations integrate virtual reality and AI to prepare personnel for diverse challenges—urban warfare and high-altitude combat for ground forces, maritime threats for naval units, and aerial dogfights and mission planning for airmen. By replicating dynamic, hybrid warfare environments, AI-based training enhances readiness, adaptability, and precision across all three services, ensuring better operational effectiveness in real-world missions.

    - **Supply Chain and Logistics**. AI optimises supply chain and logistics management across all branches of the armed forces by predicting operational requirements, streamlining transportation, and automating distribution networks. Whether it is the Indian Army operating in the challenging Himalayan terrain, the Indian Navy managing maritime supply routes across vast oceans, or the Indian Air Force coordinating aerial resupply in forward bases, AI enhances efficiency, accuracy, and responsiveness. By enabling data-driven planning and real-time tracking, AI ensures that critical supplies—ranging from fuel and ammunition to food and medical aid—reach personnel at the right place and time, thereby, strengthening operational readiness, reducing wastage, and improving mission sustainability across land, sea, and air domains.

Herein lies the inherent advantage of AI in warfare: it can free the soldier (at both the tactical and strategic level) to effectively focus solely on the most important aspect of their duties. Essentially, the adjuvant portions are outsourced to a system less prone to miscalculations and impervious to pressures of war. Such a situation is akin to multi-national corporations outsourcing auxiliary tasks to third parties to increase efficiency and reduce manpower costs.

Indian Defence Industrial Complex

In recent years, the mindset behind technological innovation and industry has seen a technological shift. The concept of 'Make in India' and *Atmanirbhar Bharat* (Self-reliant India) represent a tectonic shift in the business practices of India, aligning it more closely with the global models, where private enterprise plays a central role in national security. Prime Minister (PM) Narendra Modi had, in 2022, stated in an interview that "The Government has no business to do business".[11] Essentially meaning that the government's sole responsibility is to provide an ecosystem where businesses can thrive and not do the same itself. The idea is antagonistic to the standard practice in India, where the government itself, as of this publication, is involved in providing many services through Public Sector Undertakings (PSUs).

The above, in terms of defence manufacturing, is reflected in the creation of the Defence Innovation Organisation (DIO) and its subsidiary, the Innovations for Defence Excellence (iDEX), organisations whose *raison d'être* is to bring about innovations in defence equipment by providing funding to startups. Coupled with the drive to Make in India, the government intends to set up the Indian Defence Industrial Complex, which will essentially serve as an ecosystem for the Indian security forces akin to the one that serves the US. Wherein private players innovate and produce defence equipment for the security forces.

AI is a major component of the above. The Defence Artificial Intelligence Project Agency (DAIPA) was set up by the Ministry of Defence (MoD) with an annual budget of INR 100 cr to support AI projects. These will include development, data preparation, and capacity building. The drive towards increasing capacity in AI is part of a larger project of self-sustenance in defence production.

In 2018, the MoD, through the Department of Defence Production (DDP), instituted a task force based on whose recommendations the Defence AI Council (DAIC) and, later in 2019, the DAIPA were established.[12] The former, chaired by *Raksha Mantri* (Defence Minister), is comprised of the three Service Chiefs, the Defence Secretary, the National Cyber Security Coordinator, and representatives from the Defence Research Development Organisation, the defence manufacturing industry, and academia. The DAIC convenes bi-annually to guide, enable, and effect the development or tailoring of the operating framework, policy-level changes, and structural support.[13]

Recommendations

AI is a tool like any other. Therefore, its efficacy depends less on how advanced it is and more on how it is employed. The best technologies can fail to have a substantial impact if not properly implemented and utilised. As such, AI requires being inducted into the country's security architecture, keeping in mind its fundamentals while ensuring the final user understands them proficiently.

Within the purview of this article, the steps that the Indian Armed Forces should take along with those required by the defence manufacturing industry to make it into a juggernaut have been examined.

Integrating Artificial Intelligence into Training and Leadership Development.

- In the armed forces, senior military leaders must be as proficient in AI as they are in strategic and logistics planning, as it is increasingly shaping the future of warfare and high-stakes decision-making. To achieve this, AI education and awareness must be introduced systematically at all levels of military training, starting from the tactical tier and progressing to the strategic. The objective is to cultivate officers who are not only operationally astute but also technologically proficient capable of guiding the armed forces in next-generation of warfare.

- Promotions in the armed forces are currently based on Annual Confidential Reports (ACRs), which evaluate officers over time, and on the completion of key professional military education courses. Admission to some of these courses is merit-based, determined largely by ACR performance. Therefore, it is essential that cyber and AI training begins early in an officer's career, starting from the post-commission phase, so that those advancing through merit are already equipped with a foundational understanding of AI. As officers progress through the ranks, their exposure to AI can be deepened, thereby, ensuring that senior leadership is both strategically and technologically competent.

- The officer training pathway across the three services includes foundational and progressive courses aligned with equivalent ranks. This begins with the Young Officers Course and its equivalents in the navy and air force, followed by the Junior Staff Course or equivalent courses. Mid-career training includes the Defence Services Staff College for Majors, Lieutenant Colonels, and equivalent ranks, Senior Command for Lieutenant Colonels and equivalents, Higher Command (HC) for Colonels and equivalents, and the National Defence College (NDC) for Brigadiers and their counterparts. At all these levels, curricula and exposure must integrate advanced AI applications in ISR, command decision systems, predictive logistics, and autonomous platforms.

- At the HC and NDC levels, where learning is conducted primarily through seminars, lectures, and visits, AI use and application must be integrated through expert-led sessions by civilian technologists, defence innovators, and industry leaders. These sessions should include live demonstrations, case studies, and interactive simulations. Foreign visits should be curated to include practical exposure to AI-integrated military units or operations, enabling officers to witness first-hand use of AI in an operational context.

- Officers must be familiar with both current and emerging use of AI systems in the Indian defence ecosystem and global theatres. This is especially crucial for those attending the NDC, a gateway to three-star and higher appointments. These leaders are entrusted with strategic responsibilities—ranging from decision-making to procurement decisions to policy dialogues with the MoD. Without a sound understanding of AI capabilities and limitations, their ability to make timely, informed, and future-ready decisions will be significantly constrained. Therefore, equipping senior leadership with AI education is not optional—it is a strategic imperative.

- To institutionalise this transformation, the Headquarters Integrated Defence Staff must be tasked with the design and rollout of a comprehensive AI curriculum spanning from the post commission level to the NDC. This effort must involve collaboration with AI specialists from academia, industry leaders, friendly foreign countries, and developers of military-grade AI applications. Given that AI adoption in the Indian Armed Forces (as of Apr 2025) remains in its early stages, this is an opportune moment to shape the learning framework while the operational ecosystem remains flexible. This flexibility allows military education institutions to mould curricula that are not only reflective of operational realities but also adaptive to rapid technological change.

- To ensure the effectiveness of this initiative, assessment mechanisms must be integrated into each level of instruction. These may include AI proficiency certifications, scenario-based evaluations, and practical assignments. Furthermore, implementation challenges such as faculty development, digital infrastructure, and bureaucratic inertia should be anticipated and proactively addressed.

- By embedding AI into the formal military education structure, the Indian Armed Forces can build a future-ready leadership cadre that is capable of navigating both traditional conflict and emerging domains of warfare with equal competence.

Revamping India's Defence Innovation Ecosystem.

- The integration of AI into India's defence production ecosystem is no longer a matter of choice but a strategic necessity. AI is reshaping modern warfare, and India's ability to keep pace hinges on accelerating innovation through collaborative investment and structural reform. However, a developing economy like India cannot bear this financial burden alone. Massive investment is required to advance AI technology, and the responsibility must be shared by the private sector.

- While India has witnessed the entry of private players into defence manufacturing, the existing system remains ill-suited to fostering innovation at scale. Outside of PSUs who gain funding from the government, only large conglomerates such as Larsen and Toubro, Tata Advanced Systems Ltd, Adani Defence and Aerospace, Mahindra Defence Systems, Kalyani Group, and Reliance Strategic Business Ventures have demonstrated meaningful progress in AI-driven defence innovation. This is largely due to their financial resilience, allowing them to absorb losses in the research and prototyping stages. Very few businesses outside of those being run by multi-national corporations are able to do the same. Some like Tonbo Imaging, who have been producing optronics for the US Navy SEALs and the Israeli Defence Forces[14], are only able to do so because of their previous transactions. New players in the industry flounder due to lack of meaningful support like the one provided by China to its micro, small, and medium enterprises.[15] In contrast, smaller Indian manufacturers often struggle to survive under current mechanisms like iDEX, which offer funding only after substantial initial investment. This discourages early-stage innovation, delays product development, or forces firms to sell promising technology to foreign entities. Hence, programs like iDEX must be expanded to include pre-prototype funding, incubator support, and risk-sharing models to nurture indigenous startups.

- Furthermore, the existing defence procurement process is lengthy and cumbersome, leading to delays in the induction of indigenous AI solutions. The procedure—starting from requirement identification by service headquarters to categorisation, request for proposal issuance, trials, cost negotiations, and production—spans years. This results in the deployment of systems that are technologically outdated by the time they are inducted. A significant bottleneck is the lack of war-proven status for indigenous technologies, which forces collaboration with foreign entities and delays procurement further. To overcome this, a structured methodology should be adopted where emerging equipment and AI programs are allowed limited-scale field trials. Initially, such technologies should be tested in controlled environments like firing ranges and simulations. If successful, they should be deployed in low-risk operational settings to gather user feedback. Equipment deemed effective by field users must then be fast-tracked for induction, with manufacturers compensated at full cost to ensure profitability and incentivise future Research and Development (R&D).

- The abovementioned policy interventions could overhaul the defence production ecosystem, particularly the AI integration process. However, one of the most persistent impediments remains bureaucratic red tape. The layered chain of command—from DAIPA, DAIC, DIO, and IDEX to the DDP, the MoD, the *Raksha Mantri*, and finally the PM—slows decision-making drastically. Approvals get stalled across multiple desks, adversely impacting both the manufacturer and the armed forces awaiting critical capabilities. A practical workaround is to restructure the reporting system, allowing the DDP to report directly to the PM's Office, similar to the operational model of the Indian Space Research Organisation.[16]

- Another critical challenge is the brain drain of India's AI talent. India produces one of the largest pools of science, technology, engineering, and mathematics graduates globally, with thousands specialising in computer science, data science, and machine learning. However, many are recruited by global tech giants such as Google, Microsoft, Meta, and OpenAI, drawn by higher salaries, cutting-edge research facilities, and global exposure. This migration severely depletes India's domestic AI talent pool, weakening the innovation ecosystem in defence and allied sectors. To address this, the government could consider implementing a bond-based service model for students enrolled in premier institutions such as the Indian Institutes of Technology. Under this model, students receiving subsidised education would commit to working in Indian public sector R&D or defence innovation for a minimum of five years after completing their post-graduation. By offering competitive compensation and world-class research infrastructure, the government can retain top-tier talent and ensure that taxpayer investment in education translates into national capability building.

Conclusion

The future of warfare lies in the realm of AI. Every weapon and weapons system can be enhanced by the use of AI and, hence, it is a strategic imperative for India to innovate and implement it in the structure of the armed forces. New Delhi has setup the organisational structure and the results are showing but more needs to be done. It will still be a long road to achieving the desired results. In fact, Bharat has just started on the journey to amalgamate AI in its apparatus. The nation is operating from a position of weakness in this regard, India getting ahead of the curve is a long-term goal but the country has to first catch-up with the rest of the world. By fostering synergy between the military, industry, and government, India can not only meet its own defence needs but also emerge as a global leader in AI-driven security innovation. It is essential not only to fulfil the needs of the armed forces but also for export purposes similar to the US, which uses its indigenously produced products to expand its political and diplomatic power.

Finally, the conflicts in Ukraine, Middle East, and the Red Sea stand testament to AI reshaping the very fabric of modern warfare. Hence, the Indian Armed Forces must urgently institutionalise AI into both their operational frameworks and leadership development pathways to ensure strategic readiness in an increasingly complex security environment.

Endnotes

1 John Guilmartin and John Taylor, "Military Aircraft", *Brittanica*, accessed 20 Apr 2025 https://www.britannica.com/technology/military-aircraft#:~:text=The%20first%20use%20of%20an,in%20a %20Bl%C3%A9riot%20XI%20monoplane.

2 "Military inventions that we use every day", *North Atlantic Treaty Organization*, accessed 20 Apr 2025 https://www.nato.int/cps/fr/natohq/declassified_215371.htm?msg_pos=1

3 Dasha Smirnova, "How was the future of AI shaped in the 1940's by Turing?", *Dasha*, 10 Sep 2020, accessed 20 Apr 2025 https://dasha.ai/en-us/blog/turing-shaped-ai

4 "What is the history of artificial intelligence (AI)?" *Tableau*, accessed 20 Apr 2025 https://www.ta bleau.com/data-insights/ai/history#:~:text=Birth%20of%20AI:%201950%2D1956,it%20came%20 into%20popular%20usage.

5 "Our Mission", *DARPA*, accessed 20 Apr 2025 https://www.darpa.mil/about

6 "Artificial intelligence and the war in Ukraine", *Instituto Español de Estudios Estratégicos*, 17 Dec 2024, accessed 20 Apr 2025 https://www.defensa.gob.es/documents/2073105/2278118/la_inteligencia_ artificial_y_la_guerra_de_ucrania_2024_dieeea81_eng.pdf

7 Bethan McKernan and Harry Davies, " "The machine did it coldly": Israel used AI to identify 37,000 Hamas targets", *Guardian*, 03 Apr 2024, accessed 20 Apr 2025 https://www.theguardian.com/world/2024/apr/03/israel-gaza-ai-database-hamas-airstrikes

8 ML Cummings, "Artificial Intelligence and the Future of Warfare", *Chatham House*, Jan 2017, accessed 20 Apr 2025 https://www.chathamhouse.org/sites/default/files/publications/research/2017-01-26-artificial-intelligence-future-warfare-cummings-final.pdf

9 Ibid

10 'Enhancing Russia's Air and Missile Defense: The Arrival of the S-500 Systems Amid Global Tensions', *Debug Lies News*, 25 Apr 2024, accessed 25 Apr 2025 https://debuglies.com/2024/04/25/enhancing-russias-air-and-missile-defense-the-arrival-of-the-s-500-systems-amid-global-tensions/

11 Business Today Desk, "Government has no business to do business: PM Narendra Modi", *Business Today*, 09 Feb 2022, accessed 25 Apr 2025 https://www.businesstoday.in/latest/economy/story/government-has-no-business-to-do-business-pm-narendra-modi-322064-2022-02-09

[12] Ministry of Defence, "Enhancement of Capabilities of AI Technology", *Press Information Bureau*, 01 Aug 2022, accessed 28 Apr 2025 https://www.pib.gov.in/PressReleasePage.aspx?PRID=1846937

[13] Dr Nivash Jeevanandam, "Impact of AI in the Indian Army", *India AI*, 15 Jan 2024, accessed 28 Apr 2025 https://indiaai.gov.in/article/impact-of-ai-in-the-indian-army

[14] ISN Team, "Indian defence technology startup Tonbo Imaging raises Rs 175 crore in pre-IPO round", *Indian Startup News*, 04 Apr 2025, accessed 02 May 2025 https://indianstartupnews.com/startup-stories/tonbo-imaging-raises-rs-175-crore-in-pre-ipo-round-to-advance-infrared-and-directed-energy-tech-8925180

[15] Amit Mishra, "How Chinese 'Little Giants' Made It, And Lessons For India's MSME Sector", *Swarajya*, 03 Feb 2025, accessed 02 May 2025 https://swarajyamag.com/economy/indias-struggling-msmes-why-cant-we-imitate-chinas-success

[16] Dhiraj Nayyar, "Working on the ISRO principle", *The Hindu*, 18 Feb 2017, accessed 02 May 2025 https://www.thehindu.com/opinion/op-ed/working-on-the-isro-principle/article17321178.ece

An Analysis of the Russia-Ukraine War and Lessons for India

Mr Neelotpal Mishra, dis

Abstract

The aim of the article is to understand the geostrategic, economic, and military aspects of the Russia-Ukraine War and take lessons for India. The military aspects include all the components of a modern war and its use of fighting machine. The article also briefly touches upon the events leading up to the current war. The lessons that India should take from the war are also discussed in light of an analysis of different aspects of the war.

Introduction

The current Russia-Ukraine conflict has germinated from the United States (US), going back to the post-Germany unification promise; that the North Atlantic Treaty Organization (NATO) will not expand towards Russia.[1] Quite contrary, there was a new 'Cold War' manifested by the expansion of NATO and the European Union (EU) to amalgamate the former Soviet Union states. Ukraine and Belarus form the strategic buffer in the security calculus of Russia to counter the vulnerability of the 500-mile-wide Carpathian gap, through which invasions from Europe arrived.

Post the Bucharest NATO Summit in 2008, Russia perceived its strategic interests in Georgia being undermined by complicity of the US and launched military operations in Abkhazia and South Ossetia.[2] Unilateral abrogation of arms control and disarmament treaties and the perceived US-engineered 2014 Maidan uprising threatened the strategic interests and buffer for Russia. It launched military operations to seize control over Crimea and the Donbas region, followed by the Minsk Accords of 2014 and 2015. Subsequently, in 2015, the British military personnel were deployed to Ukraine under Operation ORBITAL for

This article has been reproduced from the USI Strategic Year Book 2025.

training the Ukrainian Armed Forces, and in 2019, the mission was extended until Mar 2023.[3]

All this compounded Russia's security concerns and threat perception of a military offensive by Ukraine to reclaim Crimea and Donbas regions. The decision to invade Ukraine stemmed from these aforementioned concerns.[4]

Overview of the War

Russia's multi-prong military blitzkrieg aimed at a quick and decisive victory, launched on 24 Feb 2022, preceded by putting nuclear forces on high readiness to deter NATO's direct intervention. The limited politico-military objectives were to deter Ukraine from joining the EU and the NATO, foist a pro-Russia regime, neutralise Ukraine's military, control the Black Sea and the Sea of Azov, a land corridor to Crimea, and elicit recognition of Donbas as an autonomous region. However, Russian planners underestimated the level of resistance from the Ukrainian Defense Force (UDF), its population, and the western support. Russia quickly learned and soon pivoted to Donbas (Donetsk and Luhansk).[5] Russia captured Mariupol by May, made slow progress in the Donbas, and captured Severodonetsk in Jun. A Ukrainian counter-offensive in 2022 captured territory in the Kharkiv and southern Kherson. From Jul to Aug 2022, the campaign morphed into classic first-world attrition warfare, resulting in a strategic stalemate. Then, Bakhmut was captured by Russia in mid-2023. Ukraine's summer offensive to recapture strategic areas in the South and East, particularly Zaporizhzhia and the land corridor connecting Russia to Crimea, ran out of steam.

Operation Interflex started in Mar 2023 in the United Kingdom (UK), continuing to train UDF soldiers in 2025, adding to the 51,000 troops and jet pilots already trained by instructors from Sweden, Norway, Netherlands, Kosovo, Australia, Canada, Finland, Romania, Denmark, New Zealand, Lithuania, and Estonia.[6,7]

On 06 Aug 2024, the UDF launched a surprise 30-kms-deep incursion into Russia's Kursk Oblast, claiming to capture 1,000 sq kms—a claim contested by Russia.[8] In Nov 2024, more than 10,000 North Korean troops were reported there[9] and in response, the US allowed the Ukrainians to use American-made long-range missiles. To retaliate, the Russians fired hypersonic missiles, and short range and air-launched ballistic missiles.[10] The UDF launched another counteroffensive in Russia's Kursk region on 05 Jan 2025[11] to presumably place Ukraine in a better bargaining position.

The Commerce War

Russia's international trade, finance, and economic growth were adversely affected by its exclusion from the Society for Worldwide Interbank Financial Telecommunications payment system, freezing of foreign reserves, and restrictions on technology import. The war has devastated Ukraine's economy with long-term social and economic instability.[12] On 17 Jul 2023, Russia terminated the Black Sea Grain Initiative (BSGI) as it objected to 'Hidden' restrictions to its exempted food and fertiliser exports and closing of the Russia's ammonia exporting Togliatti-Odesa pipeline. BSGI granted Ukraine a safe passage for 37 per cent of agricultural product exports from three crucial Black Sea ports—Odesa, Chornomorsk, and Pivdennyi. These, along with Mykolaiv and Mariupol ports, were responsible for over 90 per cent of seaport freight turnover. Companies such as US Bunge, Ukrainian Nibulon, Chinese China National Cereals, and Oils and Foodstuffs Corporation had major investments at Mykolaiv.[13,14]

Gas was sent to Germany from the Yamal-Europe pipeline through Belarus and the Nord Stream pipeline under the Baltic Sea, which were shut at the start of the war. On 01 Jan 2025, the gas supply sent to Europe via Ukraine through the Soviet-era Urengoy-Pomary-Uzhgorod pipeline across Sudzha—now under the Ukrainian control—was cut, reducing Russia's share in Europe's gas import from 35 per cent to around 8 per cent. The gas moved via Ukraine into Slovakia, where it splits into branches and takes supply to the Czech Republic and Austria. Bloomberg estimated Russia's earnings to be around USD 6.5 bn annually. Austria met almost all its demand from it, while Slovakia met approximately two-thirds. Transnistria, Moldova's pro-Russia breakaway region, was receiving supplies since 2022, which it used to generate electricity and supply to government-controlled parts of Moldova. Another gas pipeline passing through Turkiye 'TurkStream' still supplies gas to countries such as Hungary.[15]

The EU has been working on diversification of its energy supply[16] and may not face many disruptions[17], however, the curtailment has dented the European economy, increased their reliance on the US, and hiked global energy prices. The economy of Moldova would be affected adversely, leading to probably pro-Russian parties winning the upcoming elections.[18]

Russian crude oil can access western services like insurance and shipping, only if sales are capped below USD 60 a barrel, therefore, a shadow fleet of oil tankers have emerged to circumvent this[19] as Russia found alternate markets in China, India, etc.

International Support

More than 50 NATO allies have committed support for the development of the UAF in the Jul 2024 meeting of the US-led Ukraine Defence Contact Group at the US Air Force base in Ramstein, Germany.[20] Till Dec 2024, the EU has committed EUR 11.1 bn of European Peace Facility funding for military support to Ukraine.[21] The US has committed more than USD 60.7 bn since the beginning of the war.[22,23] The UK has given GBP 12.8 bn in support to Ukraine since Feb 2022, of which GBP 7.8 bn is for military assistance.[24] These include Air Defence (AD) weapons, fire control systems, tanks, armoured personal carriers, bridging systems, mine clearing systems, Unmanned Aerial Vehicles (UAVs), Unmanned Surface Vehicles (USVs), anti-armour systems, laser-guided rocket systems and munitions, naval vessels/systems, aircraft, satellite-based secure communication system, Electronic Warfare (EW) systems, drones, etc.

Geopolitical Shifts. The Ukraine war has emerged as an inflexion point in reshaping of the world order, manifesting in the 'New great game', with Eastern Europe emerging as the new frontline with consolidation of the EU and the NATO. The US is facing a challenge to balance its security commitments in Europe, West Asia, and Indo-Pacific, while Russia, China, Iran, and North Korea are forming an alliance. The non-aligned and emerging powers, such as India, Brazil, Türkiye, Indonesia, South Africa, and some other countries of the Global South, are professing neutrality.

The ensuing geopolitical contestation has seen a breakdown in confidence building measures, disarmament treaties, and the decay of the United Nations Security Council. The quest for balance of power is playing out in a volatility, uncertainty, complexity, and ambiguity world.[25]

Nature and Character of War

The Ukraine War is a classic example of new generation warfare entailing multi-domains like political, diplomatic, economic, military, informational, and critical infrastructure; and also employing a multitude of means such as states, non-state actors, kinetic and non-kinetic factors spanning new strategic frontiers like, space, cyber space, and cognitive domain.[26]

Economic Cost. Economic sanctions have a ripple effect on global markets; weaponisation of dollar and the US-centric financial transaction system have had a substantial long-term effect on the Russian economy. War caused Russia a budget deficit of USD 57 bn in Dec 2022[27] and a steep rise in unemployment. Ukraine's economy shrank, as more than USD 100 bn worth of damage has been inflicted on Ukraine and would require at least USD 486 bn to rebuild. Slowing economic growth to 2 per cent in 2025, Ukraine faces immense financial needs in the coming years, and private sector investment will be critical.[28]

Complexities of Urban Warfare. The dense urban terrain impedes the progress of operations, often resulting in high civilian casualties and destruction of infrastructure. The use of booby traps, and civilian vehicles and materials to barricade roads and create obstacles has been highly effective in restricting the use of armoured vehicles and larger units. The UDF has exploited urban terrain by using small and well-trained infantry units, highlighting importance of training in close quarter battle, fighting in built-up areas, highly precise integrated fire support in both offensive and defensive operations by targeting enemy fortifications, supply lines, and reinforcements. There is a need for a strategy that achieves military objectives and minimises civilian casualties, builds effective humanitarian corridors, and restores essential services.[29]

Importance of Intelligence, Surveillance, and Reconnaissance (ISR). The access to satellite imagery, signals intelligence, surveillance, and the use of superior drones for reconnaissance and EW has proved crucial in maintaining situational awareness and countering Russian advances. Russia has successfully used its satellite network like Persona and Bars-M; UAVs such as the Orlan-10, Forpost, Kartograf, and specialised units; EW systems like the Krasukha-4, Leer-3, and torn-mobile detection module; and long-range aviation assets like the Tu-214R and Il-20M. The war has demonstrated the value of real-time intelligence gathering, analysis, and sharing, increasing battlefield transparency as a battle winning factor.[30]

Future of Tank. The war threw up debate about the effectiveness of tank formations due to the heavy toll of Russia's armour by effective use of dispersed anti-tank teams using shoulder-fired javelin missiles and top-attack anti-tank weapons, including armoured drones. The war has, however, proved that tanks remain a formidable platform in ground warfare, as it underscored the importance of combined team operations with infantry, artillery, attack helicopters, and drones.[31,32]

The Primacy of Artillery and Missiles. Artillery systems like high mobility artillery rocket systems, precision-guided munitions, multiple launch rocket systems, and counter battery radars have been used for preparing the battlefield for ground assaults and targeting critical infrastructure. Its integration with drones as observation posts and other ISR assets for real-time targeting and post-strike damage assessments has enhanced their precision and lethality. The UDF used anti-ship Neptune, Harpoons, S-300 national advanced surface-to-air missile system, infrared imaging system—tail/thrust vector-controlled AD system, Tochka-U ballistic missiles, and cruise missiles. Russia has used missiles such as Oreshnik, Kalibr, Iskander-M, and Kinzhal, and combined drone missile attacks to great effect.[33]

Drone Warfare. Drones have acted as force multipliers for real-time intelligence, surveillance, targeting acquisition, and reconnaissance, EW, and as loitering munitions (kamikaze/suicide drones). Swarm drone attacks in depth became a regular feature of strategic targeting. Vulnerability of drones to EW, jamming, and Global Positioning System (GPS) spoofing underlines the need for resilient communication and navigation systems. A doctrinal change for integrating drones into all aspects and levels of military planning is on the cards.[34]

Aerospace Domain. Russian Air Force has played a sub-optimal role in the Ukraine War as the UDF has reaped the benefits of a layered AD strategy integrating Soviet-era systems, man-portable AD systems, the US-supplied Patriot missiles, indigenous AD networks, and radar systems. Long-range precision missiles and standoff weapons have demonstrated the effective degradation of the enemy. Satellites have played a crucial role in providing ISR in real-time, even covering missile launches. Decoys, launching salvos, and employing low-flying or stealth missiles have been used to evade or overwhelm missile defences. The conflict in Ukraine has shown the vital importance of satellite communications, positioning, navigation, and timing, and electro-optical/ ISR services to situational awareness and command and control. Ukraine has been able to offset its lack of space capabilities by buying commercial data and services from private US companies and through use of SpaceX communications. Russian attempts at jamming, spoofing, or hacking satellite networks supporting the UDF have been a feature of the war. Satellite imagery of civilian casualties increased support for the Ukrainian forces, boosting diplomatic and materiel support.[35]

Naval Domain. The UDF has effectively employed asymmetrical naval tactics by employing small/agile vessels and coastal defence systems to challenge and disrupt naval operations. USVs and UAVs have been used for ISR and for directing attacks by the UDF. Ukraine's indigenous Neptune and US' Harpoon missiles have been a key factor in deterring Russian naval operations and amphibious assaults. Vulnerability of large naval vessels has been highlighted by sinking of the Russian flagship Moskva.[36,37] Securing Sea Lines of Communications (SLOCs) is of strategic importance; thus, Russia's blockade of Ukrainian ports has exerted economic pressure and access to critical resources. To counter these, developing alternative routes, leveraging international support, and employing innovative solutions are crucial.

Cyber and Electronic Warfare. Cyber attacks on critical infrastructure have been a key component, highlighting the need for robust cyber security, electronic countermeasures, and electronic protection measures capabilities enmeshed in military strategy. Controlling the electromagnetic spectrum is essential, as EW has played a significant role in information operations by jamming/disrupting communications, GPS, and other systems.[38,39]

Logistics. This logistical failure of Russian forces slowed their advance and exposed them to the UDF counterattacks. The war has shown that maintaining robust supply chains is essential for sustaining combat operations over extended periods through protection of logistics nodes, creation of redundancies, and surge capabilities, by harnessing potential of drones and robotic vehicles in logistics operations. Efficient medical logistics, field hospitals, and medical supplies have been essential in saving lives, maintaining morale, and preserving forces.[40, 41]

Artificial Intelligence (AI). AI has emerged as the most potent disruptive technology in multi-domain warfare. AI's integration with EW makes it dynamic and effective due to quick identification of patterns, threat detection, and actionable intelligence by analyses of vast amounts of imagery and video data from satellites, drones, and other surveillance sources. AI-driven swarm drones have been used for complex operations to destroy enemy defences and conduct reconnaissance. Predictive analytics by AI-driven fusion of historical data, current intelligence, and battlefield trends is used to anticipate enemy actions and assess the likelihood of various outcomes. AI has been used for effective logistic operations by real-time tracking of supplies, equipment, and personnel. AI has been a tool in Information Warfare (IW) for creation and dissemination of disinformation by generating fake news, deepfakes, and other forms of deceptive content, to shape perceptions, control the narrative, influence public opinion, garner international support, and undermine the morale of the opponent through rapidly spreading it across social media.[42, 43]

Strategic Communication and Psychological Operations. The use of social media platforms such as Twitter, Facebook, and Telegram with the capability of reaching global audiences in real-time has been used as a tool of IW. Emotional broadcasts using coherent, clear, consistent, and timely messaging have been effective in rallying both domestic and international audiences by Ukraine.[44, 45] The use of crowdsourcing and dissemination of open-source intelligence to share battlefield updates, track troop movements, and expose disinformation is widely visible.[46] The war has highlighted the need for robust information security mechanism to protect against psychological manipulation. Even in the digital age, psychological operations remain an important tool in shaping perceptions.

Command and Control. Ukraine has deployed a combined Joint All-Domain Command and Control (JADC2) system 'Delta' for situational awareness, reflecting a single operational environment. It exemplifies software-defined warfare and provides a practical and agile approach to battlefield management, supporting frontline personnel via mobile devices. It helps commanders to maintain situational awareness of area of responsibility in real time with the help of numerous factors to support battlefield decisions.[47]

Private Armies and Foreign Fighters. The role of private military companies and foreign fighters has been significant in the war, with Russia having citizens of Nepal, Russia, Cuba, Ghana, Yemen[48] and around 10,000 North Korean soldiers. The UDF has nationals from 52 countries.[49] Integration of foreign fighters has posed significant challenges in terms of command, control, communication, and training levels as the relative lack of accountability/integration often leads to actions that may not align with broader strategic objectives. This was evident when Wagner group went rogue and turned its guns against the Russian establishment.[50]

Nuclear Deterrence. Russia's nuclear arsenal and strategy of 'Escalate to De-escalate', overt and veiled threats, and military exercises involving tactical nuclear weapons have deterred direct military intervention by the NATO. Similarly, the US deployment of nuclear weapons in the NATO partner countries and Russia's quid-pro-quo by deploying tactical nuclear weapons in Belarus have reinforced the importance of extended deterrence provided by nuclear-armed states to their allies. The war has opened new debates on review of the 'First Use' policy, nuclear postures, doctrines, effective crisis management, and communication channels, and has influenced the strategic calculations of other states.[51]

Whole-of-Nation Approach. Civil-military cooperation is of utmost importance in the modern-day wars. This has been highlighted by the fact that Ukrainian civilians have played a significant role in the defence effort by providing intelligence, supporting logistics, and engaging in direct combat. The quick repair, adaptation of damaged critical infrastructure like communications, energy, and transportation to support its war effort has demonstrated the need for close coordination between military and civilian authorities.[52]

Lessons for India

The Russia-Ukraine War has several geopolitical, economic, and military lessons for India. The lessons are mentioned below:

- **Strategic Autonomy and Multi-Alignment**. The Ukraine conflict underscores the significance of maintaining strategic autonomy in a polarised geopolitical environment. India must continue its issue-based diplomacy, aligning with partners where interests converge.
- **Buffer Zones and Regional Influence**. Proactive diplomacy, strategic partnerships, and infrastructure investments are critical to maintaining the continuing importance of denying influence by India's adversaries in its immediate sphere of influence. The immediate neighbourhood can serve either as stabilising buffers or as potential flashpoints.
- **Evolving Nature of Warfare**. India must prepare for future conflicts that span across multi-domain, non-linear warfare involving cyber, economic, informational, and conventional dimensions. Significant emphasis and investment to bolster cross-domain capabilities, a combined JADC2 strategy, effective civil-military fusion, creation of dual-use infrastructure, and use of niche and disruptive technologies.
- **Urban Warfare and Civilian Involvement**. The Indian defence effort should be bolstered by trained civilians and adaptive tactics, preparing for combat in densely populated terrain as demonstrated. India should institutionalise civil defence mechanisms for intelligence, logistics, and infrastructure support.

- **Intelligence, Surveillance, and Reconnaissance and Real-Time Battlefield Awareness**. India must rapidly enhance indigenous ISR capabilities, leveraging private sector innovation and ensuring seamless integration of space, UAVs, EW, and AI into defence strategy. The use of drones, satellites, and open-source intelligence for decisive real-time ISR is the need for the hour.

- **AI and Network-centric Warfare**. AI has emerged as a force multiplier in reconnaissance, logistics and decision-making. India should invest in AI-driven battlefield management systems like Ukraine's Delta, incorporating data fusion, predictive analytics, and swarm drone operations.

- **Cyber and Information Warfare Cyberattacks**. Narrative warfare have played key roles in the conflict. India must strengthen cyber defences, counter-disinformation mechanisms, and develop strategic communication capabilities, thus, protecting public perception and national morale.

- **Logistics and Infrastructure Resilience**. India must secure critical transport and energy infrastructure in conflict zones. Investment in drone-based logistics, high-altitude supply mechanisms, and rapid-response field medical systems is a must to avoid the logistical failures as experienced by the Russian forces.

- **Artillery, Missiles, and Drones**. The Ukraine war has reaffirmed the effectiveness of artillery systems, precision-guided munitions, and drone warfare. India should enhance capabilities in long-range artillery, counter-UAV systems, and loitering munitions. Emphasis must be placed on seamless ISR-artillery coordination and battlefield integration of drones.

- **Tank Warfare and Combined Arms Doctrine**. Despite questions about their vulnerability, tanks continue to be vital when used in conjunction with infantry, drones, and artillery. India should reinforce combined arms operations that integrate support from air, land, and cyber domains and also modernise its armoured formations.

- **Naval Strategy and Asymmetric Sea Denial**. India must enhance its coastal defences, develop asymmetric maritime tactics, and secure SLOCs by the use of missiles and USVs to deny naval superiority to the adversary, as Ukraine did.

- **Energy Security and Economic Preparedness Energy**. Disruptions and economic sanctions in Europe offer valuable lessons for India to diversify its energy imports, build strategic reserves, and secure maritime routes.

- **Nuclear Deterrence and Doctrinal Review**. The use of nuclear posturing in Ukraine has raised questions on deterrence thresholds. India should revisit its nuclear doctrine, refine its escalation control mechanisms, and enhance crisis communication frameworks to prevent miscalculations.

- **Psychological Operations and Social Media Influence**. Ukraine's adept use of social media for global influence underscores the importance of strategic communication. Strategic communication, internal security in an era of deepfake, and misinformation are other important domains to be factored in India's national security calculus. India must establish capabilities for digital influence operations, countering hostile propaganda while engaging domestic and international audiences effectively.

- **Indigenisation**. Despite India's diversification in defence imports and *Atmanirbhar Bharat* (Self-reliant India) in the defence and security sector, the reliance on Russian military equipment is significantly high, be it the production of AK203 rifles, S-400 AD systems, fighter jets, helicopters, or spares. To this end, India must strengthen the service indigenisation cells, promote technology transfers, domestic manufacturing, and supply chains.

- **Economy**. Cyber fraud losses through stock trading, and investment-based and digital arrest scams amount to approximately 0.7 per cent of gross domestic product. It is imperative to stem this tide of economic loss thorough cyber fraud to the country by developing and implementing a strategy. India has to utilise further opportunities, such as 'Crude oil refining loophole', to further its economic interests.

Conclusion

The Ukraine war offers a roadmap for India to recalibrate its military doctrine, strategic outlook, and national preparedness. From ISR and AI to cyber warfare and strategic communication, the need for holistic, future-ready capabilities is clear. The biggest leap of transformation has to come in an optimum mix of boots on ground, AI-enabled ISR, and weapon platforms to plug in gaps in India's strategic and defensive lines. By integrating civil-military responses, fostering innovation, and maintaining strategic autonomy, India can be better equipped to deter and, if necessary, fight the wars of tomorrow. Beyond doubt, India should work to usher in reforms driven by leadership and intent rather than wait for a crisis.

Endnotes

1 "Record of Conversation between Mikhail Gorbachev and James Baker", *The Digital National Security Archive (DNSA)*, The George Washington University, 09 Feb 1990, accessed 05 Jan 2025 https://nsarchive.gwu.edu/document/16117-document-06-record-conversation-between

2 Ketevan Chincharadze and Larry P Goodson, "The Enduring Impact of the 2008 Russo-Georgian War", *Army War College*, 19 Dec 2024, accessed 05 Jan 2025 https://warroom.armywarcollege.edu/articles/enduring-impact/

3 "Operation ORBITAL", *Press Release,* Embassy of Ukraine in the United Kingdom of the Great Britain and Northern Ireland, 01 May 2020, accessed 06 Jan 2025 https://uk.mfa.gov.ua/en/partnership/881-ukrajina-velika-britanija/operaciya-orbital

4 BK Sharma, "Evolving Geopolitical Dynamics of the Former Soviet Space", *Valdai Club*, 22 Nov 2023, accessed 07 Mar 2025 https://valdaiclub.com/a/highlights/evolving-geopolitical-dynamics/

5 Murat Sofuoglu, "Has Russia underestimated Ukrainian resistance?", *TRT World*, 23 Aug 2021, accessed 08 Jan 2025 https://www.trtworld.com/magazine/has-russia-underestimated-ukrainian-resistance-55417

6 "Operation Interflex is an International Effort to Train Ukrainian Soldiers", Ministry of Defence, UK, 15 Dec 2024, accessed 07 Jan 2025 https://www.facebook.com/theministryofdefence/videos/operation-interflex-is-an-international-effort-to-train-ukrainian-soldiers-instr/1330039921308346/

7 Detailed timeline of UK military assistance to Ukraine (Feb 2022-present), *Research Briefing*, UK Parliament, 22 Nov 2024, accessed 09 Jan 2025 https:/ /commonslibrary.parliament.uk/research-briefings/cbp-9914/

[8] "Ukraine in maps: Tracking the war with Russia", *BBC*, 19 Nov 2024, accessed 10 Jan 2025 https://www.bbc.com/news/world-europe-60506682

[9] Jim Garamone, "Pentagon Says 10K North Korean Troops in Kursk Oblast", *Defense*, 04 Nov 2024, accessed 08 Jan 2025 https://www.defense.gov/News/News-Stories/Article/article/3955757/pentagon-says-10k-north-korean-troops-in-kursk-oblast/

[10] "Russia has used its hypersonic Oreshnik missile for the first time. What are its capabilities?", *AP News*, 09 Dec 2024, accessed 09 Jan 2025 https://apnews.com/article/russia-oreshnik-hypersonic-missile-putin-ukraine-war-345588a399158b9eb0b56990b8149bd9

[11] Will Vernon, Amy Walker, and Patrick Jackson, "Ukraine renews attack on Russia's Kursk region", *BBC*, 05 Jan 2025, accessed 10 Jan 2025 https://www.bbc.com/news/articles/c86wz0vd1dwo

[12] Joseph Glauber, Brian McNamara, and Elsa Olivetti, "Russia terminates the Black Sea Grain Initiative: What's next for Ukraine and the world?", *IFPRI*, 20 Jul 2023, accessed 10 Jan 2025 https://www.ifpri.org/blog/russia-terminates-black-sea-grain-initiative-whats-next-ukraine-and-world/

[13] Romina Bandura, Ilya Timtchenko, and Benjamin Robb, "Ships, Trains, and Trucks: Unlocking Ukraine's Vital Trade Potential", *Centre of Strategic and International Studies*, 08 Apr 2024, accessed 10 Jan 2025 https://www.csis.org/analysis/ships-trains-and-trucks-unlocking-ukraines-vital-trade-potential,

[14] Joseph Glauber et al, 'Russia terminates the Black Sea Grain Initiative'

[15] "Russian gas flow to Europe via Ukraine stopped: Who does it hurt?", *Al Jazeera Staff*, 01 Jan 2025, accessed 05 Jan 2025 https://www.aljazeera.com/news/2025/1/1/russian-gas-flow-to-europe-via-ukraine-stopped-who-does-it-hurt

[16] "Where does the EU's gas come from?", *The European Council*, 21 Mar 2024, accessed 11 Jan 2025 https://www.consilium.europa.eu/en/infographics/eu-gas-supply/

[17] "Russian gas flow to Europe", *Al Jazeera* Staff.

[18] Sarah Rainsford, "Moldova faces energy crisis as flow of Russian gas ends", *BBC*, 01 Jan 2025, accessed 10 Jan 2025 https://www.bbc.com/news/articles/cy8ymx50kz8o

[19] "Russian oil finds its way to Europe via India; India now biggest exporter of fuel to EU", *The Hindu*, 10 Nov 2024, accessed 11 Jan 2025 https://www.thehindu.com/business/russian-oil-finds-its-way-to-europe-via-india-india-now-biggest-exporter-of-fuel-to-eu/article68852062.ece

[20] "UK to extend training programme for Ukrainian Armed Forces personnel throughout 2025", *Ministry of Defence*, UK, 06 Sep 2024, accessed 12 Jan 2025 https://www.gov.uk/government/news/uk-to-extend-training-programme-for-ukrainian-armed-forces-personnel-throughout-2025?utm_medium=email&utm_campaign=govuk-notifications-topic

[21] "Military assistance to Ukraine since the Russian invasion", *Research Briefing*, UK Parliament, 25 Nov 2024, accessed 05 Jan 2025 https://commonslibrary.parliament.uk/research-briefings/cbp-9477/

[22] "US Security Cooperation with Ukraine", Fact Sheet, *Bureau of Political-Military Affairs*, 30 Dec 2024, accessed 11 Jan 2025 https://www.state.gov/u-s-security-cooperation-with-ukraine/

[23] "US Security Assistance to Ukraine", *Defense*, Fact Sheet, 20 Nov 2024, accessed 12 Jan 2025 https://media.defense.gov/2024/Nov/20/2003590818/-1/-1/0/UKRAINE-FACT-SHEET-PDA-70.PDF

[24] "Military assistance to Ukraine", *Research Briefing*

[25] Alexander Korolev, "Demystifying the Enemy: Putin's Geopolitical Calculus and the War in Ukraine", *Georgetown Journal of International Affairs*, Walsh School of Foreign Service at Georgetown University, 28 Aug 2024, accessed 12 Jan 2025

[26] Paul Robinson, "The Russia-Ukraine Conflict and the (Un)Changing Character of War", *Journal of Military and Strategic Studies*, VOLUME 22, ISSUE 2, 12 Dec 2022, accessed 12 Jan 2025

[27] Elina Ribakova, "Sanctions against Russia will worsen its already poor economic prospects", *Bruegel*, 02 May 2023, accessed 12 Jan 2025 https://www.bruegel.org/analysis/sanctions-against-russia-will-worsen-its-already poor-economic-prospects

[28] "Overview: The World Bank In Ukraine", *World Bank*, 29 Oct 2024, accessed 12 Jan 2025 https://www.worldbank.org/en/country/ukraine/overview

[29] Anthony King, "What Does the War in Ukraine Tell Us About Urban Warfare?", *Canadian Army Journal*, Oct 2024, accessed 06 Jan 2025 https://www.canada.ca/en/army/services/canadian-army-journal/articles/2024/21-1-king-urban-warfare-in-ukraine.html

[30] Neveen Shaaban Abdalla, Philip H. J. Davies, Kristian Gustafson, Dan Lomas, and Steven Wagner, "Intelligence and the War in Ukraine: Part 1 & 2", *War on the Rocks Media, LLC*, 19 May 2022, accessed 14 Jan 2025 https://warontherocks.com/2022/05/intelligence-and-the-war-in-ukraine-part-1/

[31] Sascha Bruchmann, "Tanks take a sharp turn to remain relevant", *International Institute for Strategic Studies (IISS)*, 13 May 2024, accessed 12 Jan 2025 https://www.iiss.org/online-analysis/military-balance/2024/05/tanks-take-a-sharp-turn-to-remain-relevant/

[32] "Why have Russian tanks struggled in Ukraine?", *Imperial War Museums*, UK, 07 Dec 2022, accessed 15 Jan 2025 https://www.iwm.org.uk/history/why-have-russian-tanks-struggled-in-ukraine

[33] Vikram Mittal, "Artillery Is Still The King Of Battle In The Russia-Ukraine War", *Forbes*, 16 Jul 2024, accessed 12 Jan 2025 https://www.forbes.com/sites/vikrammittal/2024/07/16/artillery-is-still-the-king-of-battle-in-the-russia-ukraine-war/

[34] Vitaliy Goncharuk, "Russia's War in Ukraine: Artificial Intelligence in Defence of Ukraine", *International Centre for Defence and Security*, 27 Sep 2024, accessed 12 Jan 2025 https://icds.ee/en/russias-war-in-ukraine-artificial-intelligence-in-defence-of-ukraine/

[35] Theodora Ogden, Anna Knack, Mélusine Lebret, James Black and Vasilios Mavroudis, "The Role of the Space Domain in the Russia-Ukraine War", *The Alan Turing Institute*, Centre for Emerging Technology and Security, Feb 2024, accessed 05 Jan 2025

[36] John Grady, "Battles in the Black Sea Changing the Character of Naval Warfare", *US Naval Institute*, 13 Jun 2024, accessed 16 Jan 2025 https://news.usni.org/2024/06/13/battles-in-the-black-sea-changing-the-character-of-naval-warfare-experts-say

[37] Scott Savitz and William Courtney, "The Black Sea and the Changing Face of Naval Warfare", *RAND*, 31 Oct 2024, accessed 15 Jan 2025 https://www.rand.org/pubs/commentary/2023/10/the-black-sea-and-the-changing-face-of-naval-warfare.html

[38] Duncan McCrory, "Lessons for NATO Air Power Capability Development, Electronic Warfare in Ukraine: Preliminary", *Freeman Air and Space Institute*, King's College London, Journal Edition 36, Joint Air Power Competence Centre, Oct 2023, accessed 05 Jan 2025 https://www.japcc.org/articles/electronic-warfare-in-ukraine/

[39] Grace B Mueller, Benjamin Jensen, Brandon Valeriano, Ryan C Maness, and Jose M. Macias, "Cyber Operations during the Russo-Ukrainian War", *Center for Strategic and International Studies*, 13 Jul 2023, accessed 12 Jan 2025 https://www.csis.org/analysis/cyber-operations-during-russo-ukrainian-war

[40] Manuela Tudosia, "Lessons Learned from Ukraine: Logistics", *European Security and Defence*, 23 Jun 2023, accessed 13 Jan 2025 https://euro-sd.com/2023/06/articles/31845/lessons-learned-from-ukraine-logistics/

[41] Magdalena Kowalska-Sendek, Robert Sendek, Wojskowy Instytut Wydawniczy, "Wars Are Won by Logisticians", *Polska Zbrojna*, 03 Jul 2023, accessed 12 Jan 2025 https://polska-zbrojna.pl/home/articleshow/39892?t=Wars-Are-Won-by-Logisticians

[42] Samuel Bendett, "Roles and Implications of AI in the Russian-Ukrainian Conflict", *Center for a New American Security*, 20 Jul 2023, accessed 12 Jan 2025 https://www.cnas.org/publications/commentary/roles-and-implications-of-ai-in-the-russian-ukrainian-conflict

[43] Vitaliy Goncharuk, "Russia's War in Ukraine: Artificial Intelligence in Defence of Ukraine", *International Centre for Defence and Security*, 27 Sep 2024, accessed 12 Jan 2025 https://icds.ee/en/russias-war-in-ukraine-artificial-intelligence-in-defence-of-ukraine/

[44] Agnieszka Glapiak, "Implications of the war in Ukraine for the strategic communication system of the Polish", *Security and Defence Quarterly,* Ministry of National Defence, Poland, accessed 12 Jan 2025 https://securityanddefence.pl/Implications-of-the-war-in-Ukraine-for-the-strategic-communication-system-of-the,173070,0,2.html

[45] Elina Lange-Ionatamishvili and Sanda Svetoka, "Strategic Communications and Social Media in the Russia Ukraine Conflict", *NATO Cooperative Cyber Defence Centre of Excellence*, Oct 2018, accessed 13 Jan 2025 https://ccdcoe.org/uploads/2018/10/Ch12_CyberWarinPerspective_Lange_Svetoka.pdf

[46] Marian Nicu'or Stancu and George Cãzãnaru, "Psychological Operations During the Russian War of Aggression in Ukraine", *Land Forces Academy Review*, Volume 29 (2024): Issue 3 (September 2024), 19 Sep 2024, accessed 13 Jan 2025 https://sciendo.com/article/10.2478/raft-2024-0037

[47] Kateryna Bondar, "Does Ukraine Already Have Functional CJADC2 Technology?", *Center for Strategic and International Studies*, Dec 2024, accessed 13 Jan 2025

[48] "Cubans became Russians with one-year contract to fight in Ukraine war, now they can't leave as citizens", *FP Staff*, 13 Jan 2025, accessed 15 Jan 2025 https://www.firstpost.com/world/cubans-became-russians-with-one-year-contract-to-fight-in-ukraine-war-now-they-cant-leave-as-citizens-13852337.html

[49] "Ukraine says 20,000 volunteers from 52 countries sign up to fight", *The Times of Israel*, AP, 07 Mar 2022, accessed 12 Jan 2025 https://www.timesofisrael.com/liveblog_entry/ukraine-says-20000-volunteers-from-52-countries-sign-up-to-fight/

[50] A J H Bouwmeester MMAS, Thijs Cremers, "Mercenary armies in the Russo Ukrainian War", *Militaire Spectator*, 18 Nov 2024, accessed 12 Jan 2025 https:/ /militairespectator.nl/artikelen/mercenary-armies-russo-ukrainian-war

[51] Jyri Lavikainen, "Nuclear deterrence in the Ukraine war: Diplomacy of violence", *Finnish Institute of International Affairs*, Feb 2023, accessed 15 Jan 2025 https://fiia.fi/en/publication/nuclear-deterrence-in-the-ukraine-war

[52] Denise Schiavone, Nouran Ghanem, "MITRE Drives Whole-of-Nation Response for Whole of Ukraine", *Mitre Corporation*, 30 Aug 2022, accessed 14 Jan 2025 https://www.mitre.org/news-insights/impact-story/mitre-drives-whole-nation-response-whole-ukraine

The Changing Character of Warfare and its Implications for India

Colonel Umang Kumar Mittal

Abstract

This article examines the evolving character of warfare, driven by rapid technological advancements and shifting geopolitical dynamics. From ancient formations to artificial intelligence-powered and cyber-enabled conflicts, warfare has expanded into cognitive, digital, and economic domains. Recent conflicts in Ukraine, Israel, and the Caucasus illustrate trends such as drone warfare, hybrid tactics, and information dominance. Fifth-generation warfare now blends conventional and unconventional methods, making adaptability vital. For India, facing persistent threats from China and Pakistan, the implications are significant. The article highlights key challenges—technological gaps, cyber vulnerabilities, and infrastructure risks—while recommending strategic responses including investing in niche technologies, strengthening indigenous defence manufacturing, enhancing cyber capabilities, and adopting a multi-domain operational approach. India must embrace transformation to secure its sovereignty in the unpredictable future battlefield.

Introduction

The character of warfare had been changing continuously throughout history, shaped by technological advancements and consequently evolving military doctrines. The last century witnessed profound transformations of character of warfare, as technical advancement in the last 100 years has surpassed advancements witnessed in preceding 2000 years. From the disciplined ranks of ancient armies to the mechanised warfare of the 20th Century and the rise of cyber and information warfare in the modern era, the way conflicts are fought continues to change on a rapid pace. Today, warfare is no longer confined to traditional battlefields but extends into cyberspace, electronic, cognitive, and even economic domains.

The unparalleled destruction potential of nuclear weapons has forced the superpowers to adopt doctrine of deterrence, rather than active employment. Consequently, strategic focus has shifted towards the employment of other conventional means that offer greater flexibility in application to larger audience with lesser collateral damage. The blending of state and non-state actors, using both conventional and unconventional methods such as cyberattacks, has led to the emergence of hybrid warfare—a defining feature of contemporary conflicts. Technological innovations, such as Artificial Intelligence (AI), drone warfare, and hypersonic weapons, have revolutionised military strategy, enabling precision strikes and asymmetric tactics that challenge conventional notions of combat.

India is also entangled with challenges caused by continuously changing character of warfare due to unresolved borders with its both neighbouring adversaries. As the world stands on the brink of a new era of conflict, understanding these shifts is crucial for Indian military strategists, and security experts alike. This article explores the changing character of warfare, emerging trends in recent conflicts, likely future character of warfare, and implications for India including challenges and recommended strategic responses.

Generations of Warfare

The concept of generational warfare provides a framework for understanding the evolution of military conflicts over time. Warfare has progressed through four primary generations, each shaped by technological advancements, strategic shifts, and changes in military doctrine.

First-Generation Warfare. This phase began at 1648, the peace of Westphalia convention year[1], and included massed formations, line and column tactics, and conventional engagements by large-scale armies seen during the Napoleonic Wars. The use of muskets, cannons, and bayonets was prevalent, and the battlefield was relatively orderly. Discipline troops, formations, and massed firepower determined battlefield outcomes.

Second-Generation Warfare. With the advent of industrialisation, marked by technological advances like rifled weapons, artillery, and railroads, this phase emphasised indirect firepower and attrition warfare. World War I exemplified this generation with trench warfare and heavy reliance on logistics, leading to prolonged and static battles.

Third-Generation Warfare. This warfare marked a radical departure from attritional warfare. Developed by Germans in 1918[2] and characterised by manoeuvre warfare and speed, this phase sought to outflank and disrupt enemy forces rather than engage in direct attrition. The German Blitzkrieg strategy, enabled by latest technological elements during World War II epitomised this approach. Mechanised forces, airpower, and combined arms operations played a crucial role, making battles more fluid and fast-paced. Decentralised command, initiative at lower levels, and flexibility became crucial elements.

Fourth-Generation Warfare (4GW). The concept of 4GW was first introduced in 1989 by United States (US) military officers, in response to the emergence of widespread military operations that were ambiguous and non-linear, blurring the distinctions between peace and war, and between combatants and non-combatants. During Operation Desert Storm, the use of precision weapons and air supremacy proved devastatingly destructive and decisive against Iraq. This, in turn, compelled other nations and non-state actors to adopt asymmetric strategies, including insurgencies and terrorism, often targeting civilian populations and infrastructure to counter stronger adversaries. 4GW aims to undermine an adversary's societal cohesion and political will and blurs the lines between combatants and civilians, enhancing complexities of operations beyond traditional ones.[3] Non-state actors, propaganda, and hybrid tactics became key components.

Fifth-Generation Warfare (5GW). A concept still evolving, unlike previous generations of warfare, which primarily relied on kinetic force and conventional military means, 5GW is characterised by battles of narratives, influence, and perception, as witnessed in Russia-Ukraine conflict and in latest India-Pakistan scuffle in May 2025. This generation involves non-kinetic methods such as perception management, influence operations, cognitive warfare, and control of the information environment. 5GW targets the mind rather than the body, aiming to control narratives, disrupt societies from within, and achieve strategic objectives without conventional combat. State and non-state actors alike now possess the capability to influence populations, sow discord, undermine institutions, and shape the geopolitical landscape without resorting to traditional military engagement. Deepfakes, cyber sabotage, and AI-driven propaganda are tools of this new era, which has further amplified the reach and effectiveness of 5GW tactics.

Emerging Trends in Recent Conflicts

As cost of conventional war have tremendously escalated and involves huge destruction of man and material, lately nations prefer the 'Unrestricted Warfare', encompassing all kinds of means and ways to degrade adversary's comprehensive national power. However, it has not deterred the nations to wage conventional war to secure national objectives and interests. Recent conflicts highlight critical trends that redefine the conduct of warfare.

Drone Warfare Prominence in Azerbaijan–Armenia Conflict. Drone warfare has transformed battlefields, as seen in the Nagorno-Karabakh conflict (2020), where Azerbaijan achieved decisive victory by unprecedented and innovative employment of drones, which decimated Armenian armour and air defence. Azerbaijan initially employed drones to neutralise and blind the Armenian command, control, communications, computers, Intelligence, Surveillance, and Reconnaissance (ISR) structure and air defence artillery, then used armed drones—especially Turkish Bayraktar TB2 and Israeli Harop loitering munition—to destroy all mechanised platforms and troops in top attack mode.[4] The semi-autonomous targeting philosophy by drones transformed battle procedure and war fighting.

Hybrid Warfare in Israel–Hamas Episode. Hamas' well-coordinated and unprecedented attack on Israel on 07 Oct 2023 stunned the world by defeating what was considered the impregnable Israeli defence architecture, reinforced by advanced smart sensors and robust ISR grid. They overwhelmed Israel's Iron Dome air defence system by launching approximately 3,200 low-cost rockets within 20 minutes, while over 3,000 Hamas terrorists simultaneously infiltrated Israel borders using multiple modes of entry.

Israel's Multi-Domain Response. This audacious assault triggered a massive retaliation by Israeli Defence Forces (IDF), employing precision missiles strikes, airpower, and subsequently launching ground offensive on Gaza Strip.[5] To exert maximum pressure, Israel also imposed a total blockade, cutting off access to essential supplies such as food and water. The conflict witnessed IDF utilising multiple innovative operational techniques like small swarm of drones to detect enemies' hideouts, using AI tools to identify Hamas operatives camouflaged amongst civilians in dense urban operations. Additionally, the IDF targeted the Hamas leadership by striking communication devices such as pagers, which were still in use by the group. This conflict highlighted fusion of physical, digital, and cognitive domains, where non-traditional methods such as resource denial were employed alongside conventional military operations, effectively blurring the lines of modern warfare.

Russia–Ukraine War. The Russia–Ukraine conflict is a watershed event, which defied all predictions by world military thinkers about likely characteristics of modern warfare. The war has been a protracted affair with varying tempo from high to sluggish, amalgamation of characters of all previous generation of warfare from trench warfare to exploiting niche technology like AI.[6] Conflict in Ukraine showcased hybrid warfare, combining conventional military actions with cyberattacks, economic coercion, and disinformation campaigns. Satellite-based communications—courtesy Starlink satellite internet services, surveillance, and application-based intelligence gathering—transformed the targeting methodology during the conflict as under:

- **Drone Warfare**. Both sides have heavily relied on drones to execute variety of operations ranging from deep reconnaissance, surveillance, Electronic Warfare (EW) to destruction of enemy defences and fighting platforms, and even making tactical resupply difficult.[7] Ukraine employed thousands of small, commercially available unmanned aerial vehicles and raised new unmanned systems forces, which exemplified its asymmetric warfare's potential. In 2024 alone, Ukraine procured nearly two million drones, including 10,000 AI-equipped systems capable of autonomous navigation and target recognition, even under heavy jamming conditions.

- **Electromagnetic and Information Warfare**. Russian EW capabilities gained prominence targeting Ukraine drones, air defence systems, and communication entities during the conflict. Russia has targeted civilian population to wage information warfare by suppressing cellular communication and creating false mobile station to deliver propaganda messages, directly to personal devices in recent Russia–Ukraine conflict.[8]

- **Urban and Grey-Zone Warfare**. Russian increasingly fought in dense urban environments in all phases of the conflict, commencing with Battle of Kyiv to Battle of Bakhmut and Avdiivka.[9] After initial heavy losses, Russians got entangled in a series of urban conflicts with Ukrainian forces also launching counteroffensive to retrieve lost towns like Kharkiv, complicating military operations. Due to fast conurbation of urban areas and asymmetric advantages offered to the defender, it is inevitable that war and conflicts more likely to take place in urban areas. The use of private military contractor like Russia's Wagner Group and western defence contractors underscores the privatisation of warfare, offering plausible deniability to states.

- **Protracted Warfare**. The three year-long conflict necessitated a continuous process of adaptation and counter-adaptation by both adversaries, where substantial changes in the forces composition, equipment, tactics, and relative competitive advantages of the combatants were observed.[10] It highlighted not only importance of war stamina and strong defence manufacturer base to ensure uninterrupted supply of weapons and ammunition including new technology equipment, but also availability of adequate fighting force which will be a deciding factor for a favourable outcome of the conflict.

Likely Future Character of Warfare

Future Warfare Trends. The emerging trends in recent conflicts provide a glimpse of likely future character of warfare and spectrum of myriad complexities. As the world progresses deeper into the information age, the future character of warfare will be shaped by unprecedented technological advancements, the emergence of new battlefronts, and the convergence of multiple domains of conflict. Some of them are enumerated in succeeding paragraphs.

Network-Centric and Multi-Domain Operations. Future conflicts will integrate land, sea, air, space, and cyberspace under network-centric warfare. The adversaries will attempt to achieve information dominance to gain the shortest observe-orient-decide-act loop while denying same to the opponent by innovative utilisation of cyber and electromagnetic activities capability, both during grey-zone and conventional operations.[11] Real-time data sharing, AI-driven decision-making, and coordinated strikes will define battles.

AI, Quantum Computing, and Cybersecurity. AI has already changed the face of warfare by automating targeting policy as witnessed in recent conflicts. AI-driven autonomous weapons and quantum computing breakthroughs will challenge encryption, cyber defences, and traditional decision-making processes and intelligence analysis. Nations that achieve dominance in AI and quantum technologies will possess a strategic edge. However, the mass manifestation of these niche techs will also depend on global consensus on level of autonomy to be allowed to these techniques.

Directed Energy Weapons (DEWs) and Hypersonic Missiles. Russia demonstrated ineffectiveness of existing missile defences against hypersonic missile by hitting Kyiv with Zircon on 07 Feb 2024[12], which will motivate other nations to acquire same capability. Laser-based DEWs and hypersonic missiles will revolutionise strike capabilities, offering near-instantaneous attacks with high precision at low operational costs, especially against drones and electronic systems.

Swarm Warfare and Man-Unmanned Teaming. Swarm drones can overwhelm defences, conduct surveillance, and deliver precision strikes with minimal human involvement. Robotic soldiers and human–machine collaboration will further redefine battlefield tactics, reducing human casualties while enhancing overall effectiveness.

AI-Powered Psychological and Cognitive Warfare. AI-generated deepfakes, propaganda campaigns, and psychological warfare will manipulate public opinion and influence global geopolitics. The 'Battle of Narratives' will assume more importance than actual winning on the battlefield as it became evident in latest India-Pakistan conflict, where Pakistan, despite suffering heavy losses, claimed victory through their local media.

Hybrid Warfare. The increasingly use of conventional and unconventional tools in an integrated campaign, designed to achieve surprise, seize the initiative, and gain psychological as well as physical advantages, electronic and cyber operations, covert and occasionally overt military and intelligence action, and economic pressure will be norm for any future conflict. Grey-zone warfare, involving actions below the threshold of armed conflict e.g., economic coercion, cyber-attacks, and political subversion, will dominate future engagements, especially between major powers seeking to avoid direct confrontation.

Implications for India

India and the Changing Face of Warfare. The future battlefield will be complicated mosaic of grey-zone and hybrid warfare infused with niche technologies. The blurring of the traditional boundaries between the physical, digital, and psychological domains in recent conflicts offer valuable lessons for nations across the globe. For India, a country with complex and volatile security dynamics under overarching umbrella of collusivity between its two adversaries, the changing character of warfare presents both immediate and long-term challenges that demand strategic foresight, modernisation, and resilience.

Two-and-a-Half-Front Plus Threat. India continues to face a unique security predicament marked by hybrid and possible conventional threats from China and Pakistan, ongoing internal security challenges, and other neighbours due to recent political regime changes, requiring preparedness across spectrum of warfare. This scenario is further complicated by the deepening strategic collusion between China and Pakistan, including joint military exercises, technology transfers, and potential coordination in hybrid domains such as cyber and information warfare as evident during recent Operation Sindoor. The prospect of grey-zone operations, sub-conventional warfare, and possibility of simultaneous hostilities on both fronts, with covert and overt collusivity, necessitates a robust strategic posture in all domains. India must also anticipate multi-domain coercion combines with cyber disruptions and disinformation campaigns with traditional military manoeuvres.

Vulnerability of Critical Infrastructure. In the era of hybrid and grey-zone warfare, India's critical infrastructure has emerged as a key vulnerability. India's power grids, financial networks, and railway systems remains potential targets for cyber-attacks, sabotage, and information manipulation, especially during grey-zone period. The civil-military integration in the cyber domain remains weak or in the nascent stage. While government has initiated multiple efforts to bolster cyber defence capabilities, the lack of a unified national cyber command, insufficient public-private collaboration, and the absence of proactive cyber deterrence leave critical sectors exposed. There is an urgent need to build resilient digital infrastructure, enhance cyber threat intelligence sharing, and develop offensive cyber capabilities to deter and respond to potential grey-zone aggressions.

Technological Lag and Defence Modernisation. Despite notable initiatives and advancements, India's defence sector continues to lag leading military powers in many critical capabilities especially in AI, hypersonic missiles, and space militarisation. Challenges stem from:

- Limited Research and Development (R&D) ecosystem and dependence on imports.
- Inefficient defence public sector undertakings with outdated production lines and slower innovation cycles.
- Low levels of private sector participation and limited synergy between academia, start-ups, and the armed forces.

Reforming Defence Acquisition. India's drive towards *Atmanirbharta* (Self-reliance) is a strategic necessity, but it faces obstacles such as inefficient capital acquisition procedures and lack of sustained funding for high-risk innovation, which have led to widening voids in current technological capability. Hence, significant reforms in the defence acquisition ecosystem and strengthening indigenous R&D is crucial to achieve essential critical capabilities.

Geopolitical and Economic Constraints. The global geopolitical landscape adds another layer of complexity. With intensifying great-power rivalries, supply chain disruptions, and shifting alliances, India faces challenges in acquiring cutting-edge military technologies and platforms. India's efforts to diversify its defence imports also exposes her to geopolitical pressures, technology denial regimes, and potential sanctions.

Strategic Partnerships. Moreover, endeavouring to balance military preparedness with existing economic constraints requires innovative financing models, strategic partnerships, joint ventures, and technology transfers with other interested nations to achieve optimum defence modernisation.

Recommended Trajectory of Actions

Evolving Warfare. Indian military hierarchy is cognisant of evolving character of warfare and the multifaceted challenges it presents. They have already embarked on a comprehensive transformation journey under 'Decade of Transformation' to address these emerging challenges. However, given the accelerating pace of technological change, geopolitical flux, and the growing prominence of grey-zone and hybrid warfare, several additional strategic measures are essential to ensure India's security preparedness and strategic autonomy.

Defence Cooperation. To strengthen collaboration to enhance technological capabilities, India must deepen its defence cooperation with strategic partners such as the US, Israel, France, Russia, Japan, and other partners for intelligence sharing, joint R&D, joint equipment development, and technology transfers.[13] Collaborations with global defence firms and academic institution should be strengthened to build up AI-driven defence technologies, robust dual-use technology ecosystems, and hypersonic missile programs. India must also actively leverage multilateral platforms such as the Quadrilateral Security Dialogue and Association of Southeast Asian Nations' Defence Ministers' Meetings to enhance regional security cooperation in cyber, space, and maritime domains.

Develop Multi-Domain Operations Capability. India needs to develop robust cyber deterrence mechanisms and counter-disinformation strategies. A dedicated cyber command for military and national security operations needs to be established to enhance coordination between defence forces, space, and civil agencies for seamless operations. India needs to expedite the establishment of theatre commands and develop adaptive doctrines that include cyber, space, and cognitive domains. In addition, suitable structures at all levels to fight multi-domain warfare should be raised and functional. Simultaneously, public awareness programs and digital literacy initiatives must be promoted to build resilience within society.

Invest in Niche and Emerging Defence Technologies. To align with future needs, a steady increase in capital outlays for emerging warfare technologies is vital. India should accelerate indigenous drone, robotic, and unmanned combat aerial vehicles and AI-enabled decision-support systems development to enhance battlefield effectiveness.[14] Swarm drones, loitering munition systems, and battle-winner force should to be acquired to achieve precision strikes and battlefield dominance capability. A multi-layered approach to battlefield digitisation including secure communication networks, battlefield management systems, and real-time data integration is essential to facilitate faster and more informed decision-making in complex operations.

Review Military Doctrine and Training. India needs to review its existing doctrines and training philosophy to be ready as per emerging trends of warfare. It should adapt military strategies to hybrid and grey-zone warfare challenges, incorporating AI and unmanned systems. Enhancing competencies in legal warfare, information operations, and unconventional missions through elite special forces is also essential. Professional military education reforms need to continue to create technologically literate cadre capable of handling and leading future technologies. Cross-service training, civilian-military exchanges, and institutionalising practices like war-gaming and red-teaming will foster an innovation-friendly culture.

Strengthen Internal Security Mechanisms. Internal security challenges from insurgencies, terrorism, and communal strife continue to strain national security. These threats are increasingly linked to external actors and hybrid strategies. Therefore, enhanced collaboration among all security forces is vital for a unified response. Developing a national resilience framework—powered by technology-driven surveillance, big data analytics, and real-time intelligence sharing—is essential to detect and neutralise emerging threats early.

Boost Indigenous Defence Manufacturing. The geopolitical lessons of recent conflicts, where nations prioritised self-sufficiency and supply chain security, underscore the urgent need for India to build a robust indigenous defence industrial base. Hence, India needs to implement *Atmanirbhar Bharat* (Self-reliant India) initiatives more aggressively to reduce dependency on foreign suppliers for critical military hardware and develop strong defence manufacturer base by incentivising private players through introduction of attractive policies. India must focus on building dual-use technologies and defence start-up ecosystems through partnerships with India's vibrant information technology, space, and semiconductor sectors. Public-private-academic collaboration needs encouragement to fuel research in next-generation defence technologies while ensuring alignment with military requirements.

Conclusion

The character of warfare is undergoing rapid and profound changes, driven by technological advancements, geopolitical shifts, and emerging threats. For India, understanding these changes is crucial to safeguard national security and strategic interests. By investing in cutting-edge defence technologies, enhancing cybersecurity, and adapting to new conflict paradigms, India can navigate the evolving security landscape effectively. A proactive, technology-driven, and multi-domain approach will ensure India remains prepared for future warfare challenges, retaining its strategic autonomy in an unpredictable world.

Endnotes

1 Fatma Twfiak, "The Development of Warfare Through Seven Generations: Cyber- Attacks and impacts on international Relations", *International Affairs Forum*, accessed 03 Mar 2025 https://www.ia-forum.org/Files/BNMWSM.pdf

2 Ibid.

3 EBSCO, "Fourth-Generation Warfare (4GW)", *Research Starters*, 2024, accessed 05 Mar 2025 https://www.ebsco.com/research-starters/history/fourth-generation-warfare-4gw

4 Eado Hecht, "Drones in the Nagorno-Karabakh War: Analyzing the Data", *Military Strategy Magazine*, vol. 7, no. 4 (Winter 2022): 31–37, accessed 15 Mar 2025 https://www.militarystrategymagazine.com/article/drones-in-the-nagorno-karabakh-war-analyzing-the-data

[5] Maria Bordas, "Hamas-Israel War: A Brief Analysis of First Two Phases of War", *European Scientific Journal* 20, no. 11 (Apr 2024): 1, accessed 06 Mar 2025 https://www.researchgate.net/publication/380240397_Hamas_Israel_War_A _Brief_Analysis_of_First_Two_Phases_of_War

[6] Eliot A Cohen and Phillips O'Brien, "The Russia-Ukraine War: A Study in Analytic Failure", *CSIS* (analysis report), 24 Sep 2024, accessed 05 Mar 2025 https://www.csis.org/analysis/russia-ukraine-war-study-analytic-failure

[7] Jack Watling and Nick Reynolds, "Tactical Developments During the Third Year of the Russo–Ukrainian War", (London: Royal United Services Institute, 2024), pp 16, accessed 15 Mar 2025 https://rusi.org/explore-our-research/publications/special-resources/tactical-developments-during-third-year-russo-ukrainian-war

[8] Andreas Turunen, "The Broader Challenge of Russian Electronic Warfare Capabilities", in *Improvisation and Adaptability in the Russian Military*, ed. Jeffrey Mankoff (Washington, DC: Center for Strategic and International Studies, Apr 2020), pp 17, accessed 15 Mar 2025 https://csis-website-prod.s3.amazonaws.com/s3fs-public/publication/200430_Mankoff_ Russian%20Military_ web_v3_ UPDATED%20FINAL.pdf

[9] Anthony King, "What Does the War in Ukraine Tell Us About Urban Warfare?" *Canadian Army Journal* 21, no. 1 (2024), accessed 15 Mar 2025 https://www.canada.ca/en/army/services/canadian-army-journal/articles/2024/21-1-king-urban-warfare-in-ukraine.html

[10] Michael Kofman, "Assessing Russian Military Adaptation in 2023", *Carnegie Endowment for International Peace*, 08 Oct 2024, accessed 15 Mar 2025 https://carnegieendowment.org/research/2024/10/assessing-russian-military-adaptation-in-2023?lang=en

[11] James Black, Alice Lynch, Kristian Gustafson, David Blagden, Pauline Paillé, and Fiona Quimbre, "Multi-Domain Integration in Defence: Conceptual Approaches and Lessons from Russia, China, Iran and North Korea", *RAND Corporation*, RR-A528-1, 2022, accessed 13 Mar 2025 https://www.rand.org/pubs/research_reports/RRA528-1.html

[12] Reuters, "Russia Uses Zircon Hypersonic Missile in Ukraine", *Reuters*, 13 Feb 2024, accessed 12 Mar 2025 https://www.reuters.com/world/europe/russia-uses-zircon-hypersonic-missile-ukraine-2024-02-13

[13] Mercy A Kuo, "India-Israel Defense and Security Cooperation", *The Diplomat*, 19 Nov 2024, accessed 15 Mar 2025 https://thediplomat.com/2024/11/india-israel-defense-and-security-cooperation/

[14] Akshat Upadhyay, "Fighting Future Wars: Preparing India for Conflicts in the 21st Century", *Observer Research Foundation* (ORF) research brief, 2022, accessed 15 Mar 2025 https://www.orfonline.org/research/fighting-future-wars-preparing-india-for-conflicts-in-the-21st-century

Future Warfare: Will Technology Ultimately Replace the Soldier?

Colonel Mohit Kuntal, SM

Abstract

This article explores the transformative impact of Artificial Intelligence (AI), robotics, and automation on the evolving character of warfare. It traces the historical arc from the invention of gunpowder to precision and autonomous warfare, highlighting how technology has redefined combat strategy. The article examines global efforts—by the United States, China, and Russia—to develop robotic militaries and intelligent warfare systems, while showcasing current innovations like drone swarms, AI-led decision-making, and unmanned ground vehicles. It warns, however, that this technological shift raises moral, legal, and accountability concerns. Drawing from both past battles like Rezang La and speculative future scenarios, this article argues that while machines will amplify military capabilities, they cannot replace the ethical judgment, emotional intelligence, and adaptability of human soldiers—making a case for balanced man-machine integration in future conflicts.

Introduction

Warfare has always evolved with technology—from the invention of gunpowder to the deployment of nuclear weapons, each breakthrough has redefined combat. Today, Artificial Intelligence (AI), robotics, and autonomous systems are driving the next transformation in military operations. Concepts once confined to science fiction—intelligent drones, robotic soldiers, algorithm-led battles—are now shaping strategic realities across the globe. As powerful nations compete to dominate this new frontier, the very character of warfare is being reshaped. Yet amid this technological surge, a critical question persists: will machines replace the soldier, or will they remain powerful allies in a future battlefield led by human judgment?

Change is Inevitable

*Hasta La Vista, Baby (*See you later, baby*)*, a legendary dialogue from movie *Terminator II* is known to all those who believe in technological transformation of warfare. The movie showed us the future in the past i.e., in 1984. It was a bold peek into a future where humanity might one day be challenged by AI or technology. Similarly, numerous scientists, authors, and researchers have also predicted the emergence of robotic armies in the 21st Century. The initiative to integrate AI and robotics into the battlefield represents a bold endeavour that has the potential to change the future of warfare.

The adage 'Change is the only constant' resonates profoundly as the character of warfare continuously evolves, driven primarily by the advent and proliferation of technology. Throughout history, technological advancements have acted as catalysts for the transformation of warfighting. From the invention of gunpowder to the introduction of nuclear weapons, every major leap in technology has redefined the battlefield. In modern times, the rise of AI, robotics, and cyber warfare mark a paradigm shift in military operations. These advancements enable nations to conduct precise and efficient operations while minimising or eliminating risks to human soldiers.

Technology is Changing Character of War

Gunpowder Revolution. War has historically been thought of as a form of direct armed conflict characterised by violence and physical aggression. However, with the advent of technology; violence, lethality and precision have increased exponentially. Technological innovation in combat began with the invention of gunpowder. Traced back to medieval China, experiments with a medical compound enabled a 'Bullet' to be shot up to a range of 10 feet.[1] Initially, gunpowder was used for fireworks, however, its military potential was soon realised, leading to the development of rudimentary firearms and cannons. By the 14th Century, gunpowder had spread to Europe, where it revolutionised battlefields. Battles became more focused on firepower and close-quarters engagements shifted to long distance combat.

Mechanised Warfare. Industrial revolution of the early 20th Century further transformed warfare.[2] The mass production of rifles, machine guns, and artillery enhanced the battlefield lethality. With the introduction of tanks, World War I witnessed the marvel of mechanised warfare, which altered the combat dynamics. By World War II, air power, aircraft carriers, and long-range missiles added new dimensions to military strategy, making battles more mobile and less predictable.

Precision Warfare. The Gulf War of 1991 demonstrated the power of precision, where superior technology enabled swift and decisive victory. Guided missiles and smart bombs allowed for targeted strikes with minimal collateral damage. The precision weapons ensured extremely high effectiveness during the conflict, thereby, demonstrating a shift from traditional bombings with unguided munitions to targeted attacks that could neutralise critical enemy capabilities with unprecedented accuracy. The ability to hit even smaller targets accurately changed military strategy, allowing forces to conduct operations that would have been deemed too risky or impractical with conventional bombs.

Autonomous or AI Warfare. As AI, robotics, and autonomous systems continue to advance, warfare is once again on the brink of transformation. AI-powered drones, autonomous weapons, and data-driven decision-making are reshaping military strategies. AI-powered autonomous weapons and vehicles are at the forefront of military innovation. These systems are conducting reconnaissance, surveillance, and combat operations with minimal human intervention, thereby, fundamentally altering traditional combat dynamics.[3] The advancement of AI in modern warfare will forever alter the relationships between great powers like the United States (US), China, and Russia. For this reason, Beijing has committed USD 150 bn to become the world leader in AI technology, compared to the Russian spending of USD 181 mn from 2021 to 2023 and the US spending of USD 4.6 bn.[4]

Race for Intelligentised and Robotic Militaries

Quest for Technology. The US announced its 'Third Offset Strategy' in 2014, which sought to maintain US military advantage using AI and unmanned weapons. China, in 2019, announced a new military strategy, 'Intelligentised Warfare', utilising AI. In Sep 2017, Russian President Vladimir Putin said that the first country to develop true AI will rule the world.[5] The US, Russia, and China are the prominent competitors in the advancement of military robotic and autonomous systems. AI-enabled robots, due to their capabilities, can be employed across various domains like intelligence, surveillance, and reconnaissance, target acquisitions, and combat operations. The use of military robots in high-risk missions such as explosive ordnance disposal, route clearance, obstacle breaching, and Chemical, Biological, Radiological, and Nuclear (CBRN) will further decrease or eliminate the human interface. In 2022, the global military robots and autonomous systems market was valued at USD 17,575.1 mn and is expected to reach USD 19,794.0 mn by the end of 2033.[6] Countries world over, due to certain advantages, are experimenting with the employment of robots to execute high-risk tasks, presently being carried out by soldiers. The US Army is experimenting with induction of robots and wants machines in these new formations to 'Offload Risk' and provide soldiers with additional information for decision making.[7] During one such exercise 'Project Convergence', which was designed to test robots in realistic combat scenarios, General James Rainey, who leads the US Army Futures Command, articulated that the future force to be so integrated with machines that humans will face a much lower risk and said, "We will never again trade blood for first contact" but promised to deploy robots instead.[8] Details of some of the projects are as enumerated in Table 1.

Country	Project Name	Robotic System	Purpose
US	Ghost Robotics Vision 60	Quadrupedal robot	Surveillance and patrol
US	Loyal Wingman (Skyborg)	AI-powered autonomous drone	Fighter jet companion
Russia	Uran-9	Unmanned combat ground vehicle	Recon and combat support
Russia	Udar	Unmanned combat ground vehicle based on BMP 3	Udar as a 'Multi-purpose robotic platform' that can be customised with different weapons and equipment depending on the mission
Russia	Marker Robot	AI-powered combat robot	Border patrol and combat missions
Russia	Uran-9	Unmanned combat ground vehicle	Recon and combat support
China	Sharp Claw 1 and 2	Unmanned ground vehicles	Reconnaissance, patrol, and urban battle missions
China	Wing Loong Unmanned Combat Aerial Vehicle	Unmanned aerial combat vehicle	Air strikes and surveillance
Israel	RoBattle	Modular unmanned ground vehicle	Combat and reconnais-sance

Table 1: Technology Fights the Battles and Humanity Watches

Battle of Valour and Courage: Rezang La. The scene shifts back to the year 1962, unveiling the rugged, snow-covered landscape of Rezang La. Charlie Company of 13 Kumaon, comprising of 120 Indian soldiers, is braving the biting cold pierces through their woollen uniforms and the soldiers are crudely dug in trenches, reinforced with sandbags. Major Shaitan Singh stands at the forefront, scanning the horizon with binoculars.

- Nathha Singh (loading his bolt-action rifle), "*Saab* (Sir), the scouts reports movement on the eastern ridge. Chinese are advancing".
- Major Shaitan Singh, "Prepare for battle. Last man last bullet", "*Bharat Mata Ki Jai* (Hail Mother India)".
- The soldiers nod resolutely. Some check their Lee-Enfield rifles, while others sharpen their bayonets.
- Bhup Singh (smiling), "Bayonets against artillery, *saab*?"
- Major Shaitan Singh (smiling back), "Courage and grit are timeless and these do not run out like bullets".
- The Chinese soldiers in hundreds advance in tight waves, carrying modern automatic weapons.
- Major Shaitan Singh (yelling), "Hold fire! Let them come closer" (Soldiers wait keeping fingers on triggers. When the enemy is within range, Major Shaitain Singh gives the order).
- Major Shaitan Singh, "Fire!" (The soldiers unleash a volley from their rifles. Some rush forward with bayonets as ammunition dwindles, engaging in hand-to-hand combat. Smoke, shouts, and the clash of metal fill the air).

This was a scene from Battle of Rezang La, where 120 stood against hundreds, leaving a legacy of unmatched valour and courage.

Rezang La, Future Battlefield 2050. The battlefield is devoid of human soldiers. Autonomous drones hover silently, scanning the icy pass, while robotic infantry company with sleek metallic frames stand in precise formations. A command centre deep underground coordinates the operation. Screens display tactical data as AI algorithms monitor every move.

- AI Command Voice (calm, monotone), "Enemy detected at Kailash ridge. Deploy countermeasures".
- Swarm drones activate, rising in unison. They zip across the sky, emitting a faint hum. Advanced sensors lock onto heat signatures of the approaching enemy. On the opposing ridge, humanoid robots of the enemy force march forward, armed with laser rifles.

- Tactical Officer (from command centre), "AI Omega, assess threat level".
- AI Omega, "Threat level high. Enemy units 1,500. Initiating offensive defence protocol Rezang La-5".
- Autonomous turrets embedded in the mountains spring to life, firing high-energy plasma rounds. The enemy robots counter with energy shields, deflecting some shots. The battlefield lights up with bursts of energy weapons and explosions, yet not a single human voice is heard.
- In a nearby outpost, a lone human commander oversees the battle through augmented reality goggles.
- Commander (to himself), "No bravery, No fear. and No loss of life. Is this still war?" Commander removes his headset, staring at a monitor displaying a cold clinical victory.
- The rapid advancement of technology (especially in robotics) has the potential to revolutionise warfare, leading to future bloodless conflicts with no human casualties. Robotics, autonomous systems, and AI-driven technologies will take over high-risk tasks traditionally carried out by soldiers, reducing direct human involvement on the battlefield. This shift will not only decrease the operational and sustainment costs of military forces but also enhance overall efficiency and effectiveness. In addition, AI algorithms analyse vast data sets to predict enemy strategies, shortens observe, orient, decide, and act loop, thereby, ensuring enhanced and faster decision making.

Difficult Road Ahead for Robotic Militaries

Ethical and Moral Dilemma. War has traditionally raised several important ethical dilemmas. Even the great warrior Arjun refused to fight with his relatives and dear ones in Mahabharat and then, Lord Krishna had to guide him. Delegation of life and death decisions to machine or AI, which is devoid of any emotions, is not prudent.

Accountability. Military accountability is the foundation of military duty and includes the legal obligation to comply with the law of armed conflict or international humanitarian law. The potential use of machines or technology as a replacement for soldiers has raised concerns about accountability, as humans may no longer be held responsible for decisions made by machines, AI, or autonomous weapon systems during armed conflict.

Legal Challenges. International organisations have been intensifying calls for limits or even outright bans on use of autonomous or AI weapons systems. The United Nations General Assembly in Dec 2024 adopted the Resolution 79/62[9] on lethal autonomous weapons systems or killer robots, which can select and attack targets without human intervention.

Human Emotions. Soldiers are not merely fighting machines; they are individuals who experience fear, courage, and moral dilemmas on the battlefield. Robotic soldiers or technology may mitigate some risks but cannot replicate the complex emotional intelligence and moral reasoning that human soldiers bring to combat situations. In high-stress combat situations, soldiers can make nuanced decisions based on empathy and ethical considerations; these qualities cannot be replicated by machines.

Soldiers are Indispensable. Evolution of technology is as old as mankind. Every decade, every century, technology has developed and brought transformation in warfare. Gulf War I of 1990 employed the most advanced technology of its time, which today appears comparatively primitive or modest. Today, there is no doubt that technologies such as AI, unmanned aerial vehicles, autonomous weapon systems, and others are changing the contours of warfare. These technologies are serving as force multipliers and are being integrated with humans or soldiers through Man-Unmanned Teaming (MUM-T), but they are yet to replace the soldier. Machines or technology are presently not good at reacting to novelty i.e., being original. On the other hand, humans possess a strong ability to adapt to novel situations, and since adaptability is vital in warfare, the presence of humans or soldiers will always remain essential in armed conflict.

Future Prospect: Man-Unmanned Teaming

Manned-Unmanned Teaming. MUM-T is becoming a fundamental aspect of future warfare, integrating advanced technology with human decision making to enhance mission effectiveness. In near future, these systems will utilise AI-driven swarm robots, quantum-resistant networks, and adaptive machine learning to autonomously perform high-risk operational tasks, while maintaining human oversight for ethical and strategic decision-making.[10]

Technological Absorption and Human-Machine Synergy. AI-enabled autonomous systems are integrating into modern MUM-T designs for repetitive or dangerous tasks and for reconnaissance, electronic warfare, and precision attacks, while transmitting real-time data to manned command centres. Unmanned platforms like Airbus' Remote Carriers and the US Collaborative Combat Aircraft carry out risky tasks, such as breaching enemy fortifications, neutralising mines, or working in CBRN environments.[11] In contested and hazardous areas, these technologies rely on sophisticated sensor fusion and faster machine data processing, thereby, reducing human exposure to risk to a greater extent.[12]

Human Judgment in AI-Assisted Warfare. Human operators, on the other hand, maintain control over judgmental activities, which require contextual awareness like target prioritisation and proportionality evaluations under the Law of Armed Conflict and escalation management. For example, Advanced Light Helicopter Dhruv pilots during the Indian Army's Exercise *Sarvashakti* (Omnipotent) in 2025 overrode AI recommendations to avoid damaging civilian infrastructure in the Himalayan attack zone. This division of responsibilities ensures that while people choose 'Whether' and 'When' to act, machines manage 'How' to carry out tasks.[13]

Human Override and Control Mechanisms. To avoid autonomous control, MUM-T systems incorporate human-in-the-loop protocols. For instance, in dynamic battles, pilots of the US Army AH-64E Apache helicopters can switch between AI suggestions and manual control due to tiered levels of interoperability.[14] In the same way, the US Navy's unmanned surface vehicles use geofencing algorithms to prevent unauthorised human entry into politically sensitive waters. Any AI suggestion, no matter how well-planned it may be, must be reviewed by a human before it can be considered ethically. The need of moral reasoning in combat was highlighted during 2024 North Atlantic Treaty Organization's wargames, when a considerable percentage of AI-generated strike plans were rejected by commanders because of the risk of collateral damage. The use of augmented reality dashboards to simplify decision-making without overburdening operators is increasingly a priority in interface designs, with cognitive ergonomics as the primary focus.[15]

Challenges and Future Trajectories. Despite advancements, MUM-T confronts challenges with trust calibration and electromagnetic robustness. Over-reliance on AI risks making operators less sensitive to minor battlefield signs, while adversary spoofing of drone swarms remains a key weakness. Looking ahead, MUM-T will expand into urban and underwater domains, with micro-drones cleaning buildings and unmanned submersibles exploring sea beds. The speed of machines must never outpace the conscience of commanders. By balancing technological absorption with human agency, MUM-T promises to redefine multi-domain warfare while upholding ethical imperatives.

Conclusion

The increasing reliance on technology has introduced new dimensions to warfare, creating battlefields in virtual spaces and erasing traditional frontlines. As this technological landscape continues to evolve, it is crucial to ensure that advancements enhance military capabilities without compromising humanity or accountability in conflict. The future of military operations lies in balanced integration of technology and humans, where technology serves as an enabler rather than a replacement for human soldiers.

Endnotes

[1] "A Brief History of Modern Warfare Technology: From Gunpowder to Drones", *Technology Org*, 30 Jan 2018, accessed 20 Jun 2025 https://www.technology.org/2018/01/30/a-brief-history-of-modern-warfare-technology-from-gunpowder-to-drones/

[2] Walter S. Zapotoczny, "The Impact of the Industrial Revolution on Warfare", *WZAP Online*, 2006, accessed 21 Jun 2025 https://www.wzaponline.com/yahoo_site_admin/assets/docs/InductrialRevolution.292125935.pdf

[3] "Artificial Intelligence in Military Technology – 8 Applications and Examples", *Fly Sight*, 14 Jun 2023, accessed 22 Jun 2025 https://www.flysight.it/artificial-intelligence-in-military-technology-8-applications-examples/

[4] Kristian Humble, "War, Artificial Intelligence, and the Future of Conflict", *Georgetown Journal of International Affairs*, 12 Jul 2024, accessed 22 Jun 2025 https://gjia.georgetown.edu/2024/07/12/war-artificial-intelligence-and-the-future-of-conflict/

[5] Koichiro Takagi, "Artificial Intelligence and Future Warfare", *Hudson*, 23 Nov 2022, accessed 23 Jun 2025 https://www.hudson.org/defense-strategy/artificial-intelligence-future-warfare

[6] "Military Robotic and Autonomous System (RAS) Market—A Global and Regional Analysis, Focus on Application, Platform, Operation Mode, and Country—Analysis and Forecast, 2023–2033", *BIS Research*, 2025, accessed 24 Jun 2025 https://bisresearch.com/industry-report/military-robotic-autonomous-systems-market.html

[7] Jen Judson, "The Robots Are Coming: US Army Experiments with Human-Machine Warfare", *Defense News*, 25 Mar 2024, accessed 25 Jun 2025 https://www.defensenews.com/unmanned/2024/03/25/the-robots-are-coming-us-army-experiments-with-human-machine-warfare

[8] Ibid.

[9] "Killer Robots: UN Vote Should Spur Treaty Negotiations", *Human Rights Watch*, 05 Dec 2024, accessed 25 Jun 2025 https://www.hrw.org/news/2024/12/05/killer-robots-un-vote-should-spur-treaty-negotiations

[10] Gp Capt (Dr) DK Pandey (Retd), "Manned-Unmanned Teaming: Enhancing Lethality", *CENJOWS*, 09 Jan 2025, accessed 29 Jun 2025 https://cenjows.in/manned-unmanned-teaming-enhancing-lethality/

[11] Gp Capt (Dr) D.K Pandey (Retd), "MUM-T v/s A2/AD: Exploring to Dominate in a Contested Environment", *SYNERGY*, vol. 2, no. 2 (Sep 2023), accessed 25 Jun 2025 https://cenjows.in/wp-content/uploads/2023/10/Ch-06-Dinesh-Kumar.pdf

[12] Thomas K. Adams, "Future Warfare and the Decline of Human Decision Making", *Parameters* 41 (2001), accessed 25 Jun 2025 https://press.armywarcollege.edu/cgi/viewcontent.cgi?article=2058&context= parameters

[13] Anamika Dutta, "Indian Army Breaks New Ground with MUM-T Capability in Northeast: Trishakti Corps Leads the Way", *Times Now*, 09 Apr 2025, accessed 26 Jun 2025 https://www.timesnownews.com/india/indian-army-breaks-new-ground-with-mum-t-capability-in-northeast-trishakti-corps-leads-the-way-article-151354669

[14] Mark Currass, "The Future of Manned-Unmanned Teaming (MUM-T) Opportunities and Challenges", *LinkedIn*, 23 Apr 2024, accessed 24 Jun 2025 https://www.linkedin.com/pulse/future-manned-unmanned-teaming

[15] Monte Erfourth, "Blending AI with Human Judgment, Man, Machine, and the Battlefield in Modern Warfare", *Strategy Central*, 08 Dec 2024, accessed 28 Jun 2025 https://www.strategycentral.io/post/blending-ai-with-human-judgment

Artificial Intelligence: Disrupting the Character of Warfare

Colonel Neeraj Mann

"By far the greatest danger of artificial intelligence is that people conclude too early that they understand it"

—**Eliezer Yudkowsky**

Abstract

Artificial Intelligence (AI) and its applications are bursting through the seams. While optimists believe that it will herald a new era of prosperity, there are growing concerns about the common future in the absence of any established ethical and moral rules of its research or application. The restrictions earlier constraining its growth have all but disappeared with the availability of phenomenal computing power, lightening internet speeds, and enormous data. With the shackles now gone, the animal that is AI does seem to have a malignant side as well. While there is a general sense that these threats are well understood, the reality is that future developments may unfold in ways vastly different from current expectations and preparations. National security and security, in general, are vulnerable to potential ulterior motives driven by AI. Some of these threats have been highlighted to encourage further research on the subject.

Introduction

Artificial Intelligence (AI) is everywhere—in the news, teatime conversations, mobile and internet applications, and movies. It is already affecting most aspects of everyone's daily routine in new and profound ways. In the last decade, AI has been able to break the ceiling, and the acceleration it has achieved is expanding to the other domains, horizontally as well as vertically. It is already being touted as the 'Cambrian Explosion' of technology.[1] The last few years have seen a burst of applications and use cases of AI that have brought transformative changes to fields like learning, medicine, marketing, and supply chain management, amongst a few. In this emerging landscape, the military cannot stay isolated from its effects for long. The security, both at organisational and national level, will face major challenges in the very near future because the growth of AI, both in scale and complexity, is so rapid that it will overwhelm the painfully slow bureaucratic system of threat assessment.

Evolution of Artificial Intelligence: Principal Factors

When Alan Turing proposed the concept of a universal machine in 1936[2], he would not have thought that 60.42 per cent of the world's population (4.88 billion in actual numbers) would be owning 'Pocket-sized Supercomputers' aka smartphones in 2024.[3] With such reach and availability of super high-speed internet, there is little that even a marginally powerful AI cannot achieve. This is highlighted as under:

- **Computational Power**. The evolution of computational power has been nothing short of revolutionary. While AI research saw intermittent successes, a major public breakthrough came in 1997 when International Business Machines' Deep Blue defeated world chess champion Garry Kasparov.[4] The limitations in processing capabilities were overcome by rapid advancements in microchip technology that were driven by commercial industries. While Moore's Law, which predicted the doubling of transistors in dense integrated circuits every two years[5], has begun to slow down, the industry has responded with new innovations such as 2.5- and 3.0-dimensional chip integration. With the rise of AI-specialised chips like Google's tensor processing unit and NVIDIA's latest graphics processing units, computing power continues to surge beyond what was predicted decades ago. The advent of quantum computing is set to further redefine these limits, promising exponential gains in processing capability. In 1985, the CRAY-2, a supercomputer, set a record with a peak performance of 1.9 gigaflops, dwarfing the Apollo-11 Guidance Computer. Fast forward to today, even a flagship smartphone can surpass that performance by over 5,000 times.[6]

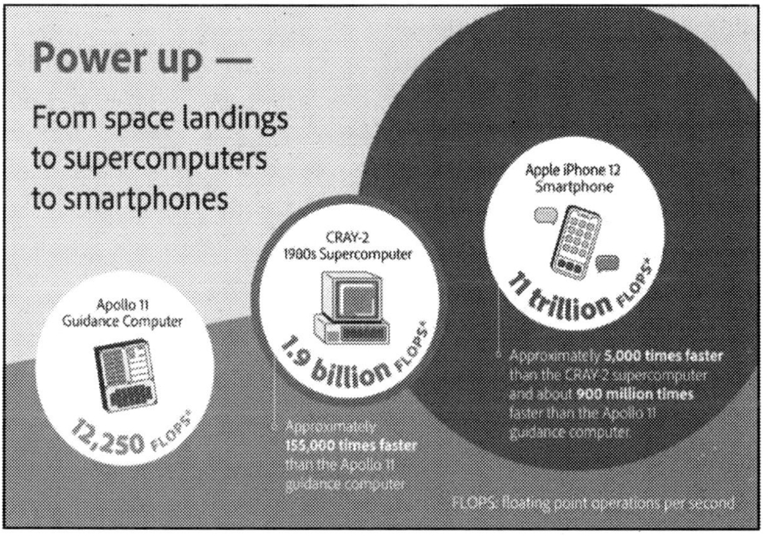

Figure 1: Comparison between CRAY-2 and iPhone 12
Source: Adobe Blog[7]

❑ **Internet Speeds**. These have also undergone a meteoric rise. When AI concepts were being explored for the first time, networking was virtually non-existent, and it was not until 1995 that the internet became commercially available. Dial-up connections struggled at 14.4 Kbps, but by the early 2000s, broadband and Wi Fi transformed accessibility.[8] As of 2024, the global average wired internet speed exceeds 150 Mbps, growing at an annual rate of nearly 20 per cent.[9] Similarly, mobile internet has progressed from the rudimentary wireless application protocol services of 1999 to today's 5G networks, offering gigabit-level speeds. Nearly every digitally capable individual has access to high-speed internet at historically low costs, laying the groundwork for widespread AI integration.

❑ **Data Availability**. Perhaps the most significant enabler of AI's rapid development is the explosion of data. From a mere 0.054 ZB (10 GB[10]) in 2000,[11] global data volume is projected to exceed 200 ZB by 2025—an increase of nearly 4,000 times.[12] The rise of cloud storage and big data analytics has enabled corporations to harness vast amounts of user-generated information, often buried within complex 'Terms of Service' agreements that only a few read. AI research is gaining more traction from private corporations as compared to academic institutions, where commercial agendas often dictate the pace of innovation. The ethical and security challenges this poses are profound—AI is no longer a tool reserved for governments or elite organisations but is available to anyone with the necessary skills and intent. The rapid commercialisation of AI has outpaced regulatory frameworks, raising urgent questions: who will oversee its ethical deployment, and where should the boundaries be drawn? The defence industry and national security, in general, cannot stay insulated from this growth. AI is going to affect security in ways previously unimagined, as it slowly transforms the way of life. The true disruption is yet to happen, it is visible, and one can feel it like a jungle fire, but the security planners may not be truly comprehending its true force or velocity and may soon get engulfed in its fury.

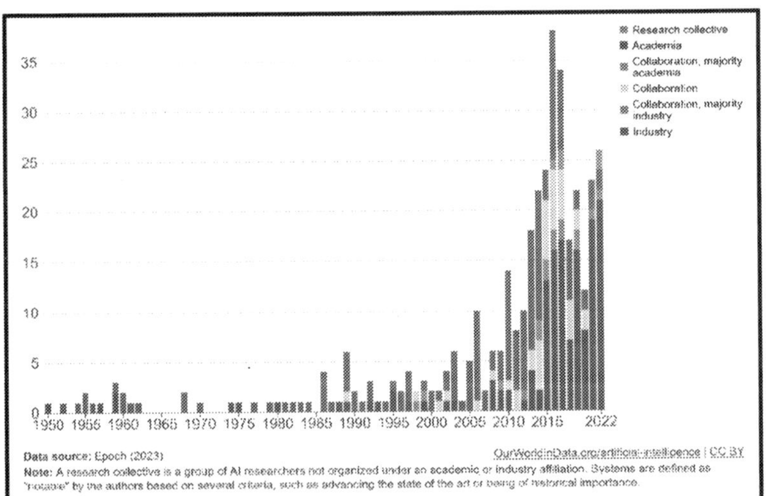

Figure 2: Affiliation of research teams involved in building artificial intelligence models.

Source: Our World in Data[13]

Threat Paradigms: Artificial Intelligence

Let us tackle the obvious first. Security over the past century has been seen as a structure that revolves around the security forces viz., military, and in that too, it is weighed against factors of surveillance, intelligence, target identification, acquisition, and eventual neutralisation by a weapon of choice. How AI poses as a threat in these realms is amplified by the way it could be employed in other innate paradigms that seem innocuous now but, with the application of AI, could turn into major security challenges for any sovereign state.

Surveillance. There is quite a difference between how defence personnel view 'Surveillance with AI' and how the AI experts and social scientists understand 'AI Surveillance'. Both can pose an adequate threat.

- Military surveillance is undertaken by using fixed radar stations, patrol aircraft, drones, long-range cameras, electronic tracking, and satellites. These sources provide voluminous amounts of information about enemy movements that may reveal threatening and anomalous intentions. However, it is difficult to humanly process such large amounts of information to identify the smallest of pattern changes.[14] AI, on the other hand, could be trained to detect even the seemingly insignificant pattern changes, making it extremely difficult for any large-scale movement of troops to remain undetected even if attempted by taking concealed measures.

- AI surveillance, on the other hand, is a term used to describe the utilisation of various AI tools by a state or organisation to monitor, track, and survey nationals and employees.[15] AI surveillance is growing fast and as on date, at least 74 out of 176 countries globally are actively using AI technologies like smart city platforms, facial recognition systems, and policing.[16] Most of the equipment for these platforms is being sourced from limited manufacturers, majority of which are China-based, thereby, hinting that the unethical access and utilisation of such data cannot be ruled out. This, coupled with covert access to the commercial security cameras and real-time tracking of social media accounts of the personnel (even if only 20 per cent have been compromised) and the amount of data available for a decent AI program, is enough to forewarn the adversary of any planned movement. This makes 'Surprise and Deception' a difficult proposition.

Intelligence. The biggest threat comes from the capability of AI to sift through vast data to cull out relevant intelligence. AI is already being used extensively by countries like the United States (US), China, and Israel to sift through satellite images and drone video feeds to provide crucial intelligence with respect to location of major weapons systems, command elements, and logistic installations that can and will enable faster decision making. The attack of 07 Oct 2023 in Israel raises questions on the efficacy of it but initial reports suggest the failure was more attributable to organisational and systemic issues than the actual concept itself. But as brought out earlier as well, it is not only in the realms of the military that AI will provide crucial intelligence. It is the social intelligence about the population that can be exploited by the adversary or non-state actors to have second or third order impact on the military forces. As of updated status on 23 Feb 2025, 402.74 million TB of data is created globally each day.[17] At the right price, all data is potentially up for sale, and a suitably programmed AI can identify vulnerabilities within any organisation or state. For example, all diagnostic centres across the country are now mostly digital and all medical reports are uploaded on the web, from where a customer accesses them. This data itself can provide the crucial health profiling of a country by region, age, sex, profession, etc., indicating the vulnerabilities of its population to a particular genome or a simple lifestyle change.

Target Identification and Acquisition. AI can make target identification more accurate and faster in any combat environment. It can achieve this by analysing not just the reports, documents, and inputs of the various sensors but also feed from news, social media accounts of local population, and other forms of information. It can aggregate and scrutinise a plethora of data sets from all these sources much faster than humans can. AI systems could be trained to predict enemy actions, identify vulnerabilities, assess weather and environmental conditions, and finally acquire targets.[18] In a test conducted during an exercise in the US, it was observed that AI algorithms narrowed down initial sets of data, later vetted by human analysts. The AI-tipped inputs reached an accuracy of 95 per cent in target identification and reduced the time taken from 320 minutes to under an hour.[19]

Autonomous Weapon Systems. While a Terminator T-800[20], a fictional cyborg assassin featured prominently in *The Terminator,* is not yet a reality, the pace of development in the field makes it very likely soon.

Lethal Autonomy. As early as 2010, South Korea deployed a fully autonomous sentry robot SGR-A1 in the demilitarised zone made by a subsidiary of Samsung Electronics in collaboration with Korea University.[21] While it was capable of firing, surveillance, and tracking, it included an onboard speaker and microphone to enable identification of friend or foe, allowing own troops to deactivate it on approach. Alarms would be sounded if someone whose voice was not in the system approached, which would be followed by non-lethal rubber bullets first and real bullets subsequently.[22] What is scary here is the independence of a machine to decide whom to fire at or that an electronics company readily manufactured a deadly machine or the involvement of academia in its creation.

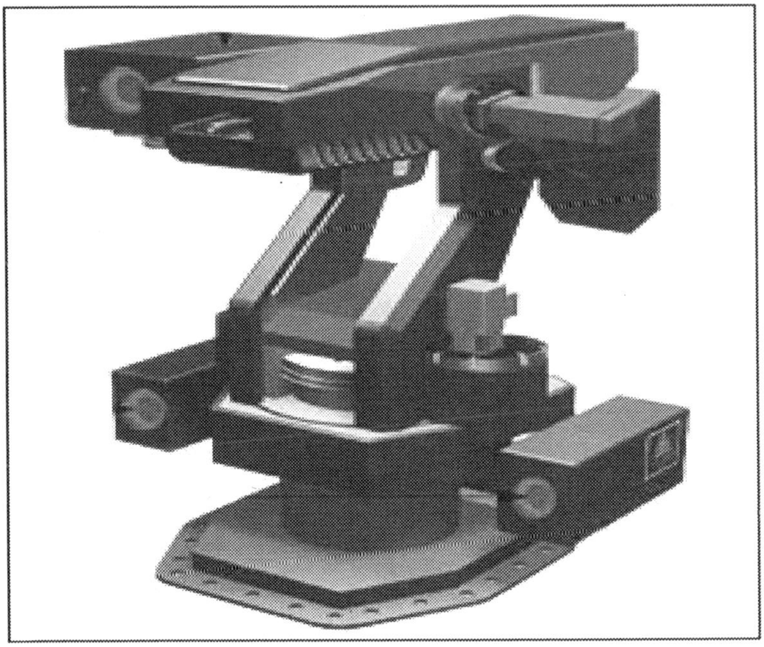

Figure 3: SGR-A1, developed by Samsung Techwin (now Hanwha Defense) in collaboration with Korea University
Source: The Register[23]

❑ **Killer Drone Risks**. In 2019, a fictional video called 'Slaughter Bots' was uploaded on YouTube by 'Dust', a scientific entertainment brand. The graphic fictional video depicted scary futuristic scenario where swarms of killer palm-sized quadcopters armed with explosive charges could kill anyone by exploiting AI. The aim of the producers was to draw public attention to a very likely future, where development of lethal autonomous weapons could wreak havoc on societal law and order across the globe.[24] How challenging is it to develop a lethal drone capability in today's context? This section examines the requirements for such a system and assesses the technologies currently available:

- **Mini Quadcopter Technology**. Easy, since college students make these as their projects.
- **Ammunition**. The requirement can be met by any small arms ammunition bought off the shelf.
- **Swarm Technology**. Thanks to the computational power available at a modest cost, tutorials, and basic programming kits available on internet as open source, modifying it suitably is not difficult.
- **Network and Data**. 5G is enough to enable the drone swarm to gather data on the go without requiring any input from the home server.
- **Delivery Systems**. A swarm of micro drones to cause major casualties could be launched from the back of a truck.

❑ **Drones**. The employment of loiter ammunition and strike drones in Russia–Ukraine conflict has proven beyond doubt how these cheap alternatives could be used successfully to blunt or destroy more expensive and critical weaponry and infrastructure. Adding AI to the mix, such drones with autonomous capability could render range restrictions invalid.

❑ **Cyber**. Though AI has been used in the past few years for creating more resilient cyber security systems that exploit machine learning and deep learning algorithms to identify anomalies and plug the gaps, it is to be remembered that AI is a double-edged sword. Attackers can use generative AI and large language models to undertake large-scale attacks of unimaginable complexity. Programs like DeepSeek and ChatGPT can and are already being used to write code for basic programs. Recently, a researcher found a loophole in ChatGPT and created a nearly undetectable complex data-theft executable that had the sophistication of malware created by a state-sponsored actor.[25] If this is possible now, the futuristic and more powerful AI tools may allow individuals and/or organisations with mala fide intent to create vicious malware like an advanced malicious bot.

Manipulation of Online Information Environment

This is by far one of the scariest scenarios that is every bit likely to manifest if adequate control strategies are not implemented at a global level. AI tools are very proficient at providing propagandists with capabilities that were beyond imagination till only a few years back. Even though humans are highly complex beings, advancements in AI tools are being made to cater just that—handle and decode complex systems. The data being generated by everyone with a mobile or internet, whether on social media, shopping, or just plain simple browsing, provides a sea of data points that is enough for making a psychological profile. Till now, it was not humanly possible to create such profiles at scales and complexity that AI can do today very easily, given the right coding and training.[26] One can envision what such a system might be capable of achieving. A completely automated AI bot created just for furthering a narrative or propaganda could use the immense online data, like the freely and cheaply available marketing databases, to create an individual's personality that would include political preferences, religious affiliation, and other interests. It would track the websites and social-media platforms one uses. It would be able to dynamically create content as per the need, whether just a comment on one's or their friends' profile or a complete article on one of their interests. These would be explicitly designed to exploit one's specific thought process to further hidden motives. The curated content could be true, complete lie, or just the right mix to convince someone and condition their thinking. This could be done in multiple languages to the extent that even the dialect and accent would be copied. It would interact through multiple platforms and present compelling evidence to persuade an individual.

If nothing else succeeds, it may use one's identified and captured weakness to troll or, at worse, extort them.[27] The security forces are made of the same people that make up the society. The families and extended families are all vulnerable to such influences.

Miscellaneous

While the above mentioned are the prominent and recognised threats to national security, there are other fears spurred by the rapid advancement in AI that may have secondary or tertiary effects. As robotics evolves further with AI, making the machines smarter and more capable, many tasks that humans do today may get shifted to machines, adversely affecting employment options. Though more jobs would be created to manage AI systems and machines, but the skill gap between the jobs being taken and those being offered may be difficult to bridge.[28] Since AI systems work on training data and algorithmic design, these can inadvertently accentuate societal biases as the data being utilised for forming the base may be biased.[29] Taking a cue from the latest trend in popular cinema and television, the creation of Artificial General Intelligence (AGI) that outdoes human intelligence may actually threaten the human existence as glorified in such movies. Such AGI could result in catastrophic consequences, as these AI systems may not necessarily align with what we consider correct or important.

Mitigation Measures

To alleviate the AI-driven threats, some of which are still conceivable and mentioned above, India must adopt a multifaceted strategy by integrating technological, regulatory, and strategic countermeasures. It must nurture organisations and culture that can predict the future cases of this technology to enable preparatory measures well in time. Some of these are:

- **Surveillance and Intelligence**. The first and foremost measure is to reduce dependence on foreign AI surveillance systems. Investing in indigenous AI-powered reconnaissance and surveillance platforms that are integrated with secure domestic data networks will enhance adequacy towards desired national security. Efforts are required in developing counter-AI measures that can detect and deceive adversarial AI surveillance. Some of these are algorithmic camouflage, signal obfuscation, and decoy tactics that can also help in retaining operational secrecy. To prevent espionage, there is a need to institute stricter policies on data collection, storage, and transfer, especially for companies using foreign AI surveillance infrastructure.

- **Information Manipulation**. AI is the best countermeasure against itself. Therefore, development and deployment of AI-driven disinformation detection tools to counter deepfake content and propaganda in real time is a prime necessity. India must integrate AI into strategic communications to proactively counter adversarial influence campaigns by identifying and neutralising online threats before they gain traction. It is the need of the hour to put adequate efforts towards educating both the public and armed forces on AI-generated misinformation. This can help reduce vulnerability to cognitive attacks and psychological operations.

- **Cybersecurity Measures**. India must invest in design and development of AI-powered cyber defence systems capable of predicting threats, generating rapid response options, and undertaking limited automated countermeasures. Simultaneously, an AI-enhanced offensive cyber strategy could be used as a deterrent. Research into post-quantum cryptography is necessary to not only ensure data integrity against future AI-augmented cyber threats but also to stay at par with India's adversaries.

- **Autonomous Weapons and Warfare**. Drones are the new normal and their proliferation will increase in days to come. Therefore, developing AI-based anti-drone systems capable of detecting, jamming, and neutralising autonomous swarms is critical in mitigating future threats. AI deployment in military operations must retain human oversight to prevent unintended escalation in operational situations.

- **Economic and Technological Resilience**. India must endeavour to develop AI-driven economic monitoring systems to detect and counter foreign AI manipulation of financial markets and supply chains. Strengthening AI-powered epidemiological surveillance and genomic research can protect against potential

AI-guided biological threats. Use of AI for satellite monitoring and anti-satellite capabilities can ensure dominance in space-based strategic assets.

- **Policy and International Outreach**. The whole world is struggling to come to common ground with respect to the legal framework around AI. The earlier the better that a robust legal framework is established for AI ethics, cybersecurity, and military AI applications to ensure responsible AI deployment. Therein lies the need to collaborate with like-minded strategic partners to s ape international AI regulations. The government must st ve to create AI research hubs, increase AI-focused defen e funding, and foster AI exper

  e within the armed forces to secure long-term national AI capa ility.

Conclusion

The proliferation of AI, as it is taking place at present, may already be beyond the control of any one nation or organisation. The sheer simplicity and availability of the tools to create and deploy AI models makes it almost impossible to control. It is like a paper plane that anyone can make, only it is more dangerous than a fighter aircraft, if intended for such a use. The means to counter AI themselves lie in AI and a global effort to lay down strict ethical and moral guidelines on research and application of AI tools.

Endnotes

[1] Can Kasapoðlu and Baris Kýrdemir, "Wars of None: Artificial Intelligence and the Future of Conflict", *Foreign Policy and Security 2019*, Centre for Economics and Foreign Policy Studies, accessed 20 Jun 2025 https://www.scribd.com/document/550639944/WARS-OF-NONE-ARTIFICIAL-INTELLIGENCE

[2] Mark Rollins, "The History and Evolution of Artificial Intelligence: A Journey Through Time", *LinkedIn Post*, 07 Jun 2023, accessed 21 Jun 2025 https://www.linkedin.com/pulse/history-evolution-artificial-intelligence-journey-mark

[3] S Gill, "How Many People Own Smartphones in the World? (2024-2029)", *Priori Data*, 01 Jan 2025, accessed 13 Jun 2025 https://prioridata.com/data/smartphone-stats/

[4] Team CHESScom, "Kasparov vs. Deep Blue | The Match That Changed History", *Chess.com*, 12 Oct 2018, accessed 18 Jun 2025 https://www.chess.com/article/view/deep-blue-kasparov-chess

[5] "What is Moore's Law?–Is Moore's Law Finally Ending?", *Synopsys*, 2023, accessed 15 Jun 2025 https://www.synopsys.com/glossary/what-is-moores-law.html

[6] Adobe Acrobat Team, "Fast-forward — comparing a 1980s supercomputer to the modern smartphone", *Adobe Blog*, 11 Aug 2022, accessed 20 Jun 2025 https://blog.adobe.com/en/publish/2022/11/08/fast-forward-comparing-1980s-supercomputer-to-modern-smartphone

[7] Ibid.

[8] "Who Invented the Internet? History of The Internet", *Plusnet*, 2023, accessed 18 Jun 2025 https://www.plus.net/broadband/discover/history-of-the-internet/

[9] W Fox, "Global average Internet speed, 1990-2050", *Future Timeline*, 2023, accessed 20 Jun 2025 https://www.futuretimeline.net/data-trends/2050-future-internet-speed-predictions.htm

[10] Steven Feldstein, "The Global Expansion of AI Surveillance", *Carnegie Endowment for International Peace*, Sep 2019, accessed 21 Jun 2025 https://carnegie-production-assets.s3.amazonaws.com/static/files/files__WP-Feldstein-AISurveillance_final1.pdf

[11] S Sinha, "Data as the New Oil: Unravelling Equitable Value Across Geographies", *HGS,* 10 Jul 2023, accessed 15 Jun 2025 https://hgs.cx/blog/data-evolution-prehistoric-times-to-modern-era/

[12] Kevin Bartley, "Big Data Statistics: How much data is there in the world?", *Rivery,* 28 May 2025, accessed 25 Jun 2025 https://rivery.io/blog/big-data-statistics-how-much-data-is-there-in-the-world/

[13] "Affiliation of research teams building notable AI systems, by year of publication", *Our World in Data,* accessed 21 Jun 2025 https://ourworldindata.org/grapher/affiliation-researchers-building-artificial-intelligence-systems-all

[14] Dr Peter Svenmarck, Dr Linus Luotsinen, Dr Mattias Nilsson, Dr Johan Schubert, "Possibilities and Challenges for Artificial Intelligence in Military Applications", *Swedish Defence Research Agency,* accessed 21 Jun 2025 https://www.sto.nato.int/publications/STO%20Meeting%20Proceedings/STO-MP-IST-160/MP-IST-160-S1-5.pdf?__cf_chl_tk=ZCwke1Ni_AgAbfD_rn0AhAbmTC8Eq9X4HNbdibymvAE-1751272544-1.0.1.1-_ktUxk120T4loY7kwbaVjD2BgswzLcRue5xeX0TiHjU

[15] Feldstein, "The Global Expansion"; Ibid.

[16] Fabio Duarte, "Amount of Data Created Daily", *Exploding Topics,* 24 Apr 2025, accessed 24 Jun 2025 https://explodingtopics.com/blog/data-generated-per-day

[17] Ibid.

[18] "The Most Useful Military Applications Of AI In 2024 And Beyond", *Sentient Digital, Inc.,* 2024, accessed 21 Jun 2025 https://sdi.ai/blog/the-most-useful-military-applications-of-ai/

[19] Amanda Miller, "In DOD Experiments, Target Identification Gets Faster, More Accurate With AI", *Air & Space Forces Magazine*, 29 Oct 2021, accessed 29 Jun 2025 https://www.airandspaceforces.com/dod-experiment-artificial-intelligence-target-identification/

[20] Scoot Allen, "Every Terminator From The Franchise, Ranked By Advances In Technology", *CBR*, 27 Jan 2022, accessed 28 Jun 2025 https://www.cbr.com/every-terminator-technology-advancement-ranked/

[21] Eli Shayotovich, "Everything We Know About Samsung's Machine Gun Robots", *Slashgear*, 01 Feb 2023, accessed 11 Jun 2025 https://www.slashgear.com/825074/everything-we-know-about-samsungs-machine-gun-robots/

[22] "SGR-A1", *Robotics Today*, accessed 25 Jun 2025 https://www.robotics today.com/robots/sgr-a1-description

[23] Lewis Page, "South Korea to field gun-cam robots on DMZ", *The Register,* 14 Mar 2007, accessed 27 Jun 2025 https://www.theregister.com/2007/03/14/south_korean_gun_bots/

[24] Glenn McDonald, "'Slaughterbots' Video Depicts a Dystopian Future of Autonomous Killer Drones", *Space.com*, 18 Nov 2017, accessed 18 Jun 2025 https://www.space.com/38820-slaughterbots-video-depicts-a-dystopian-future-of-autonomous-killer-drones.html

[25] "AI in Cyber Security: Risks of AI", *Malwarebytes*, accessed 21 Jun 2025 https://www.malwarebytes.com/cybersecurity/basics/risks-of-ai-in-cyber-security

[26] Matt Chessen, "The MADCOM future", *Atlantic Council*, 26 Sep 2017, accessed 26 Jun 2025 https://www.atlanticcouncil.org/in-depth-research-reports/report/the-madcom-future/

[27] Matt Chessen, "Artificial intelligence chatbots will overwhelm human speech online; the rise of MADCOMs", *Medium,* 17 Mar 2017, accessed 18 Jun 2025 https://medium.com/artificial-intelligence-policy-laws-and-ethics/artificial-intelligence-chatbots-will-overwhelm-human-speech-online-the-rise-of-madcoms-e007818f31a1

[28] Mike Thomas, "15 Risks and Dangers of Artificial Intelligence (AI)", *Built In*, 13 Jun 2025, accessed 16 Jun 2025 https://builtin.com/artificial-intelligence/risks-of-artificial-intelligence

[29] Bernand Marr, "The 15 Biggest Risks Of Artificial Intelligence", *Forbes,* 02 Jun 2025, accessed 12 Jun 2025 https://www.forbes.com/sites/bernardmarr/2023/06/02/the-15-biggest-risks-of-artificial-intelligence/

Leveraging Artificial Intelligence for Securing Cyberspace

Colonel Harpreet Singh

Abstract

The emergence of niche disruptive technologies like Artificial Intelligence (AI) is going to transform the cyber security landscape across the globe. Cyber Security is becoming more-and-more important as the world moves into the era of 'Internet of Things' or 'Internet of Military Things'. The evolution as well as maturing of the 'Network Centric Warfare' is accompanied by a similar rise in the vulnerabilities as well as threats. Traditional cyber security measures often fall short of expectations to address these challenges. Apropos, there is a need to leverage technologies like AI to handle cyber security aspects.

Introduction

To understand the significance of Artificial Intelligence (AI) in cyber security, it is important to explore these individual domains as well as their inter-se relation with each other.

- **Artificial Intelligence**. AI, a field focussed on the pursuit to replicate human cognitive functions, has come a long way since its inception. Alan Turing introduced the concept of machines that could emulate human intelligence in his seminal 1950 paper.[1] Since then, there have been numerous advancements in the field of AI to include machine learning, compute vision, and neural networks. One of the most important sub-sets of AI is machine learning, which facilitates the learning from data without explicit programming. This has enabled the development of various other sub-fields of AI to include deep learning, artificial neural networks, natural language processing, social media analytics, and computer vision, etc.

Image 1: Command and Control in Cyber Warfare

❑ **Cyber Security**. Importance of cyber security has grown exponentially in the ongoing digital age. The digital battlefield of today relies more on the computer systems with network linkages between sensors, shooters, and decision makers. Traditional security mechanisms (such as firewalls and antivirus software) are inadequate in safeguarding against the sophistication of modern cyber-attacks. Thus, the evolution of cyber security is under a transition from reactive to proactive measures. While early approaches focused on preventing known threats, contemporary strategies emphasise more on threat detection and prediction. The increasing reliance on inter-connected systems, the proliferation of mobile devices, and the advent of the Internet of Military Things (IoMT) have expanded the attack surface during military operations. Defence forces are, thus, challenged to secure their digital landscape, which is highly dynamic and complex.

- **Role of AI in Cyber Security**. The astronomical amount of data generated in the digital domain nowadays makes it virtually impossible for human operators to carry out manual analysis of data for identification of the potential cyber security threats. AI's ability to process and analyse vast datasets in real-time presents a solution to this problem. AI is increasingly being employed in cyber security for threat detection and monitoring as well as response. Machine learning algorithms can identify patterns of behaviour that deviate from the normal, thereby, signalling potential security breaches. Also, AI-driven automation can perform routine tasks more efficiently and with fewer errors, thereby, reducing the burden on human cyber security teams.
- **Cyber-Space as a Domain of Warfighting in the Contemporary Digital World**. Cyber-space is increasingly being recognised as a new domain of warfighting. State-sponsored actors, hacktivists, and criminal organisations are active participants in this digital domain. Nations have been developing offensive and defensive cyber warfare capabilities to protect their interests and engage in cyber-attacks against other nations. These attacks can target critical information infrastructure, military systems, and even disrupt the functioning of a nation's government. The Stuxnet malware is a well-known example of a cyber weapon used for strategic purposes. Furthermore, cyber espionage can have across-the-board implications for national security and diplomacy as it involves the theft of sensitive information and intelligence from other nations. State-sponsored hacking groups engage in rampant espionage activities to gain leverage in political, economic, and military matters.

Applications of AI in Cyber Security

The amalgamation of AI with cyber security has led to the creation of many innovative applications which can enhance cyber security. AI can be utilised to fortify military computer networks, detect threats, and streamline cyber security operations, as covered in the succeeding paras.

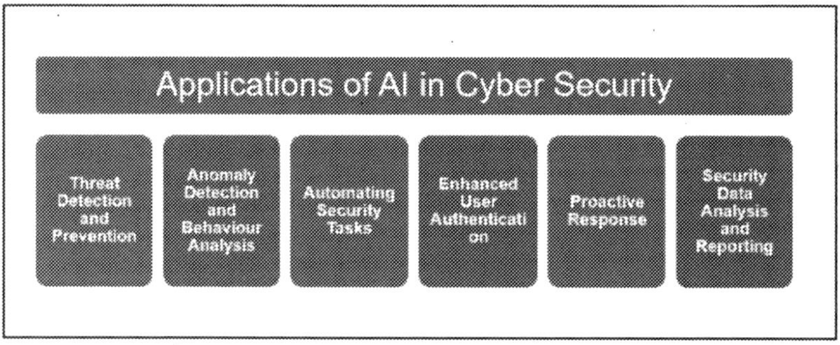

Figure 1: Applications of Artificial Intelligence in Cyber Security

❑ **Threat Detection and Prevention**. One of the most critical applications of AI in cyber security is threat detection and prevention.[2] Traditional methods of cyber security rely on the known attack patterns, threat-signatures, and rule-based systems. However, modern cyber threats are dynamic and ever evolving, which make these methods inadequate. AI, especially machine learning, excels in identifying unknown or zero-day cyber threats. AI systems have the capability to identify potential cyber security threats in real time as they can process large quantum of data quickly to flag unusual network traffic and user behaviour, and pinpoint the anomalies for further analysis.

❑ **Anomaly Detection and Behaviour Analysis**. AI is proficient at anomaly detection which is an important component of cyber security.[3] It establishes a threshold for normal network or user behaviour, thereby, identifying any deviations from it in real time. Same is invaluable for identifying insider threats, such as employees abusing their privileges as also any compromised accounts. Additionally, AI can analyse the characteristics of malicious code or email content to flag potential threats. This proactive approach in identifying attacks before they execute themself is a significant asset in cyber security.

❑ **Automating Security Tasks**. AI's automation capabilities can streamline routine security tasks, thereby, allowing human operators to focus on more complex issues.[4] AI-driven tools can handle tasks like patch management, vulnerability scanning, and incident response with speed and accuracy. Therefore, the probability of human error is greatly reduced and the cyber security operations are becoming more agile. AI-driven platforms can also coordinate incident responses across various systems.

- **Enhanced User Authentication**. AI is transforming user authentication and access control mechanisms.[5] Traditional username and password-based authentication systems are prone to breaches, more so when users choose weak or easily breakable passwords. AI-based authentication use biometrics, such as fingerprint or facial recognition, to ensure a more secure identity verification. AI can monitor the user behaviour by comparing with historical data. This will enable the identification of suspicious behaviour and prompt the system to automatically initiate supplementary authentication checks.

- **Proactive Response**. Machine learning algorithms can facilitate analysis of data with respect to the historical cyber-attacks. This facilitates the proactive response from own side. Also, AI-based cyber security platforms can analyse data from many sources and provide real-time updates on likely cyber security threats.[6]

- **Security Data Analysis and Reporting**. AI can process vast amounts of security logs and generate meaningful insights. AI-driven dashboards and reporting tools provide actionable information to make informed decisions and respond to security incidents[7] in near real time.

Challenges and Ethical Concerns

While the integration of AI into cyber security offers immense potential, it also raises a host of challenges and ethical concerns as discussed in the following paragraphs.

- **Bias and Fairness**. The incorporation of AI in cyber security faces a major ethical concern: the potential for both deliberate and unintentional biases in AI algorithms. Historical data on which the AI systems are trained may contain inherent biases. If these biases are not addressed, AI could inadvertently fail to detect threats that do not conform to past patterns.[8]

❑ **Security of AI Systems**. The security of AI systems is a critical challenge. If AI systems are themselves compromised, they could become tools for the enemy rather than own forces. Attackers might manipulate AI algorithms to evade detection or launch more sophisticated attacks.[9] Therefore, AI systems need to be protected with strong cyber security measures.

❑ **Data Privacy and Data Protection**. AI-based cyber security systems must rely on large quantum of data, which is sensitive in nature. Ensuring the privacy and protection of this data is a significant ethical concern.[10] Thus, following of data protection regulations is a must.

❑ **Interaction Between Humans and Computers**. AI has the potential to automate many cyber security tasks. However, the relationship between humans and AI is still not mature enough. The decisions made by AI should be transparent and understandable to humans. For example, the reasons for flagging a user's behaviour as suspicious should be clearly comprehensible to human operators.[11]

❑ **Covering Gaps in the Skills through Education**. The role of AI is continually increasing in the field of cyber security. This has resulted in gaps in the skills required to manage and operate AI-driven cyber security systems. Therefore, there is a need to train the personnel to understand and use the AI-based cyber security tools in an effective manner.

❑ **Gaps in Legal and Regulatory Frameworks**. The legal and regulatory frameworks in the domain of AI in cyber security are still in the process of evolving. Laws that govern the use of AI in cyber security are still fragmented and do not tackle the emerging challenges in the requisite manner.[12] Therefore, the need for up-to-date and internationally consistent regulations is unavoidable.

❑ **Accountability Issues**. Actions taken by AI-based systems in the field of cyber security are very complex and marred by the accountability issues. If an AI system wrongly identifies a legitimate user as a threat or misses an actual threat, pinpointing of responsibility[13] becomes an issue. Therefore, establishing clear accountability and consequently arising liability is an aspect that needs to be taken care of.

Future Trends

The inter-linkages between AI and cyber security continue to evolve at a very rapid pace. Therefore, it is important to crystal gaze to correctly identify the emerging trends that will bring requisite synergy in the domain of AI in cyber security, as follows:

- **Explainable AI**. As AI becomes more-and-more amalgamated into the cyber security, need for transparency becomes important. The research in the field of 'Explainable AI' is most suited to address this aspect.[14] It aims to make AI algorithms as well as their decision-making processes more understandable to the human operators and, thus, increases their trustworthiness.

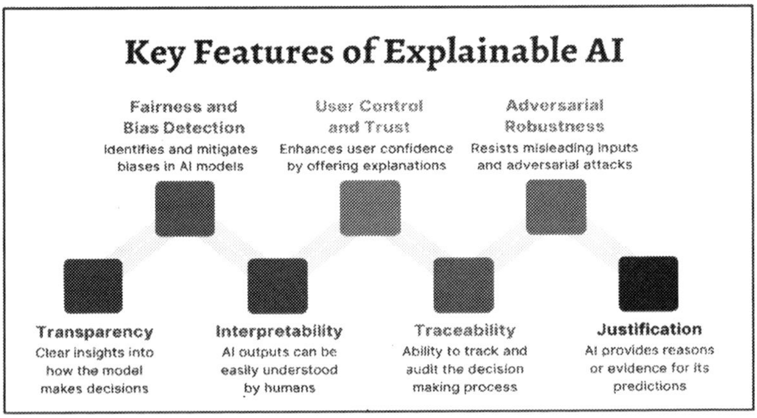

Figure 2: Key Features of Explainable Artificial Intelligence[15]

- **Autonomous Cyber Security Systems**. The advancements in the field of autonomous cyber security systems will enable responding to cyber threats with minimum human intervention.[16] These systems will also learn and adapt to the ever-evolving cyber threat vectors. This will have a great impact in reducing the response times to enhance the cyber security posture.

- **Quantum Computing and Post-Quantum Cryptography**. Advancements in field of quantum computing have resulted in opportunities as well as challenges. Quantum computers have the potential to break existing encryption algorithms and methodologies. This has made the research and development in the field of post-quantum cryptography[17] inescapable. Undoubtedly, AI is playing a critical role in research and further designing of the quantum-resistant encryption algorithms for requisite cyber security.

- **Proactive Cyber Security**. AI will enable defence forces to proactively detect and tackle the cyber security threats. Rather than of relying on the automated alerts, AI-based proactive tools will sense the network for threats and vulnerabilities[18] and take remedial actions accordingly.

- **Cyber Security for Edge Devices**. As the use of IoMT devices grow, the world needs to carry out localised processing at the network edge duly utilising the AI. AI at edge can increase the security of IoMT devices by locally analysing the data. This reduces the need to transmit sensitive information to the central servers[19] for further processing, thereby, increasing the speed and efficiency.

- **AI-based User Authentication**. AI will undoubtedly play a significant role in developing the behaviour-based metrics for fool-proof user authentication. A user's unique behaviour patterns can be identified by using aspects such as typing speed and pressure on the keyboard keys. This will enable bolstering of the cyber security measures while providing a seamless user experience simultaneously.[20]

Recommendations

Integration of AI into the cyber security has immense potential. However, it also requires that users adhere to best practices at the same time. Some of the recommendations to harness the power of AI while maintaining robust cyber security are discussed as follows:

- **Reskilling and Upskilling of the Workforce**. It is imperative to plan and invest in continuous education and training for cyber security professionals in the defence forces. This assumes importance as AI evolution is happening at a very rapid pace which makes it essential to stay updated on the latest AI-based tools.[21]

- **Handling of Biases**. There is an inescapable requirement tackle the biases in the AI algorithms, as well as in the data being used to train the AI. Same necessitate periodic audit of the AI-based cyber security systems. Aim is to ensure that all such systems are fair and transparent.[22]

- **Data Protection**. AI agents should be designed and developed through methodical research, with the aim of ensuring that their architecture and design do not violate data protection rules and regulations at both national and international levels.
- **Red Teaming**. There is a need to conduct vulnerability and penetration testing of AI-based cyber security systems duly utilising various red-teaming tools. Simulation of real-world cyber-attacks through red-teaming will assist to identify the shortcomings and, thereafter, take remedial steps to improve the AI-based cyber security systems.[23]
- **Collaboration in Research**. There is a need to collaborate with the national as well as international cyber security community including academia and industry. This will help to stay current on the latest cyber security threats as also on the latest AI-driven cyber security innovations.
- **Ensuring Security of AI Infrastructure**. It is imperative that the security of AI infrastructure is ensured. The AI models as well as data is required to be protected to prevent them from becoming targets for inimical elements.
- **Collaboration Between Humans and AI**. There is a need to have a collaborative approach, wherein AI complements the human capabilities in the field of cyber security, rather than replacing them. This is because humans can provide overall context and ethical judgment that AI may possibly lack.[24]

Conclusion

The cyber security environment today is continuously evolving and is also becoming increasingly sophisticated. Integration of AI with cyber security will lead to transformation in the current war-fighting methodologies. AI not merely automates various tasks but is a game-changer which can empower the defence forces to proactively defend against the cyber threats. AI-based cyber security systems do not have the limitations of human operators and can continuously check for the cyber security threats and take remedial actions.

However, the usage of AI for cyber security comes with its own challenges including ethical concerns. Issues related to bias, data privacy, and accountability need to be taken care of. The rapidly evolving AI technology and its ongoing integration into cyber security mandates that the cyber security professionals are always updated. The research and development of explainable AI and autonomous cyber security systems will go a long way to have a good cyber security posture of Indian armed forces. The advancements in the field of quantum computing and post-quantum cryptography makes it more important to have AI-based cyber security systems. Proactive actions to mitigate cyber threats and edge AI for IoMT security are some of the emerging applications of AI in this field.

The role of AI in cyber security is not a just a convergence of two technologies. It has the potential to shape the future of digital security and to bring in the next revolution in military affairs. Therefore, the future of cyber security is intertwined with AI and together both hold the key to defend against the challenges of the present and futuristic digital age.

Endnotes

1 Alan M Turing, "Computing Machinery and Intelligence", *Mind* 59, no. 236 (1950), pp 433–460, accessed 14 Mar 2025 https://doi.org/10.1093/mind/LIX.236.433

2 Peter M. Mell and Timothy Grance, "The NIST Definition of Cloud Computing", *NIST Special Publication,* pp 800-145, Gaithersburg, MD: National Institute of Standards and Technology, 28 Sep 2011, accessed 15 Mar 2025 https://nvlpubs.nist.gov/nistpubs/Legacy/SP/nistspecialpublication800-145.pdf

3 T. Lane, C.E. Brodley and V. Honavar, "Temporally Expressive Reasoning for Intrusion Detection" in *Proceedings of the 14th National Conference on Artificial Intelligence (AAAI-97)*, vol. 97, pp 3–10. Providence, RI: AAAI Press, 1997, accessed 15 Mar 2025 https://www.aaai.org/Papers/AAAI/1997/AAAI97-001.pdf

4 H. Kim and J. Feinberg, "A Consumer Perspective on RFID and Privacy: The Behavioural Intention Model", *International Journal of Production Research* 44, no. 18–19 (2016), pp 3915–3938, accessed 15 Mar 2025 https://doi.org/10.1080/00207540600635155

5 A.K. Jain, A. Ross, and S. Prabhakar, "An Introduction to Biometric Recognition", *IEEE Transactions on Circuits and Systems for Video Technology* 14, no. 1 (2004), pp 4–20, accessed 14 Mar 2025 https://ieeexplore.ieee.org/document/1262027

[6] X. Gu and D. Bridge, "A Probabilistic Model for Real-Time Threat Detection Using Bayesian Networks", *Computers & Security* 29, no. 4 (2010): pp 385–400, accessed 13 Mar 2025 https://doi.org/10.1016/j.cose.2010.01.001

[7] Bruce Schneier, *Data and Goliath: The Hidden Battles to Collect Your Data and Control Your World,* New York: W. W. Norton & Company, 2015, accessed 15 Mar 2025 https://www.schneier.com/books/data-and-goliath/

[8] Solon Barocas, Hardt Moritz, and Arvind Narayanan, *Fairness and Machine Learning.* 201, accessed 25 Mar 2025 http://fairmlbook.org

[9] Battista Biggio, Blaine Nelson, Pavel Laskov, and Giorgio Giacinto, "Poisoning Attacks Against Support Vector Machines" in *Joint European Conference on Machine Learning and Knowledge Discovery in Databases*, pp 146–161, Berlin: Springer, 2012, accessed 14 Mar 2025 https://doi.org/10.1007/978-3-642-33460-3_10

[10] European Union, "General Data Protection Regulation (GDPR)", Regulation (EU) 2016/679, *Official Journal of the European Union* L119/1, 04 May 2016, accessed 14 Mar 2025 https://eur-lex.europa.eu/eli/reg/2016/679/oj

[11] Raja Parasuraman, and Victor Riley, "Humans and Automation: Use, Misuse, Disuse, Abuse", *Human Factors* 39, no. 2 (1997), pp 230–253, accessed 14 Mar 2025 https://doi.org/10.1518/001872097778543886

[12] European Union Agency for Cybersecurity (ENISA), "Regulation (EU) 2019/881 on ENISA (the 'Cybersecurity Act')", *Official Journal of the European Union* L 151, 07 Jun 2019, accessed 14 Mar 2025 https://eur-lex.europa.eu/legal-content/EN/TXT/?uri=CELEX%3A32019R0881

[13] Deborah G. Johnson, and Thomas M. Powers. "Computer Systems: Moral Entities but Not Moral Agents", *Ethics and Information Technology* 10, no. pp 2–3 (2008): 77–88, accessed 24 Mar 2025

[14] Velez Doshi, Finale, and Been Kim, "Towards a Rigorous Science of Interpretable Machine Learning", *arXiv*, 28 Feb 2017, accessed 13 Mar 2025 https://arxiv.org/abs/1702.08608

[15] Ammar Asim, "Explainable AI (XAI): The Next Step in Building Trustworthy Artificial Intelligence," *Data Science Dojo* (blog), 18 Feb 2025, accessed 14 Mar 2025 https://datasciencedojo.com/blog/explainable-ai-xai/

[16] Gagandeep C. Deka, Saurav Sur, and Anupam Baruah, "Autonomous Intrusion Detection System Using Data Mining Techniques", *Procedia Technology* 23 (2016): 660–667, accessed 16 Mar 2025 https://doi.org/10.1016/j.protcy.2016.03.073

[17] Michele Mosca and Douglas Stebila, "Post-Quantum Key Exchange for the Internet and the Open Quantum Safe Project", *IEEE Security & Privacy* 14, no. 1 (2015), pp 57–63, accessed 14 Mar 2025 https://doi.org/10.1109/MSP.2015.7

[18] Da Silva, D. R., and R. C. de Oliveira Albuquerque, "Cyber Threat Hunting with Open-Source Intelligence: An Exploratory Study" in *Proceedings of the 50th Hawaii International Conference on System Sciences (HICSS)*, 2017, accessed 27 Mar 2025 https://hdl.handle.net/10125/41742

[19] Li, En, Zhi Zhou, and Xu Chen, "Edge Intelligence: On Demand Deep Learning Model Co Inference with Device Edge Synergy" in *Proceedings of the Workshop on Mobile Edge Communications (MECOMM 2018)*, 20 Jun 2018, accessed 15 Mar 2025 doi:10.1145/3229556.3229562

[20] Michael R. Frank, Fabian Monrose, and Samuel E. Schechter, "Keyboard Acoustic Emanations Revisited" in *2013 IEEE Symposium on Security and Privacy*, 3–18. Washington, DC: IEEE, 2013, accessed 15 Mar 2025 https://doi.org/10.1109/SP.2013.7

[21] SANS Institute, "Security Awareness Training", 2020, accessed 15 Mar 2025 https://www.sans.org/security-awareness-training

[22] Ibid.

[23] Michael E. Whitman and Herbert J. Mattord, "Management of Information Security", Boston, *Cengage Learning*, 2013, accessed 15 Mar 2025 https://www.cengage.com/c/management-of-information-security-5e-whitman

[24] Raja Parasuraman, and Victor Riley, "Humans and Automation: Use, Misuse, Disuse, Abuse", *Human Factors* 39, no. 2 (1997): ppm 230–253, accessed 14 Mar 2025 https://doi.org/10.1518/001872097778543886

Drone Warfare: Tactical Shift in Land Warfare

Colonel Abhishek Chauhan, VSM

"India's drone revolution is not about catching up—it is about leapfrogging into a future where technology defends our borders and empowers our people"

—Raksha Mantri Rajnath Singh

Abstract

This article explores the transformative role of tactical drones in modern land warfare, highlighting their evolution, operational advantages, and strategic significance. From loitering munitions to first-person view and modified commercial drones, these technologies offer unprecedented intelligence, precision, and lethality at sub-unit levels. The article traces the journey of drone warfare from early innovations to today's artificial intelligence-enabled, swarm-capable systems, demonstrating their growing importance in intelligence, surveillance, and reconnaissance, mechanised operations, and counter-insurgency roles. It also examines India's indigenous drone capabilities and evolving regulatory framework. Emphasis is placed on countermeasures, including electronic warfare and directed energy weapons. This article concludes by positioning tactical drones as force multipliers that demand continual innovation and adaptive strategies to remain effective amidst evolving threats and increasingly complex battlefields.

Introduction

Lighter, cheaper, and simpler to deploy than the medium-altitude long endurance-class Unmanned Aerial Vehicles (UAVs), small drones are a force multiplier and provide an unpresented tactical edge in modern land warfare. With the rise of drones, the battlefield is no longer just about boots on the ground but also about eyes in the sky. Drones have transformed contemporary conflicts into a chessboard, where speed, surprise, and Electronic Warfare (EW) dictates victory. They provide militaries real-time intelligence, precise targeting, and the ability to strike enemies without risking soldiers' lives. These drones have demonstrated the ability to effectively disrupt heavy armoured movements, neutralise long-range artillery assets, and significantly influence battlefield outcomes in a cost-effective manner.[1]

Drones are reshaping land warfare in several ways. Attack drones, including loitering munitions and First-Person View (FPV) drones, give small units an unprecedented ability to destroy high-value targets. At the same time, the widespread availability of modified Commercially-off-the-Shelf (COTS) drones has blurred the lines between state and non-state actors, making modern battlefields more unpredictable.

Evolution of Drone Warfare

From making a very humble beginning in 1839, when Austrians attacked the town of Venice using unmanned hot air balloons filled with explosives, to the modern targeting marvel, the MQ1 Predator employed by the United States (US) and North Atlantic Treaty Organization forces, the journey of the evolution of drones has been a very exciting one. Drone warfare has evolved from the rudimentary hot-air balloons deployed by the Austrian Army in 1849 to modern precision-guided autonomous systems developed by technologically advanced nations such as the US, Israel, and China.

Thereafter, UAV technology improved throughout World War II and into the Cold War as well, but they were largely seen as unreliable and expensive novelties. Modern drone warfare can be traced back to 1982, when Israel integrated battlefield UAVs with manned aircraft to attack the Syrian fleet. The future is already knocking on the door in the form of Artificial Intelligence (AI) and robotics taking drones to a new level of warfare. Modern militaries are already in the process of commissioning swarms of autonomous drones which are enabled by AI and can collaborate in both the spheres of surveillance and targeting.[2]

Tactical Drone Warfare

Tactical Transformation with Drones. Drone warfare conducting military operations remotely is not entirely a new concept. Tactical drone missions date back to the Yom Kippur War, where UAVs such as the Israeli 'Scout' and 'Mastiff' drones flew reconnaissance and combat missions. Today, precision drone strikes have become a routine and preferred option in all modern battlefields. Introducing drones at brigade level and even lower has fundamentally transformed the tactical battle area by drastically shortening observe–orient–decide–act loop and significantly increasing the lethality of engagements.[3]

Commercially-off-the-Shelf Drones | *First-Person View Drones* | *Loitering Munitions*

Image 1: Types of Kinetic Drones

Drones and the New Revolution in Military Affairs (RMA). An RMA refers to transformations in how wars are fought, involving major changes in military tactics, techniques, and procedures. Such a shift is currently underway due to the tactical integration of drones. Small commercial drones (modified commercial drones) are reshaping infantry combat by effectively targeting enemy troops in open and urban environments. FPV drones, used even by small infantry troops, have demonstrated capabilities to completely halt armoured columns. Simultaneously, Loitering Munitions (LMs) are autonomously destroying high-value targets, reshaping the tactical battlefield.[4] Outlined below are three primary types of kinetic drones that are practical for use at the brigade level and below.

Modified COTS Drones. Modified COTS drones have become vital in today's battlefield due to their affordability and ease of customisation. Examples include civilian drones adapted for tactical use, such as the Dà-Jiâng Innovations series drones modified and innovated by frontline units for reconnaissance and small-scale precise attacks. Ukraine and Russia both effectively use modified commercial drones to enhance battlefield intelligence and strike targets. These drones are reshaping tactical engagements by providing ground units with rapid reconnaissance and highly accurate strike capabilities.[5]

FPV Drones. FPV drones are inexpensive, easy to operate, and highly effective, especially when equipped with explosives. Their low cost compared to traditional systems like the Javelin missile makes them an attractive option. FPV drones allow small teams to launch accurate attacks against armoured vehicles and fortified locations. Controlled by operators, these drones have successfully destroyed tanks and heavily armoured formations, demonstrating substantial effectiveness and precision in conflict scenarios.

Loitering Munitions. The idea behind LMs is not entirely new, but recent advancements in sensors and autonomy have dramatically improved their effectiveness.[6] LMs are categorised based on their tactical use and deployment methods.

- ❑ **Mini LMs**. Small and portable, these drones can be operated individually by soldiers for targeting infantry or light armoured vehicles. Examples include AeroVironment Switchblade/ 300, UVision HERO 90, Rotem, Warmate, and STR-35 'Silent Thunder'. They provide infantry units with flexible and precise striking capabilities.
- ❑ **Tactical LMs**. These drones usually need vehicle-based launch systems and possess longer endurance and better sensors compared to mini variants. They can conduct both surveillance and precision strikes, proving useful at tactical formation levels. Examples include Switchblade 600 and similar systems.
- ❑ **Operational LMs**. Larger variants, like the Harpy and Harop, have higher endurance, better sensors, and capability to autonomously target strategic enemy assets such as radar

installations. However, not all LMs offer recovery options or the extensive surveillance endurance typical of traditional UAVs.

Tactical Indian Drones

India is gradually keeping pace with the drone revolution by developing its own tactical drones to bolster the capability of the fighting formations. These drones play a key role in multiple domains and assist Indian Armed Forces to stay ahead in modern battlefields.[7] Some important developments include:

- **NETRA 5 (Idea Forge)**. It is a lightweight and rugged drone built for real-time surveillance and reconnaissance in challenging terrains. It provides troops with an aerial view of the adversary sub-unit weapon deployment and troops disposition, hence, reducing risks before contact battle.
- **SWITCH V2**. Designed for long-endurance operations, this drone offers situational awareness to tactical commanders. It can be deployed for surveillance, target tracking, and battlefield assessments without exposing troops. It is ideal for high-altitude warfare and quick deployment in semi-held or conflicts zones.
- **Archer (Defence Research and Development Organisation [DRDO])**. It is a weaponised surveillance drone that blends intelligence gathering with offensive capabilities. It can identify enemy movements, guide its own artillery fire, and is even capable of undertaking precision strikes.
- **Abhyas (DRDO)**. It is a high-speed aerial target drone used to simulate enemy UAVs and missiles. It helps in testing air defence systems and training troops to counter aerial threats.

Tactical Advantages of Drones

Tactical Edge Through Aerial Eyes. Tactical commanders will agree with the fact that the biggest limitation they face is the organic ability to look over the hill, for which they have to rely on higher headquarters and other agencies. Intimate knowledge of terrain, enemy disposition, and its weapons systems are battle-winning factors. Rather than relying on intelligence inputs, if a tactical commander can obtain the intelligence inputs by having an eye in the sky, he will be able to make much better plans and be more confident of executing them. All this, if achieved by having integral resources which can be tasked, operated, and analysed without having to look over his shoulders, will result in a high level of battlefield transparency. Having a scout in the air to look ahead and to keep one out of danger, in any form of operation, is a major force multiplier. That is the reason that Unmanned Aerial System (UAS) is one of the most popular pieces of equipment at sub-tactical levels.

Intelligence, Surveillance, and Reconnaissance. Having eyes in the sky, which can be tasked and operated, and the feed obtained directly by the tactical commander, is a great asset. The entire effort of how much force to use, weapons matching, and timing of operation can be, thereafter, suitably modified to carry out effect-based operation. Availability of this force multiplier at the tactical level will invariably result in reducing the number of manpower and weapons required to complete a particular task.

Precision Strikes. Tactical drones can be effectively used not only for surveillance but also to target the objective which has been identified near real time. This gives a tremendous boost to the fire power resources at tactical and operational level. LMs (also known as kamikaze drones) can hover over a battlefield and attack time-sensitive targets with pinpoint accuracy.

Mech Forces. By virtue of the peculiarity of the nature of operations, drones can address most of the vulnerabilities of mechanised columns and can act as a potent vanguard to the advancing forces. Initially, they can be used to provide advance information by flying ahead and, thereafter, targeting enemy tanks and emplacements. All can be conveniently achieved by monitoring the operation from a ruggedised module from inside the safety of a tank.

Counterinsurgency/Counterterrorism (CI/CT) Operations. The most versatile use of the drones is in the CI/CT environment. In addition to acting as an excellent weapon platform, they also eliminate the danger to the lives of the security personals. Small drones like Black Hornet from Norway, weighing just 32 gms, are hand launched to slip through a window or door, making them ideal for house clearance, room, intervention, and hostage rescue.

Logistic Operation. Drone can be used effectively for provisioning of the essential supplies in the battle zone, reducing the risk to the human convoy. They can also provide essential rations, medical supplies, and equipment spares to the frontline troops, thereby, ensuring the longevity of the operation.

Psychological Warfare and Deterrence. Persistent buzzing noise of a drone flying high in the sky intimidate enemy forces and reduces their combat effectiveness. The mere presence of the drone in a tactical area can force adversity to alter the strategies, limiting their mobility and decision making. This causes extensive external psychological distress among the enemy troops and, thus, act as a non-lethal deterrent effect when used persistently.

Countermeasures Against Tactical Drones

India's Drone Policy. India's regulatory framework for drones' operations has evolved significantly to accommodate technological advancements and industry needs. Initially, the UAS Rules, 2021, published by the Ministry of Civil Aviation, were criticised for being overly restrictive, requiring extensive paperwork and multiple permissions for each drone flight. In response to stakeholder feedback, the Drone (Amendment) Rules, 2024, were introduced recently, offering a liberalised regulatory environment. These new rules apply to all entities involved in drone operations in India and exempt most drones from the stringent provisions of the Aircraft Rules, 1937, except for those exceeding 500 kgs. This shift has enhanced India's drone ecosystem, fostering innovation, ease of operation, and greater integration of UAVs in defence, commercial, and research sectors. This article focuses only on tactical drones, and the medium and large drones fall under strategic applications and, hence, are not covered in this article. The Indian classification of drones is mentioned in the article. However, with the development of the drone systems, the measures to counter these are also developing at a rapid pace. There still exist inherent limitations to drone technology that can be leveraged to construct countermeasures. The vulnerabilities include adverse weather condition along the borders, limited time both in terms of flight as well as payloads, and soft and hard kills that will get the bird down without even the operator knowing about it. The primary tactic to neutralise a drone is to shoot it while its air-borne, however, another effective approach is to stop the drone even before it takes off. Preventing drones from launching in the first place can often be simpler and more efficient than trying to hit them once it is in air.[8] Countermeasures against drones can involve a range of technologies and tactics that continue to evolve in response to advancements in drone capabilities. A few examples are outlined below:

- **EW**. Drones are extremely susceptible to EW, which can be used to disrupt or jam the signals that control them. This can cause drones to lose communication with their operators and can even be taken over by the adversary. These rogue drones can then be used against friendly forces in a devastating manner.

- **Shotguns and Tactical Weapons**. Drones are so fragile that almost anything that hits them or touches them is likely to cause them to crash or lose orientation. While higher flying drones would be beyond the range of weapons normally available at the unit and sub-unit level, tactical drones may be within range. Shotgun, snipers, and automatic weapons used with tracer round can be employed against them.

- **Physical Barriers**. Simple structures like nets or metal grids can protect vehicles and equipment from drone attacks. These barriers can cause drones to detonate prematurely or prevent them from reaching their targets. Creating a kind of bubble barrier for the vulnerable areas and points in the tactical area will be useful against the aerial threats.

- **Directed Energy Weapons**. Technologies like high-power microwave systems and lasers can disable drones by targeting their electronic components or structural integrity. These also include lasers and high-powered beams that can destroy a drone's electronic circuit. While potentially expensive to develop, they may have a low cost per shot.[9]

- **Global Positioning System (GPS) Spoofing as a Countermeasure**. GPS spoofing is an effective EW countermeasure that misguides enemy drones by transmitting new GPS coordinates, leading them to stray off course or land in unintended locations. This method is particularly useful against drones reliant on satellite navigation for targeting and flight path correction. Militaries can deploy mobile or stationary spoofing systems to protect critical assets from drone attacks.

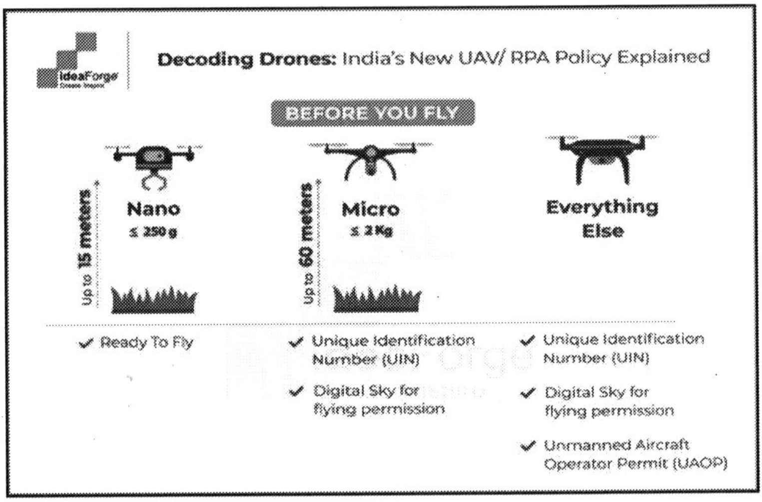

Figure 2: India's New Unmanned Aerial Vehicles and Remotely Piloted Aircraft
Source: ideaForge[10]

Category	Weight Cl	Regulatory Provision
Nano	≤ 250 grams	Exempted from most regulations
Micro	250 g – 2 kg	No security clearance required for operations
Small	2 kg – 25 kg	Requires UIN registration and remote pilot license
Medium	25 kg – 150 kg	Requires security clearance and operational approval
Large	> 150 kg	Falls under Aircraft Rules, 1937

Table 1: Drone Categories and Regulatory Requirements in India

Future Trends in Tactical Drone Warfare

The future development of the drone technology revokes both dreams and nightmares. As these become cheaper and easier to obtain, the skies are open to those who once saw flying as unattainable. Although today's technology yields some conclusion about how drones will affect future decision making, the technology of tomorrow brings with it, the possibility of even further acceleration of these trends. Hence, drones are unlikely to remain in their present form for long, and technological development will radically alter their future development. The following undermentioned technological development, in particular, will intersect with drone technology and change their operation in remarkable way with consequences for tactical choice surrounding their use.[11]

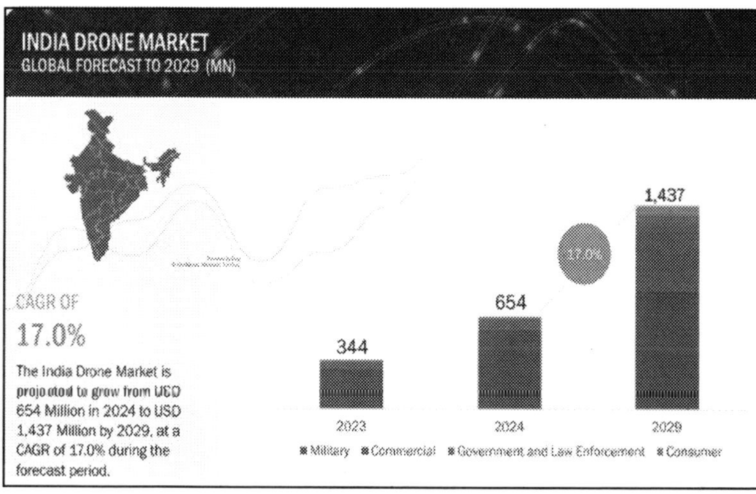

Figure 3: Indian Drone Market, Global Forecast

Source: insideFPV[12]

- ❑ **AI**. Perhaps the greatest potential change in how drones operate will come from the rise of AI. Future tactical drones are expected to operate autonomously, which means that they can decide how to handle complex missions with minimum human input. These drones can drastically cut response time in high pressure situation. An autonomous drone could be programmed to function as a scout, carrying out recce of the forward zone ahead of the defences.

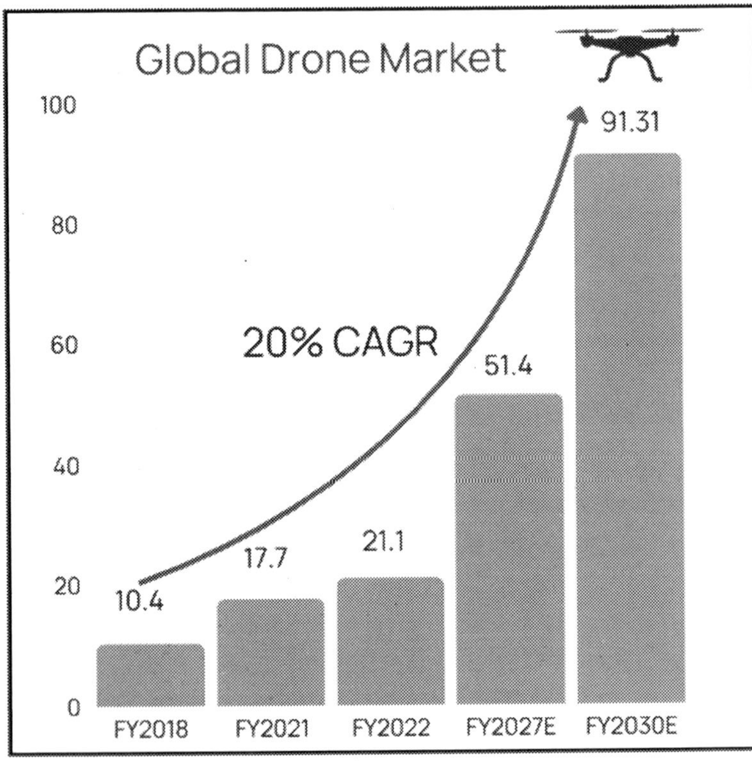

Figure 4: Global Drone Market
Source: WrightResearch[13]

- **Swarm Technology**. The development of swarming drones is another potential game changer. Recent advances in AI and robotic have offered new opportunities for drones to fly together and coordinate as part of a swarm to overwhelm defensive locality is a low-hanging fruit for drone technology. These drone swarms can perform complex missions more efficiently than individuals and sub-units.[14]

- **Miniaturisation**. This perhaps is the well-established trend of making the drones to a smaller size every year since the Predator made its debut. The existing prototype of these miniaturisation like Raven, Black Horner, and Switchblade can conveniently be carried by a soldier in their backpack on the battlefield for speedy and stealthy deployment. This trend will continue with modern drone going even further to nano drones, no bigger than a bird or even insects. These can be a major gamechanger as they will be able to conduct surveillance without even being noticed.

- **Resilience to Countermeasures**. As EW becomes more prevalent, drones are being designed to withstand jamming and other disruptions. Innovations include using fiber-optic cables for secure communication and AI systems that allow drones to continue missions even when traditional controls are compromised.
- **Integration of Directed Energy Weapons**. The use of lasers and microwave weapons on drones themselves is being explored, enabling them to disable enemy electronics or other drones. This integration could provide a tactical advantage by neutralising threats swiftly and efficiently. Companies like Epirus are developing high-power microwave systems, such as the Leonidas, capable of disabling drone swarms and other electronic threats.

Conclusion

Drones are no longer an experimental tool of the future; they are a decisive factor in today's battles. Their development has reached a stage comparable to tanks in the early years of mechanised warfare. While drone-enabled asymmetry can tilt the scales of battle, its impact depends on who wields it more effectively. High-end drones may face increasing challenges due to cost and countermeasures, making their sustained deployment uncertain. However, tactical drones, particularly those that are low-cost and adaptable, provide an unprecedented force multiplier at the smallest levels of unit and sub-unit. Their ability to deliver intelligence, precision strikes, and rapid mobility at minimal risk gives tactical commanders an edge, disproportionate to their investment. At the same time, counter-drone tactics must evolve in parallel, ensuring that the advantage remains with those who can both exploit and neutralise this technology in a rapidly shifting battlefield.

Endnotes

[1] Paul Scharre, "Army of None: Autonomous Weapons and the Future of War", (New York/London: W. W. Norton & Company, 2018), accessed 25 Jun 2025 https://ftp.idu.ac.id/wp-content/uploads/ebook/tdg/MILITARY%20 PLATFORM% 20DESIGN/Army%20of%20None%20Autonomous% 20Weapons%20and%20 the%20Future%20of%20War.pdf

[2] Laurence R. Newcome, "Unmanned Aviation: A Brief History of Unmanned Aerial Vehicles", (South Yorkshire: Pen & Sword Aviation, 2004), accessed 26 Jun 2025 https://arc.aiaa.org/doi/book/10.2514/4.868894

[3] Mira Patel, "The Use of Drones in International Warfare over the Years", *The Indian Express*, 25 Oct 2024, accessed 16 Jun 2025 https://indianexpress.com/article/research/the-use-of-drones-in-international-warfare-over-the-years-9638393/

[4] US Air Force. "Small-Unmanned Aircraft Systems Guide and Reporting Procedures", *US Department of State*, 14 Mar 2022, accessed 16 Jun 2025 https://media.defense.gov/2022/Mar/14/2002956018/-1/-1/1/SUAS%20IDENTI FICATION%20AND%20REPORTING%20GUIDE.PDF

[5] "How cheap commercial drones are changing the face of war in Ukraine", *The Economist*, 05 Feb 2024, accessed 24 Jun 2025 https://www.economist.com/interactive/science-and-technology/2024/02/05/cheap-racing-drones-offer-precision-warfare-at-scale

[6] Eric Schmidt, "Ukraine Is Losing the Drone War", *Foreign Affairs*, 22 Jan 2024, accessed 25 Jun 2025 https://www.foreignaf-fairs.com/ukraine/ukraine-losing-drone-war-eric-schmidt

[7] "India's ides Forge unveils new NETRA 5 drones", *Asia Pacific Defence Reporter*, 09 Feb 2025, accessed 24 Jun 2025 https://asiapacificdefencere porter.com/indias-ideaforge-unveils-new-netra-5-drone/

[8] Arushi Singh, "Future Countermeasures for Drones and Drone Swarms: India as a Case in Point", *The Cove*, 13 Oct 2023, accessed 24 Jun 2025 https://cove.army.gov.au/article/future-countermeasures-drones

[9] Frantzman, Seth, *Drone Wars*, New York: Bombardier Books, 2021, accessed 25 Jun 2025 https://www.simonandschuster.com/books/Drone-Wars/Seth-Frantzman/9781642938317

[10] "India's Drone Policy Explained", *ideaForge*, accessed 23 Jun 2025 https://ideaforgetech.com/blogs/indias-drone-policy-explained

[11] Zachary Kallenborn and Marcel Plichta, "Drone, Counter drone, counter counter drone: Winning the unmanned Platform innovation cycle", *Modern War Institute*, Sep 2024, accessed 25 Jun 2025 https://mwi.westpoint.edu/drone-counterdrone-counter-counterdrone-winning-the-unmanned-platform-innovation-cycle/

[12] "InsideFPV: India Drone Market Forecast to 2029", *insideFPV,* accessed 23 Jun 2025 https://insidefpv.com/blogs/blogs/insidefpv-poised-for-growth-in-indias-booming-drone-market?srsltid=AfmBOopEERzGn9yNv895Nqwl5Jjg_iyl56e2r0LKe0zDTQjZzJlJwR44

[13] Naman Agarwal, "Chapter 1: Overview of the drone Industry", *WrightResearch*, 20 Sep 2024, accessed 20 Jun 2025 https://www.wrightresearch.in/encyclopedia/chapter-report/chapter-1-overview-of-the-drone-industry/

[14] Peter Bergen, Melissa Salyk Virk and David Sterman, "World of Drones — Who Has What: Countries Developing Armed Drones", *New America*, 30 Jul 2020, accessed 25 Jun 2025 https://www.newamerica.org/future-security/reports/world-drones/who-has-what-countries-developing-armed-drones/

Logistics: Lessons from the Ukraine Conflict and its Impact on Indian Military Logistics

Colonel Deepak Kumar

"Leaders win through logistics. Vision, sure. Strategy, yes. But when you go to war, you need to have both toilet paper and bullets at the right place at the right time. In other words, you must win through superior logistics"

—Tom Peters

Abstract

Military force has always been a display of power, from the swords of Alexander's Day to the mechanised formations of 'Operation Iraqi Freedom', and contemporary warfare using drones and precision missiles. However, behind these pictures of the battlefield are the invisible military logisticians who toil day and night to keep everything running. On 24 Feb 2022, Russia, a former Cold War superpower, began its onslaught against Ukraine with the goal of winning quickly. But nine months later, Ukraine began counteroffensives in addition to holding its ground. What led to this disparity in operations? Military logistics hold the key to the solution. Although planning is the last resort, a strong logistical foundation is essential for success. History demonstrates that strategic failures and adversary counteroffensives can result from any neglected logistical deficiency. This article examines the role of Russian military logisticians in the ongoing conflict, key lessons learnt, and implications for Indian Military Logistics in context of future warfare.

Figure 1: Map of Russia and Ukraine

Introduction

Russia's takeover of Crimea in 2014[1] was a watershed moment in European security, paving the way for the continent's biggest war since World War II.[2] Numerous diplomatic attempts including Ukraine, North Atlantic Treaty Organization (NATO), the United States (US), and Russia over the course of the following eight years were unsuccessful in ending the situation. In the meantime, Russian President Vladimir Putin had already started planning for a more significant conflict by using a sophisticated hybrid warfare strategy in the Donbas region. He saw NATO's relentless eastward expansion as an existential threat to Russia's strategic interests, and his main goal was to stop it. Tensions increased because of the West's continuous expansion in Eastern Europe despite Moscow's repeated warnings.

Russia began what it called a 'Special Military Operation' on 24 Feb 2022 with the goal of 'Denasifying' and demilitarising Ukraine.[3] The original Russian plan was for a brief, decisive campaign, similar to a blitzkrieg, in which Russian forces would quickly seize Kyiv, topple the Ukrainian government, and establish rule.[4] Concurrently, efforts in the east and southeast concentrated on fortifying the Donbas area and creating a vital land route that connected the Donbas[5] to Crimea. But this idea did not work out as planned. As the months went by, Ukrainian resistance turned out to be more formidable than expected, entangling Russian soldiers in an expensive and protracted conflict. By the ninth month, many of Russia's initial advances had been undone by Ukraine's successful counter offensives.

Many military analysts blame Russia's logistical failures for the conflict's protracted duration. Russian progress was halted by supply chain interruptions, inadequate coordination, and an underestimate of Ukrainian tenacity. Russia has always depended on its 'Three Generals'—General Winter, General Fuel and Gas, and General Food and Grains for strategic support. The war has emphasised the importance of operational logistics in maintaining military campaigns and worldwide consequences of interrupted food and energy supplies.

Russia's War Objectives

As the second most populous and powerful country in the Soviet Union after Russia, Ukraine was a pillar of the organisation. It was essential to the Soviet economy, making a substantial contribution to defence industry, agricultural output, and military resources, including the Black Sea Fleet and some of the nuclear arsenal. Ukraine's 1991 decision to break off relations with the Soviet Union dealt a serious blow to the already waning superpower.

Russia proposed a political partnership with Ukraine in response to NATO's ongoing border expansion, offering conditional agreements to guarantee open and cooperative border policy.[6] But the Ukrainian government turned down these suggestions. Tensions increased because of President Volodymyr Zelenskyy's insistence on joining NATO, which strengthened Russia's determination to oppose what it perceived as a direct danger to its strategic interests.

Strategic Objectives

The acknowledgment of Crimea as Russian territory was one of Moscow's primary demands, even though Ukraine and most of the international community believed that its annexation in 2014 was illegal. It also called for Donetsk and Luhansk to be recognised as independent states, a demand that was mostly denied. Furthermore, Russia insisted that Ukraine pledge to remain neutral and non-NATO, a position Ukraine contemplated during the early stages of the 2022 conflict but now pursues for security grounds.[7]

Military Objectives

Russia began its 'Special Military Operation' on 24 Feb 2022, with the primary goals of securing the Black Sea coastline, isolating Donbas, and exerting military pressure on Kyiv to increase its geopolitical clout. Kharkiv's capture was essential for future invasions and logistical advantages. To maintain its power and change Ukraine's geopolitical affiliation, Russia also sought to overthrow the country's current government and establish a pro-Russian one.

Russian Logistics During the War

Russia took control of the abandoned Chernobyl power facility on Ukraine's northern border on the first day of hostilities.[8] Russia's seizure of the facility was ambiguous in motive, but leverage over the asset would be seen as strategic even though the motive for the seizure was not entirely clear because the plant still needs active maintenance to prevent future disasters, providing Russia significant leverage over Ukraine. Additionally, Belarus, a country that backs Russia and its Soviet Union claims in the area, is not far from the site. As a result, Russia gained its first foothold in northern Ukraine and established a northern approach route to Kyiv on the Dnieper River's western bank. Since then, the Russian military has taken control of several other vital assets, such as seaports, airports, and the Zaporizhzhia Nuclear Power Plant, the biggest facility in Europe. As a result, Russia has been able to seize control of a sizable amount of Ukraine's domestic power-producing capacity and effectively isolate the country by water. Russia has also launched missile attacks against Ukrainian military installations.

Ukraine Actions on Russian Logistics

Ukraine aimed to keep vital logistics infrastructure out of Russian hands, just as Moscow has attempted to take control of it. Ukrainian Railways declared the destruction of all rail connections between Russia and

Ukraine on 26 Feb 2022. This appeared to be an attempt to prevent Russian military usage. Since then, Russia has been beset by obvious logistical problems, such as the suspension of whole military convoys for days at a time. There have also been reports of military vehicles running out of petrol while traveling to Kyiv. Due to its heavy reliance on rail for military force projection, Russia was forced to rely on automobiles and road systems. As a result, Russian supply network was disrupted and Russian columns were physically removed from supply locations.

Following the incident, Ukraine began aggressively attacking logistics vehicles. Russia changed its strategy to pass off fuel vehicles as freight versions, but Ukraine soon figured it out. Additionally, Ukrainians were hiding in the intricate urban landscapes and attacking Russian convoys at night, which made it possible to target vital logistical vehicles. This strained Russian supply lines and interfered with communications with higher headquarters. On the other hand, Russia does not now have the luxury of an active global supply chain or the receipt of arms and munitions from other countries, which Ukraine does. The war between the two nations disrupted the global supply chain of fuel, gas, and other essential commodities.[9]

Weather and Environment

Former US President Joe Biden said that Putin might be holding off on starting activities until the ideal freeze conditions are met. The winter season in Ukraine lasts from Dec to Feb. In Jan, the average temperature drops below zero, causing a lot of the ground to freeze. The average temperature reached low single digits (Celsius) by Mar. Much of the land defrosts and turns to muck during this springtime. With weights under 50 tonnes, the Russian T72B3, T80-U, T90-A, and T14 Main Battle Tanks (MBTs) are among the lightest MBTs in operation today. Most NATO military MBTs weigh more than 60 tonnes, prompting fears that war in Eastern Europe would be extremely difficult not only due to the ground conditions, but also the many bridges unable to hold the load of a NATO MBT.

Figure 2: Inhospitable Weather Conditions

These conditions are nothing new to the Russian military, which trains in a variety of weather situations all year long. Despite this, numerous instances of Russian tanks and supply vehicles becoming stuck in mud have been documented, either during pre-conflict training or during actual combat. Although a lot of critics have said that this shows inadequate preparation for the invasion's schedule, it might mean something else. The fight was designed to be won quickly, not because Putin and his generals mistimed the invasion. According to some military analysts, Russia's plan called for an instant triumph, anticipating that Ukraine would either give up or fall apart in a matter of minutes or hours. With the thaw well and truly set in, it seems that the window for Russia to achieve a swift ground victory may be closing.

Complexities in Logistics Management.

- **Planning and Vulnerabilities.** Given its extensive size (6,000 miles across) and dependency on pipelines and railroads, Russia's logistical standstill was prearranged. These networks, however, spread into Ukraine, leaving them exposed during times of conflict. When advancing forces exceeded supply lines, the Russian Transport Corps, a combination of military and civilian fleets, experienced logistical difficulties due to mobility restrictions on border routes.

- **Limitations**. Due to its low trucking capacity, Russia's logistics were primarily depended on rail. Only about 400 vehicles were used by each Material Technical Support Brigade, which was not enough for deep offensives. Like the Gulf War's 100 hour-stop, the initial three days blitzkrieg demonstrated how the operational plan exceeded logistical capabilities. Resupply and battlefield adaptability were impacted by a strict command structure that decreased flexibility.

- **Key Failures**. Logistics were hindered by long distances, inadequate convoy security and a dispersed command organisation. Due to the paucity of support staff, Russian forces experienced supply shortages, frostbite instances from ill-equipped equipment, and antiquated food. Operational sustainability was further undermined by inadequate medical treatment, car problems, and cyber risks.

Logistical Failures of Russia in the Ukraine Conflict. During the battle in Ukraine, Russia experienced serious logistical setbacks, including inadequate coordination, fuel shortages[10], and supply chain problems. Troops' mobility, resupply attempts, and overall operational effectiveness were all negatively impacted by these problems.[11] The following are some of the key lessons learned:

- **Over-Reliance on Rail-Based Logistics**. Russia's capacity to maintain long-range operations was constrained by its reliance on railroads for military supply. Although this strategy worked well inside Russian borders, it became a disadvantage in Ukraine when Ukrainian forces targeted rail networks. The transportation of vital resources like food, ammunition, and fuel was slowed significantly by the inability to set up alternate supply routes.

- **Inadequate Trucking and Supply Chain Flexibility**. Russia did not have enough military trucks to move supplies efficiently more than 90 miles from railroad stations. As a result, troops were obliged to work with fewer food and fuel, and supply routes were congested. Operational momentum was severely hampered by the abandoned and stranded convoys caused by the lack of logistical transport vehicles.

Figure 3: Movement of Tanks and Fuel by Rail

❑ **Poor Road Infrastructure and Mobility Issues**. Heavy military traffic was not appropriate for Ukraine's road system, especially in rural areas, which resulted in traffic jams and breakdowns. Due to muddy terrain, destroyed roads, and their reliance on well-known routes, Russian forces found it difficult to move and were, therefore, at risk of being ambushed by Ukrainian forces. Poor planning and maintenance problems caused the notorious 40-mile convoy north of Kyiv to become a symbol of logistical immobility.

Figure 4: Poor Road Infrastructure Hindered Mobility

❑ **Weak Logistics Convoy Protection**. Due to their lack of protection, Russian supplies convoys were prime targets for Ukrainian ambushes employing light infantry, artillery, and drones. Russian logistics units suffered severe casualties and interruptions because of their frequent isolation and lack of proper force protection, in contrast to Western military that combine supplies with combat troops.

Figure 5: Movement of Convoy

- **Centralised and Rigid Logistics Planning**. Top commanders had to approve resupply missions in Russia's highly controlled logistics system, which caused delays and inefficiencies. In contrast to NATO's decentralised logistics strategy, which enables battlefield flexibility, Russian forces found it difficult to react to shifting operational circumstances, which resulted in shortages of supplies during crucial times.
- **Inadequate Winter Gear and Medical Support**. Due to subpar winter gear, many Russian soldiers experienced exposure and frostbite, underscoring logistical shortcomings in apparel and personal gear. Over time, the lack of adequate field hospitals, medical supplies, and evacuation systems increased losses and decreased combat efficiency.

Figure 6: Harsh Winter Conditions

- **Fuel and Ammunition Shortages**. Absence of a sustainable supply of ammunition and fuel was one of the worst mistakes. Fuel shortages often resulted in abandoned Russian armoured units. Due to irregular ammunition supplies, troops were forced to limit their firepower, which made it harder for them to maintain extended confrontations.

- **Communications and Coordination Failures**. Inadequate communication systems further hindered logistical efforts. Ukrainian forces were able to intercept communications because Russian forces used unprotected radio channels and even civilian mobile networks. Ineffective coordination between fighting units and logistics resulted in operational disarray and misplaced supplies.

- **Intelligence Failures and Underestimation of Ukrainian Resistance**. Russia misjudged the success of its original blitzkrieg approach and underestimated the tenacity of Ukrainian soldiers. Early supply exhaustion resulted from logisticians' failure to take into consideration the necessity of maintaining a protracted fight. Logistics planning and execution were made even more difficult by the absence of real-time combat intelligence.

- **Strategic Consequences of Logistics Failures**. Russia was obliged to give up on early goals, like taking Kyiv and switch to an attrition-based campaign in eastern Ukraine because of these logistical setbacks. The inability to sustain rapid offensives caused operational pauses, which allowed Ukraine to regroup and mount a successful counteroffensive. These logistical problems exposed deeper weaknesses in the Russian military's ability to maintain long-term, large-scale operations.

- **Significance of Mobility and Flexibility**. Supply systems lacked flexibility and mobility, offensive operations were hindered, and food, gasoline, and ammunition deliveries were severely disrupted. Because Russian forces heavily depend on fixed supply routes, they were vulnerable to Ukrainian attacks against logistics convoys and facilities. On the other hand, Ukraine successfully employed decentralised logistics, mobile supply units, and adaptable tactics to sustain its forces. This fight shows how effective military logistics require resilience, quickness, and agility to overcome operational challenges.

- **Redundancy and Resilience in the Supply Chain**. Russia's logistics were particularly vulnerable to Ukrainian attacks because of its reliance on centralised supply channels, which led to acute shortages on the front lines. In contrast, Ukraine kept its forces moving by using dispersed networks, alternative forms of transportation and rapid response. This disagreement demonstrates the importance of strong supply chains with built-in redundancy for maintaining operational effectiveness in high-risk scenarios.

- **Long Distances to the Objectives**. Initially, Russia believed that if Kyiv was overrun swiftly, President Zelenskyy would be ousted, but this did not occur. Significant logistical challenges were exposed by the extended conflict, particularly about sustaining supply lines across long distances. Because military movement was hindered by reliance on narrow roads and little control over key rail hubs, resupply efforts were slow and ineffectual.

- **Critical Supply Chain Disruptions**. Russia's logistical issues severely hampered the resupply of frontline troops, depriving them of basic supplies like food and fuel. Some soldiers experienced frostbite from wearing inadequate cold-weather gear, while others carried supplies that had been out of date since 2002. Intercepted communications revealed that troops near Kyiv were hurriedly requesting food, water, and fuel. There were numerous incidents of theft due to food shortages and Russia even requested rations from China.

- **Excessive Wear and Tear of Vehicles**. Since the start of the assault, Russia has reportedly lost more than 2,000 vehicles, including more than 300 tanks. Some were just left behind, while others were destroyed or taken by Ukrainian forces. Some of the tanks were old versions, including ones from the Soviet Union that had been manufactured more than 50 years ago.

Implications of Russia and Ukraine War on Indian Military logistics. The war between Russia and Ukraine highlighted the need for domestic defence industry[12] and diversified supply networks. The conflict also emphasised the need for strategic reserves and reducing dependency on outside sources. Some of the consequences of the conflict are enumerated in the following paragraphs:

- **Disruption in Supply Chains**. Majority of the Indian Armed Forces equipment including fighter jets, tanks, and missiles are produced in Russia. Delivery of ammunition and critical spare parts to India were delayed due to the conflict between both the nations. India decided to find alternate sources of supply and increase domestic manufacture under the scheme *Atmanirbhar Bharat* (Self-reliant India).[13]

- **Importance of Reserves and Self-Reliance**. The conflict highlighted the importance of reserves for essential military supplies before the commencement of a war. India noticed the issue of becoming overly dependent on one source of supply as Russia struggled to maintain its own war effort. This aspect emphasised the necessity of developing a home-grown defence sector and finding alternate sources of supply for vital military hardware.

- **Impact of Reduced Ammunition Reserves**. Prolonged fierce fighting in Ukraine demonstrated the extent of ammunition use, particularly for artillery shells and missiles. India has considered of the same and reassessing its war inventories, increasing local manufacture, and improving logistical planning to maintain operational preparedness in the event of conflict.

- **Vulnerability of Fuel Supply Chain and Energy Security Risks**. There was a severe impact on world's oil price and supply chain due to the war which affected fuel availability and prices. Fuel plays a vital role in all the military operations, India is focusing on diversifying its energy sources, securing long-term supply contracts and enhancing storage infrastructure to reduce reliance on uncertain foreign markets.

- **Complexities of Supply Chain in High-Intensity Conflict**. The difficulties faced by Russia in logistics operations highlighted the need for adaptable and a robust supply chain. India is putting these lessons into practice by investing in modern logistical infrastructure, enhanced transportation networks, and robust military trucking capabilities to sustain operations across a variety of terrains.

- **Technology in Logistics Optimisation**. Conflict made it evident that how important Artificial Intelligence (AI), satellite photography, and real-time tracking are to the effectiveness of logistics. To improve military logistics resilience and response time, India is implementing blockchain-based inventory management, AI-driven smart warehousing, and predictive maintenance.[14]

- **Civil-Military Integration: A Strategic Imperative**. The necessity of civil-military fusion was brought to light by Ukraine's successful use of commercial transportation, private sector assistance, and civilian logistics throughout the conflict. To ensure better coordination between military and civilian supply chains, India is attempting to use the private sector in defence logistics.[15]

- **Considerations for Air and Sea Logistics**. The conflict highlighted how crucial airlift and naval supply routes are during conflict. Therefore, India is improving its fast deployment capabilities, focussing on the development of naval logistics infrastructure and strengthening its strategic airlift capability to preserve operational flexibility in the times of crisis.

- **Focus on Theaterised Logistics**. The necessity of well-coordinated, integrated logistics across military branches was emphasised by the logistical difficulties in Ukraine. To provide a simplified, centrally managed supply system that improves efficiency throughout the army, navy, and air force, India is focussing on theaterised logistics.

- **Strengthening Logistics for a Dual Challenge**. India may have to fight with China and Pakistan on a two-front conflict. The necessity of sustainable logistics in protracted battles was brought to light by the Russia-Ukraine War. To guarantee ongoing warfighting capability in both the northern and western sectors, India is concentrating on improving forward stocking, border infrastructure, and fast mobilisation.

Logistics Lessons Learnt from Other Contemporary Conflicts

- **US-Afghanistan War**. The conflict's protracted duration highlighted how difficult it is to maintain long-term supply chains in hostile, mountainous environments. To avoid rebel attacks on ground convoys, especially along dangerous routes like the Khyber Pass, a heavy dependence on air logistics became necessary. Self-reliant logistics is a crucial lesson for future battles because the war also brought to light the dangers of an excessive reliance on private contractors and host-nation infrastructure.[16]

- **Israel-Hamas Conflict**. Israel's capacity to maintain high-intensity operations against Hamas demonstrated the need for quick mobilisation and pre-stockpiling of essential supplies. Tunnel networks and urban combat created special logistical problems that called for flexible replenishment techniques. Furthermore, integrating real-time intelligence with logistics planning was essential for foreseeing breakdowns and guaranteeing prompt restocking of fuel, ammunition, and medical supplies.[17]

- **Armenia-Azerbaijan Conflict**. Rapid logistical support affected battlefield momentum during the conflict, underscoring the significance of strategically placed supply depots and effective resupply chains. Targeting logistics infrastructure and revealing weaknesses in conventional supply chains were key outcomes of drone warfare. This shows that to safeguard vital assets, decentralised and mobile logistics networks are required, along with enhanced camouflage and counter-drone capabilities.[18]

Conclusion

India's defence readiness has learned a lot from the Russia-Ukraine war, which has highlighted the critical role logistics play in maintaining military operations. Over-reliance on foreign suppliers, ineffective supply chains and the urgent need for flexible, tech-driven logistics have all been exposed by the conflict. This is a wake-up call for India to boost strategic stocks, improve civil-military cooperation for wartime logistics, and speed indigenisation under programs like Make in India. Given India's complicated operational environment and the potential for a two-front battle, it is also becoming increasingly clear that AI-driven inventory management, better transportation infrastructure, and robust supply chains are necessary. By incorporating these lessons, India can strengthen its military logistics to guarantee long-term operational preparedness, quick force mobilisation, and an independent defence ecosystem that can successfully handle upcoming challenges.

Endnotes

[1] "Conflict in Ukraine", *Global Conflict Tracker*, Council on Foreign Relations. 27 May 2025, accessed 01 Jul 2025 https://www.cfr.org/global-conflict-tracker/conflict/conflict-ukraine

[2] "A brief history of the Russia-Ukraine war | Explained", *The Hindu*, 06 Mar 2025, accessed 01 Jul 2025 https://www.thehindu.com/news/international/a-brief-history-of-the-russia-ukraine-war-explained/article69294264.ece

[3] "Russia-Ukraine War", *The New York Times*, 30 Jun 2025, accessed 01 Jul 2025 https://www.nytimes.com/news-event/ukraine-russia

[4] John W. Deni, "Russia's War in Ukraine: Identity, History, and Conflict", *Institute for National Strategic Studies, National Defense University*, Mar 2022, accessed 01 Jul 2025 https://inss.ndu.edu/Publications/View-Publications/Article/3010403/russias-war-in-ukraine-identity-history-and-conflict/

[5] The Editors of Encyclopaedia Britannica, "2022 Russian Invasion of Ukraine", *Encyclopaedia Britannica*, 18 Jun 2024, accessed 01 Jul 2025 https://www.britannica.com/event/2022-Russian-invasion-of-Ukraine

[6] Jack Watling and Nick Reynolds, "Russian Military Objectives and Capacity in Ukraine Through 2024", *Royal United Services Institute (RUSI)*, 17 Jan 2024, accessed 01 Jul 2025 https://www.rusi.org/explore-our-research/publications/commentary/russian-military-objectives-and-capacity-ukraine-through-2024

[7] Rupali R. Kasabe, "A Study of Russia-Ukraine War and Its Impact on Indian Economy", *IOSR Journal of Business and Management* 24, no. 11 (2022), pp 1–11, 05 Nov 2022, accessed 02 Jul 2025 https://www.iosrjournals.org/iosr-jbm/papers/Vol24-issue11/Ser-1/A2411010111.pdf

[8] Ibid.

[9] Freightify, "Russia-Ukraine War: Global Supply Chain Problems", *Freightify Blog*, n.d., accessed 03 Jul 2025 https://www.freightify.com/blog/russia-ukraine-war-global-supply-chain-problems

[10] Manuela Tudosia, "Lessons Learned from Ukraine: Logistics", *European Security and Defence* (Euro SD), 23 Jun 2023, accessed 03 Jul 2025 https://euro-sd.com/2023/06/articles/31845/lessons-learned-from-ukraine-logistics/

[11] Ronald/ Ti and Christopher/ Kinsey, "Lessons from the Russo Ukrainian Conflict: The Primacy of Logistics over Strategy", *Defence Studies* 23, no. 3 (2023), pp 381–398, 21 Jul 2023, accessed 03 Jul 2025 https://kclpure.kcl.ac.uk/portal/files/224102580/Lessons_from_the_Russo_Ukrainian_conflict_the_primacy_of_logistics_ over_strategy.pdf

[12] "Impact of Russia Ukraine War on India and World", *ResearchGate*, n.d., Mar 2024, accessed 03 Jul 2025 https://www.researchgate.net/publication/378842058_Impact_Of_Russia-Ukraine_War_On_India_And_World

[13] "Russia–Ukraine War and Its Implications in Global Politics", *International Journal of Political Science and Governance* 6, no. 1 (2024), 06 Jun 2023, accessed 03 Jul/ 2025 https://www.journalofpoliticalscience.com/uploads/archives/5-1-81-193.pdf

[14] Force India, "From Setback to Opportunity", *Force India Cover Story*, Jun 2025, accessed 03 Jul 2025 https://forceindia.net/cover-story/from-setback-to-opportunity/

[15] Lt/ Gen/ (Retd.) Anil/ Kapoor, "Random But Relevant Lessons for OP Logistics Planning from the Russia Ukraine War", *Centre for Joint Warfare Studies (CENJOWS)*, 26 Apr 2023, accessed 03 Jul/ / 2025 https://cenjows.in/wp-content/uploads/2023/05/Lt_Gen_Anil_Kapoor_Web_Article_May_2023.pdf

[16] Paul/ Cornish, David/ Livingstone, Dave/ Clemente, and Claire/ Yorke, "On Cyber Warfare", *Chatham House*, Nov 2010, accessed 03 Jul 2025 https://www.chathamhouse.org/sites/default/files/public/Research/International%20Security/r1110_cyberwarfare.pdf

[17] Gilles/ Paché, "Israeli Palestinian Conflict: Towards a Major Logistical and Environmental Crisis?", *Technium Social Sciences Journal* 53, accessed 03 Jul/ 2025 https://www.researchgate.net/publication/377263406_Israeli-Palestinian_conflict_towards_a_major_logistical_and_environmental_crisis

[18] "Russia–Ukraine Conflict Logistics Analysis", *Bulletin of the National Defence University–Carol I* (Revista UNAP) 5, 2023, accessed 03 Jul/ / 2025 https://revista.unap.ro/index.php/bulletin/article/download/1674/1625/5599

Israel-Hamas War: Military Logistics Lessons for India

Colonel Neeraj Kotwal, SM

Abstract

This article examines the pivotal role of military logistics in the Israel-Hamas conflict and distils key lessons for India's defence preparedness. Through detailed analysis of urban warfare, drone deployment, artificial intelligence-enabled logistics, and rapid mobilisation strategies, it illustrates how Israel's logistics apparatus adapted under high-intensity, multi-domain warfare. It highlights the Israeli Defense Forces' success in sustaining operations through forward supply bases, multi-modal delivery, autonomous drones, and resilient stockpiling—despite infrastructure losses and embargoes. Hamas's asymmetric logistics, dependent on tunnels and low-cost drones, exposed vulnerabilities but inflicted disproportionate costs. Drawing on these insights, the article outlines strategic recommendations for India, including decentralised execution, tri-service joint logistics, pre-positioned reserves, anti-drone capabilities, and wartime financial planning. It argues that in future conflicts—urban or hybrid—the ability to keep forces mobile, supplied, and adaptive will determine operational success. This article underscores the timeless axiom: in war, logistics is not a support function—it is the strategy.

Introduction

The recent Gaza conflict between Israel and Hamas has underscored the critical role of military logistics in modern warfare. Fighting in a densely populated urban terrain presented protracted unique challenges for supply chain management, transportation of troops, material, and an overall logistics strategy. Both the Israeli Defense Forces (IDF) and Hamas had to adapt rapidly to disruptions from destroyed infrastructure to constant attacks while managing resources under intense pressure. The 2023 Israel-Hamas War was a high-intensity conflict that tested military logistics under surprise attack and combat. Israel's rapid mobilisation and sustained operations in Gaza highlighted several critical logistics lessons. Each lesson offers valuable takeaways for India's defence preparedness, given India's own security challenges and the possibility of high-intensity or prolonged conflicts. This article analyses key logistics lessons from the conflict, including how modern urban combat and asymmetric threats influenced planning.

Supply Chain Resilience and Adaptability

The Israel-Hamas war highlighted the importance of resilient, flexible logistics.[1] Facing multi-front operations and constant rocket attacks, the IDF adopted a multi-modal supply strategy—establishing forward bases, using airlifts, sea routes, and rerouting convoys in real time despite early setbacks and arms embargoes.[2] Israel's Logistics Command adapted by conducting over 2,000 supply missions across 14 months, including operations from six forward bases, some inside Gaza. This agility ensured consistent delivery of essentials like ammunition, food, and fuel even under disrupted conditions.[3]

Rapid Mobilisation and Deployment Strategies

Israel's response to the Hamas attack demonstrated the importance of swift mobilisation and deployment in the face of surprise offensives. Within hours of the 07 Oct assault, Israel began calling up reservists on an unprecedented scale. In just a few days, 3,60,000 reservists (about 04 per cent of Israel's population) were mobilised, effectively tripling the size of the IDF and many were at the frontlines within days.[4] Key to this speed was pre-planned mobilisation infrastructure and preparedness. This agility in force generation helped Israel stabilise the situation and launch counter-offensives within days of the initial shock.[5]

Urban Warfare Logistics

Fighting in Gaza's dense urban environment presented severe logistics challenges. Urban warfare is resource-intensive, troops need continuous resupply of ammunition and water in city combat, casualty rates can be high, requiring medical evacuation and the terrain itself can block traditional supply convoys. The IDF faced these issues in Gaza's cities and refugee camps, where Hamas's extensive tunnel network and booby traps compounded the difficulties.[6]

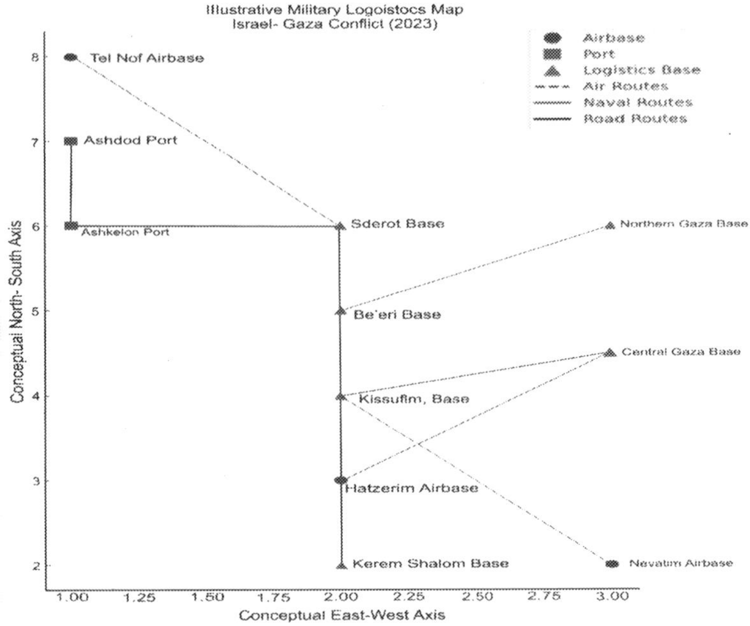

Figure 1: Illustrative Military Logistics Map: Israel-Gaza Conflict (2023)

Forward logistics bases were established inside Gaza once areas were secured, reducing the distance for delivering supplies to frontline units. The IDF also revitalised aerial resupply tactics on multiple occasions, the Israeli Air Force air-dropped supplies directly to troops deep in urban battle zones that were too risky for ground convoys. In one instance, a C-130J transport aircraft dropped 16 tons of ammunition, fuel, water, and food to an IDF division operating in southern Gaza.[7] In a short span, at least five such airdrop operations delivered around 60 tons of equipment to forces cut off by urban combat.[8] Additionally, engineering units with armoured bulldozers cleared rubble to open corridors for supplies and armoured ambulances were used to evacuate wounded under fire.

Drone Warfare Logistics

The conflict saw an unprecedented scale of drone usage by Hamas and Israel, adding a new dimension to battlefield logistics. Hamas employed cheap, commercially available drones for reconnaissance and attacks, including dropping small bombs on Israeli troops and even on tanks. In one recorded instance, a simple quadcopter drone deployed by Hamas dropped an explosive on a USD 3 mn Israeli Merkava tank, exploiting its top vulnerability and destroying it.[9] This highlighted how low-cost drones, if used cleverly, can impose disproportionate costs on a modern army.

Logistics also evolved to use drones as delivery platforms. Over the course of the war, Israel stood up a new Multi-Dimensional Supply Division dedicated to aerial supply, including the use of 'Logistical Drones'. For the first time, the IDF deployed autonomous drones to carry loads of equipment to forward positions, complementing traditional supply lines. They even experimented with automatic parachute systems that self-navigate to their drop zones, guided by Global Positioning System (GPS), to deliver supplies with high precision.[10]

Use of Artificial Intelligence (AI), Automation, and Precision Logistics

The Israel-Hamas conflict, like the concurrent war in Ukraine, has been a catalyst for greater use of technology in military logistics. The IDF incorporated automation and AI-driven tools to improve efficiency for example, the aforementioned self-navigating parachute drops which likely use GPS guidance and algorithms to land supplies precisely where needed. Additionally, the scale of Israel's operations forced them to analyse huge amounts of logistics data to predict needs and pre-position stocks accordingly. The conflict also saw automated systems like drones and robots taking on supply roles.[11]

Strategic Stockpiling and Logistics Planning for Prolonged Conflicts

Israel had to prepare for a potentially prolonged, multi-front war, highlighting the critical importance of deep strategic stockpiles. A major advantage was the United States (US)-maintained War Reserve Stockpile–Israel (WRSA-I), which allowed the IDF to access essential munitions like 155mm shells and precision-guided bombs without delay.[12] This pre-positioned reserve significantly reduced response times when rapid resupply was vital. However, the high intensity and extended duration of operations quickly depleted stocks, prompting urgent calls for additional supplies such as Iron Dome interceptors and artillery rounds. In some cases, partial embargoes or delays from allies forced

Israel to seek alternative sources or boost domestic production. The war underscored that national endurance in conflict depends not just on weapons but also on comprehensive stockpiling—fuel, spares, medical supplies, and even food—for both military and civilian needs.[13]

Coordination Between Military Branches for Logistical Efficiency

The Israel-Hamas war highlighted the vital role of tri-service coordination in sustaining effective logistics. While the Israeli Army led ground operations in Gaza, the Israeli Air Force conducted airstrikes and supply drops, and the Israeli Navy secured coastal routes and ferried supplies when roads were compromised. A key enabler was Israel's centralised Logistics Command, which worked closely with all services, especially the air force, to ensure timely support across fronts. This joint approach prevented delays and optimised resource use.[14]

Data Analysis of Gaza Conflict

Logistic Element	Quantity / Details
Duration of Conflict	16 months (Oct 2023–Mar 2025)
Number of Forward Logistic Bases	6 (2 inside Gaza, 4 near border)
Supply Missions (Total)	2,000+
Airlift Operations	250+ (fixed wing and helicopter)
Airdrop Operations	5 major operations
Total Supplies Airdropped	Approx. 60 tons (ammunition, water, food)
Naval Shipments Conducted	40 plus shipments
Artillery Shell Consumption	Approximately 1,50,000 shells
Iron Dome Missile Usage	3,000+ interceptors fired
UAV or Drone Operations	800+ sorties
Casualties Evacuated (Medical)	2,000 plus
Fuel Consumption (Daily average)	5,00,000 litres
Ammunition Expenditure (155mm Shells per day)	1,500–2,000 shells per day

Table 1: Logistic Data of Israel (Oct 2023-Jan 2025)

The logistic operations of the Gaza conflict underscore several critical insights:

❑ **High Intensity and Resource Consumption**.

- **Ammunition and Fuel**. Israel's high ammunition expenditure highlights the immense resource demands of modern high-intensity warfare.
- **Air and Drone Operations**. Extensive airlift and drone sorties show reliance on airborne logistics due to risks and restrictions on ground supply lines. The five major precision airdrop operations provided critical resupply when conventional routes were compromised.

Logistic Aspect	Details and Estimates
Primary Logistics Infrastructure	Underground tunnels, urban storage
Estimated Number of Tunnels Used	500+
Storage Locations	Over 100 (hidden caches in urban areas)
Rocket Inventory at Start	Approximately 15,000-20,000 rockets
Rocket Launches	9,000+ rockets fired
Drone Operations	300+ (Reconnaissance and Attack)
Logistics Routes	Primarily underground tunnels, some civilian routes
Fuel Reserves (est.)	Limited (~30-40 days' operational reserve)
Ammunition Stockpile	Estimated 1-2 months of intense combat
Medical Capability	Limited, reliant on civilian infrastructure
Food and Water Supplies	Civilian-dependent, limited long-term reserves
Casualty Management	Field hospitals, limited evacuation capabilities
External Resupply	Severely restricted due to blockade
Main Supply Challenges	Israeli airstrikes, tunnel detection, border blockade
Key Logistic Vulnerabilities	Reliance on fixed infrastructure (tunnels), limited external resupply

Table 2: Logistic Data of Hams: Gaza Conflict

- **Medical Logistics**. Evacuation of casualties emphasises the necessity of robust, responsive medical evacuation infrastructure under combat conditions.
- **Logistics of Hamas: Gaza Conflict**. Here is a representative illustrative logistic data table on Hamas during the 2023 Gaza conflict.

Logistic Analysis

Fragile Logistics Under Pressure. Hamas relied heavily on underground tunnels and urban caches for its logistics network, which, while offering concealment, became key targets for Israeli airstrikes once detected. This disrupted supply flows and exposed a major vulnerability. With limited stockpiles of ammunition and fuel, Hamas's ability to sustain high-intensity combat was constrained to about one-two months, forcing conservation of resources. To offset traditional logistics limitations, Hamas employed around 300 commercial drones for reconnaissance and attacks, creating low-cost disruptions for Israeli forces. However, their dependence on fixed infrastructure made their logistics fragile under sustained Israeli pressure, requiring constant and risky rebuilding efforts.

Foreign Logistic Assistance: Quantity and Financial Support (Israel vs Hamas). Here is a detailed comparative table showing approximate quantities, financial costs, and financial aid associated with the foreign logistic assistance received by Israel and Hamas during the conflict.

Analysis

Israel. Israel benefited from substantial US support, receiving USD 3.8 bn annually in defence aid, plus an additional USD 1 bn in emergency wartime assistance. This funding helped sustain high-intensity operations despite the high cost of modern logistics—such as USD 50,000 per Iron Dome interceptor—contributing to an estimated USD 6 bn in total war expenses.

Logistic Aspect	Israel	Hamas
Primary Foreign Suppliers	US, Germany, United Kingdom	Iran, Syria
Type of Supplies	Ammunition, Precision-guided bombs, Iron Dome missiles, Fuel	Rockets, small arms, drone components, explosives
Estimated Quantities Supplied	1,50,000+ artillery shells, 3,000+ interceptor missiles, thousands of guided bombs	Approximately 15,000-20,000 rockets, thousands of small arms, ~300+ drones
Key Logistic Stockpiles	US WRSA-I: 3,00,000 artillery shells initially earmarked for Ukraine; about half transferred to Israel (1,50,000 shells)	Several hundred tons of rockets and munitions smuggled over years (primarily pre-war)
Logistics Routes	Air (Ben Gurion, Tel Aviv), Sea (Ashdod, Haifa ports)	Smuggling tunnels from Sinai, small sea shipments
Estimated Financial Cost of Supplies	Approximately USD 3-4 bn	Approximately USD 50-100 mn
Financial Aid Received	Approximately USD 3.8 bn annual US military aid; additional emergency aid (~USD 1 bn extra approved post-conflict)	Estimated USD 100-200 mn per year from Iran (military and financial aid combined)
Approx. Cost of Key Items	Iron Dome interceptor (USD 40,000 each) 155mm shells (~USD 2,000 each)	Short-range rockets (USD 2,000-5,000 per unit)
Estimated Total Financial Cost (War)	~USD 6 bn (military logistics and armaments)	~USD 500 mn (munitions, rockets, drones, infrastructure)

Table 3: Logistical Profiles: Israel and Hamas (Suppliers, Quantities, Routes, Financials)

Hamas. Hamas relied on limited but steady support from Iran (~USD 100–200 million annually) and used low-cost weapons like improvised rockets and drones, enabling it to maintain pressure despite spending only about USD 500 million. Their cost-effective tactics created an economic imbalance, forcing Israel to spend disproportionately on defence.

Logistics Lessons for India

Multi-Route Supply Networks and Real-Time Logistics Management. India must diversify supply routes—road, rail, air, and sea—and establish forward logistics hubs near borders. Integrating real-time tracking systems and AI-based logistics software will allow battlefield commanders to monitor movements and rapidly re-route supplies in response to disruptions. This mirrors the IDF's multi-route supply strategy and the US logistics approach seen in Ukraine and Gaza.

Domestic Resilience and Local Resource Utilisation. India must enhance its indigenous defence manufacturing and maintain buffer stocks of critical supplies. Leveraging civilian infrastructure—fuel, transport, and warehousing—during emergencies ensures continuity even if global supply lines are disrupted or embargoed, as seen in Israel's self-reliance model.

Rapid Mobilisation and Surge Preparedness. India should implement a digitised call-up system for reservists and paramilitary forces with clearly defined protocols and conduct regular large-scale exercises to identify logistical bottlenecks. Emulating Israel's mobilisation agility will help India respond swiftly to crises like a two-front war or sudden terror strikes.

Prepositioning Equipment and Alliance Logistics Support

Prepositioned War Reserves. Drawing from Israel's experience, India should preposition war reserves, including weapons, vehicles, ammunition, and fuel near likely flashpoints along the Western and Himalayan borders. Secure storage facilities close to these regions can dramatically reduce response times during emergencies. Additionally, India should proactively establish logistical exchange agreements with friendly nations, allowing reciprocal access to supplies during prolonged conflicts. Strategic prepositioning and alliance-based logistics create depth and flexibility, especially, if diplomatic or external logistical channels become constrained in wartime.

Mobilisation Logistics and Civil-Military Coordination. Effective mobilisation requires pre-established frameworks for requisitioning civilian transport—railways, buses, airlines—during emergencies. Drawing from Israel's example, India should integrate local infrastructure into logistics planning, ensuring rapid troop and material movement.

Specialised Logistics for Urban Operations. Urban combat scenarios require specialised logistics strategies, emphasising prepositioning supplies close to built-up areas prone to conflict. Drawing lessons from the Gaza conflict, India should develop mobile supply units capable of establishing forward depots even within partially secured urban terrain. Traditional ground logistics methods may prove inadequate in densely populated areas, thus, exploring innovative delivery methods such as drone or helicopter drops becomes crucial. Regular urban logistics exercises, mirroring India's experience in Kashmir or potential urban engagements, will ensure readiness for sustained operations in complex city landscapes.

Protected Logistics and Engineering in Combat. Logistics troops must be trained and equipped for high-risk operations, especially in urban battlefields. This includes armoured supply vehicles, combat engineering support for obstacle clearance, and armoured medical evacuation platforms. Israel's experience highlights the need to protect and empower frontline logistics teams.

Comprehensive Drone Management. The growing threat from enemy drones, as evidenced by Hamas's effective use against high-value Israeli targets, necessitates comprehensive anti-drone capabilities within Indian Armed Forces. India must deploy radar systems, drone jammers, and Electronic Warfare (EW) measures as standard protective equipment at bases and along critical supply routes. Simultaneously, India should establish dedicated logistical support structures for its drone fleet, including forward maintenance workshops, stocked critical components such as rotors, batteries, and optics, along with specialised training for technicians. Employing drones for logistics, particularly in challenging terrains such as mountainous regions or dense urban areas, further enhances operational agility and reduces vulnerabilities in conventional supply lines.

Investing in Logistics Technology and Automation. AI and automation can revolutionise logistics by enabling predictive maintenance, smart inventory management, and guided delivery systems—such as drone or parachute-based drops—that reduce delays and enhance precision. Warehousing automation using robotic systems can accelerate response during high-tempo operations.

Cyber Security and Robust Communication Networks. With increased digitisation, logistics systems are vulnerable to cyber-attacks. India must fortify its information technology infrastructure, establish backup protocols, and retain human expertise to manage systems manually during outages—replicating the Israeli focus on cyber-secure logistics.

Ample War Wastage Reserves (WWR) and Strategic Stocks. India must review and scale its WWR to ensure ammunition and fuel are available for high-intensity, short-duration conflicts. Spares for imported systems and missiles must be stockpiled in dispersed, secure locations to withstand strikes or supply disruptions.

Joint Logistics Structures and Integrated Planning. Establishing joint logistics nodes and conducting regular tri-service exercises can streamline coordination between the army, navy, and air force. A joint logistics framework ensures optimal resource sharing, faster response, and better operational synergy.

Centralised Coordination, Decentralised Execution. India must adopt centralised logistics planning at theatre levels with decentralised execution authority. Logistics units should have flexibility to make real-time decisions in dynamic combat zones, supported by interoperable systems across all three services.

Miscellaneous Aspects

- **Airborne Logistics**. Enhance helicopter and aircraft-based resupply systems for remote and high-altitude areas.
- **Medical Evacuation**. Invest in armoured and airborne medical evacuation systems for casualty management under fire.
- **Balanced Investments**. Avoid over-dependence on costly technologies, invest in cost-effective countermeasures like EW and drone defence.
- **Strategic Financial Planning**. Allocate budget reserves for rapid wartime procurement and boost local production of critical systems.
- **Alliance Leverage**. Strengthen formal logistics partnerships with allies like the US, France, Israel, and Japan for wartime interoperability and supply assurance.

Conclusion

The Israel-Hamas War offers a vivid case study of modern military logistics under duress. From it, India can draw a comprehensive set of lessons to enhance its own readiness. Supply chains must be resilient and flexible, able to overcome shock disruptions. Mobilisation must be swift and supported by prepositioned resources. Urban warfare demands novel supply solutions and hardened logisticians. Drone warfare is now a staple, requiring both support for India's own unarmed aerial vehicles and defences against enemy drones. Technology—AI and automation—can give a decisive edge in managing the complexity of wartime logistics, but only if embraced and secured. Stockpiling and long-term planning are insurance for when wars drag on longer or hotter than expected. Finally, jointmanship in logistics is essential, victory in modern war will favour those who can marshal all elements of national power in a coordinated, efficient manner. For India, investing in these areas will strengthen its military posture against potential adversaries and unforeseen crises. The adage that amateurs discuss strategy while professionals study logistics has been proven true once again and India would do well to heed the logistical lessons from Israel's experience to ensure its own forces are never found wanting in the hour of need.

Endnotes

1 Council on Foreign Relations, "Israeli-Palestinian Conflict", *Global Conflict Tracker,* 2024, accessed 15 Mar 2025 https://www.cfr.org/global-conflict-tracker/conflict/israeli-palestinian-conflict

2 "Expert Analysis: Logistics and Supply Chain Lessons from Israel-Hamas War", *Locate2U*, 10 Nov 2023, accessed 15 Mar 2025 https://www.locate2u.com/logistics/expert-analysis-logistics-and-supply-chain-lessons-from-israel-hamas-war/

3 LMA Consulting Group, "Israel-Hamas War and the Impact on Global Supply Chains", *LMA Consulting Group*, 30 Mar 2024, accessed 16 Mar 2025 https://www.lma-consultinggroup.com/israel-hamas-war-impacts-on-the-supply-chain/

4 Jeffrey Heller, "Israel's Reservists Drop Everything and Rush Home", *Reuters*, 12 Oct 2023, accessed 15 Mar 2025 https://www.reuters.com/world/middle-east/israels-reservists-drop-everything-rush-home-following-hamas-bloodshed-2023-10-12/

[5] Rachel Chason and Meryl Kornfield, "Israel's Massive Mobilization of 360,000 Reservists Upends Lives", *The Washington Post*, 10 Oct 2023, accessed 13 Mar 2025 https://www.washingtonpost.com/world/2023/10/10/israel-military-draft-reservists/

[6] Congressional Research Service, "Israel and Hamas Conflict in Brief: Overview", *U.S. Policy, and Options for Congress*, Report No. R47828, 2024, accessed 15 Mar 2025 https://crsreports.congress.gov/product/pdf/R/R47828

[7] The Times of Israel, "IDF Airdrops Supplies to Troops in Southern Gaza," *The Times of Israel*, 17 Jan 2024, accessed 15 Mar 2025 https://www.timesofisrael.com/liveblog_entry/idf-airdrops-supplies-to-troops-in-southern-gaza/

[8] Ibid.

[9] Defence Blog, "Hamas Drone Drops Grenade on Israeli Merkava Tank", *Defence Blog*, 07 Oct 2023, accessed 15 Mar 2025 https://defence-blog.com/hamas-drone-drops-grenade-on-israeli-merkava-tank/

[10] The Jerusalem Post, "Inside the IDF's New Logistics Division to Bring Soldiers Supplies", *The Jerusalem Post*, 07 Nov 2024, accessed 15 Mar 2025 https://www.jpost.com/israel-news/article-827928

[11] TWZ, "Guided Parachute System Used by Israel for First Time in Gaza", *The War Zone*, 12 Dec 2023, accessed 15 Mar 2025 https://www.twz.com/guided-parachute-system-used-by-israel-for-first-time-in-gaza

[12] Congressional Research Service, "Israel and Hamas October 2023 Conflict: Frequently Asked Questions*(FAQs)*", *CRS Reports*, Report No. R47754, 2024, accessed 15 Mar 2025 https://crsreports.congress.gov/product/pdf/R/R47754

[13] *The Guardian*, "Gaza War Puts US's Extensive Weapons Stockpile in Israel under Scrutiny", 27 Dec 2023, accessed 13 Mar 2025 https://www.theguardian.com/world/2023/dec/27/gaza-war-puts-us-extensive-weapons-stockpile-in-israel-under-scrutiny

[14] The Jerusalem Post, "IDF Logistics Command Overcomes War Challenges, Improves Supplies and Medical Response", *The Jerusalem Post*, 26 Nov 2024, accessed 14 Mar 2025 https://www.jpost.com/israel-news/article-830737

Joint Operations and Interoperability: Insights from Ukraine

Colonel Rajesh Kumar Ranjan

Abstract

This article examines the strategic and operational lessons emerging from the ongoing Ukraine conflict, with a specific focus on joint operations and interoperability. It explores how Ukraine's military effectively combined land, air, cyber, and intelligence capabilities, leveraging both legacy platforms and modern technologies like drones, precision-guided munitions, and electronic warfare. The article highlights implications for India, as it advances towards theatreisation and seeks deeper defence cooperation with global partners. It addresses India's internal challenges—siloed command structures, doctrinal divergence, and technical integration issues—as well as external interoperability hurdles with foreign militaries. The article offers practical recommendations to strengthen jointness through organisational reform, joint doctrine, technology standardisation, and international collaboration. It concludes that India must institutionalise jointness and strategic partnerships to navigate future conflicts effectively.

Introduction

The world today continues to witness conflicts of varying intensity across the globe. Military planners and practitioners have a tough task at hand. They are busy analysing and refining their doctrines and strategies to ensure that their forces are well prepared to face any eventualities based on the lessons being learnt. The ongoing conflict in Ukraine has in many ways underscored the critical importance of joint operations and interoperability in modern warfare. The large-scale conventional war over the last three years has seen the integration of land, air, and cyber capabilities by the defending forces, enabled in part by extensive Western support and intelligence-sharing.[1]

This conflict provides a rich source of operational and strategic lessons. Today, the Indian Armed Forces are in process of transformation. With theaterisation on the horizon, the lessons from Ukraine provide valuable insight to joint operations challenges and opportunities.

Integrated Multi-Domain Operations and Tactics

The war in Ukraine has vividly demonstrated the effectiveness of integrated multi-domain operations. Ukraine's military, though outmatched in size by Russia, leveraged joint operations to blunt and counter Russian offensives. Small, agile Ukrainian units used a network of drones, sensors, and Precision-Guided Munitions (PGMs) to direct artillery fire and conduct targeted strikes, blurring the lines between traditional service domains like during the defence of Avdiivka.[2] Indeed, analysts have called the Russia-Ukraine war 'The first full-scale drone war', where unmanned aerial systems became ubiquitous for reconnaissance and attack.[3] From cheap quadcopters spotting targets for artillery to long-range loitering munitions striking high-value assets, drones proved indispensable in Ukraine's defence. This underscores that in modern warfare, achieving battlefield success requires seamless coordination across domains—air, land, sea, and even the cyber or information sphere—rather than siloed, single-service efforts.

Combined Arms at the Tactical Level

The urban battles and trench warfare in Eastern Ukraine illustrated the enduring need for combined arms tactics. Russian forces often massed armour and mechanised units, only to be ambushed by Ukrainian infantry armed with anti-tank guided missiles and supported by drone-directed artillery, as was seen in Russia's Kursk Oblast.[4] Ukrainian units learned to operate in dispersed, flexible formations including drones even at the platoon level, practising true combined-arms cooperation. This is reminiscent of lessons from past wars but updated with modern technology. As one Indian analysis noted, despite high-tech advancements, traditional elements like 'Boots on the ground' in fortified positions remain crucial, meaning militaries must be prepared for both high-tech and conventional tactics.[5]

Cutting Edge Technology and Legacy Platforms

In Ukraine, neither cutting-edge technology nor legacy firepower alone decided battles. Instead, it was the creative combination of both. Western-provided precision artillery, such as the High Mobility Artillery Rocket System, delivered long-range strikes, while local territorial defence units held ground in cities using simple yet effective tactics—for example, rocket-propelled grenade and Molotov attacks on armoured columns in Kyiv's suburbs in 2022. The key takeaway is that integrating capabilities, old and new, yields a force multiplier effect. Military observers have emphasised that Ukraine's 'Tactical innovation from the bottom up' stemmed from adaptive soldiers combining technologies in novel ways, rather than any single 'Super-Weapon' deciding the outcome.[6] For instance, off-the-shelf drones modified to drop grenades became tank killers when used in concert with ground manoeuvre units. The successful defence of Kyiv and the later counter-offensives were products of joint planning.

Military Technology and Innovation

Technology has been at the forefront of the Ukraine conflict, offering salient lessons, innovations, and opportunity for cross-domain applications.

- ❑ **Drones**. Drones enabled persistent eyes in the sky and rapid targeting cycles. They turned artillery into a precision tool by providing real-time targeting coordinates. Commercial quadcopters and drones allowed even small infantry units to detect enemies, fundamentally changing tactics.[7] Moreover, Ukraine's creative use of loitering munitions and explosive laden drones to hit tanks and air defence systems caught Russia off guard. Russia's initial neglect of drone warfare proved costly, whereas Ukraine's rapid adaptation exemplified the agility of a military that embraces new technology. As a result, both sides now face 'Swarms' of cheap drones in the skies, complicating traditional notions of air superiority. North Atlantic Treaty Organization's (NATO) observers note that achieving uncontested control of the air may be impossible when 'Cheap and plentiful drones' saturate the battlespace.[8] Instead, future conflicts will involve contesting the air with a mix of manned and unmanned systems, a lesson keenly relevant to the Indian Air Force's doctrine.

❑ **Precision-Guided Munitions**. The Ukraine war reaffirmed that precision strikes can have strategic effects. Ukrainian forces, using Western-supplied PGMs, achieved notable successes such as the sinking of Russia's Black Sea flagship Moskva.[9] This demonstrated how a smaller military could level the playing field by striking high-value targets precisely rather than relying on massed firepower. On the flip side, Russia's use of long-range missiles against Ukrainian critical infrastructure highlighted the threat of strategic bombardment in modern war. The integrated duel of strike and counterstrike in Ukraine underscores the need for both offensive precision capabilities and robust air defences.

❑ **Electronic Warfare (EW) and Cyber Domain**. Russia has formidable EW units that have jammed global positioning system signals, communications, and drone control links on the battlefield. Ukraine, with Western support, countered by hardening its communications—using satellite links like SpaceX's Starlink—and dispersing its command and control. Both sides also engaged in cyber operations, destructive malware attacks, intelligence hacks, and propaganda campaigns. A parallel 'Shadow War' in the cyber and information domain has been waged alongside kinetic fighting.[10] This hybrid aspect where hacking of military networks, disruption of satellites, and info-war on social media demonstrates that cyber warfare is now inseparable from conventional warfare. For instance, at the outset of the invasion in 2022, a major cyber-attack on Viasat's satellite internet service disrupted Ukrainian communications, illustrating how an opening salvo in cyberspace can accompany or even precede missile strikes.[11]

❑ **Perseverance and Adaptability**. The conflict highlights that adaptation is not just a necessity but a determinant of success. Both Ukraine and Russia have demonstrated an ability to learn from battlefield experiences and adjust their tactics accordingly. Whether through EW innovations evolving drone countermeasures or operational deception, this war offers valuable lessons for military planners worldwide on how adversaries can adapt rapidly in a high-stakes environment.[12]

Intelligence Sharing and Coalition Support

One of the most striking aspects of the Ukraine conflict has been the extensive intelligence-sharing and coalition support provided to Ukraine, which offers lessons on the power of alliances and information superiority. NATO officials' credit 'Shared intelligence among allies, especially from the United States (US)' as a foundational reason why the collective response in 2022 was far more unified and effective than in 2014.[13] This real-time intelligence-sharing model was so effective that when there were temporary pauses, such as a brief US policy halt on certain intel due to political considerations, experts warned it could seriously 'Blind' Ukraine on the battlefield.[14] In tandem, Ukraine has been bolstered by a broad coalition of support from NATO countries and other allies. This ranges from lethal aid (tanks, artillery, air defence systems) to non-lethal aid and training. By early 2023, Ukraine was operating a diverse array of Western-supplied equipment. Managing this influx required a high degree of interoperability and adaptability on Ukraine's part (e.g., training crews quickly on different platforms, establishing new supply chains for ammunitions).

Logistics

The logistics coordination among allies itself was a formidable joint operation. NATO established coordination cells (like the International Donor Coordination Centre in Stuttgart) to align the supply of weapons and avoid gaps or redundancies.[15] A notable strategic initiative has been the creation of a NATO-Ukraine Joint Analysis and Training Centre to systematically gather lessons and improve Ukraine's interoperability with NATO standards.[16]

Information Warfare

The Ukraine War has also been a prime example of modern Information Warfare (IW). Ukraine, despite being the underdog, largely won the information war on the global stage, courtesy of savvy use of strategic communications, open-source intelligence, and social media to tell its story and maintain Western public support. Russia employed propaganda and disinformation (some of it aimed at its domestic audience, some globally) but found limited success outside of certain regions. Both sides also engaged in cyber-enabled information operations. Hacktivist collectives like 'Information technology Army of Ukraine' or pro-Russian groups leaked information, defaced website and flooded social networks with content to influence opinion.[17] The unity of effort for synergising the effort in IW is lesson for all militaries across the globe.

Internal Joint Operation and Interoperability Challenges for India

The Indian Armed Forces need to take note of the ongoing development on the battlefield in Ukraine as well as the complete operational environment. The aftereffects and impacts in each domain need a deep analysis. Certain key lessons specific to joint operations and interoperability are enumerated in the succeeding paragraphs.

- **Organisational Silos and Command Structure**. One of the long-standing challenges for the Indian Armed Forces has been the fragmented command structure. They often have overlapping geographic areas but without a unified command in those areas. The coordination between them depended on ad-hoc measures rather than an integrated chain of command. This can slow decision-making and create interoperability issues in fast-paced operations. The Kargil conflict of 1999 famously highlighted coordination issues. To address this, India has embarked on establishing Integrated Theatre Commands, a major reform to unify forces under joint commanders for specific theatres. Progress has been made—with the appointment of a Chief of Defence Staff in 2019 and the creation of structures like the Integrated Defence Staff—but implementation has faced some inter-service disagreements. The Indian government in 2023-24 pushed further, declaring a 'Year of Reforms' to accelerate consensus on theatre commands. The challenge lies in ironing out concerns of each service.

- **Cultural and Doctrinal Differences**. Each service in India has its own doctrine, culture, and training ethos, which can impede joint action. The services historically trained mostly within their domains, with limited joint exercises until the 2000s. Bridging this gap is a work in progress. Joint training exercises have increased, and institutions like the Defence Services Staff College and War Colleges ensure officers of different services learn together early in their careers. Still, achieving true interoperability means developing a generation of military leaders who think 'Jointly' first.

- **Technical and Logistical Interoperability**. The Indian military's diverse inventory poses an internal interoperability challenge. India operates equipment from various countries and indigenous sources. Integrating these into one cohesive network is not straightforward. Different communication systems, data link protocols, and weapon interfaces complicate joint operations. The forces have been working towards this. But more effort is needed to establish truly joint command, control, communications, computers, intelligence, surveillance, and reconnaissance systems where, say, an army missile battery can receive targeting data from an air force unmanned aerial vehicle or a naval warship's radar in real time. Logistically, each service has its own supply chain; the joint logistics nodes are currently evolving and are in a nascent stage.

External Joint Operations and Interoperability Challenges for India

When it comes to operating with foreign militaries, India's unique geopolitical stance of non-alignment and strategic autonomy has meant it has no formal alliances and, thus, less institutionalised interoperability with other nations. However, India does conduct numerous bilateral and multilateral exercises and is deepening defence ties with partners. There are multiple challenges in this realm.

- **Standardisation and Protocol Differences**. Different countries use different military standards i.e., from equipment calibres to map grid systems to jargon. NATO allies, for instance, have spent decades standardising these through standardisation agreements. India, not being part of an alliance, must bridge standards on a case-by-case basis. These are being addressed through exercises, but it is a slow process. The more India procures Western-origin equipment, the more it naturally aligns with NATO standards. But India also has legacy Russian equipment, which a

NATO partner may not be familiar with. Achieving smooth interoperability might require India to gradually shift towards common standards with its primary partners.

- **Political and Secrecy Constraints**. True interoperability often requires sharing sensitive information and technology. Allies like the US are cautious about sharing certain technology unless trust and agreements are in place. Even then, some advanced intelligence might be shared only sparingly. From India's perspective, there is also caution in sharing too much operational information with another country, no matter how friendly. Building trust to the level of real-time wartime coordination is a challenge.

- **Balancing Relationships**. India's case is complicated by its diverse friendships. It has significant defence relations with Russia (its long-time supplier) as well as growing ties with the US and the Western bloc. This can create interoperability dilemmas. These issues must be navigated diplomatically and technically. India's unique position means it is not fully embedded in any single bloc's military architecture, so interoperability improvements must be pursued in a nuanced, context specific way rather than via a treaty framework.

- **Communication and Language**. Indian Armed Forces working with foreign forces must overcome language barriers and differing operational terms. English is commonly used, and Indian officers are fluent, so that helps with Western partners. With others, language could be a barrier in joint operations, mitigated by liaison officers and translators, in case forced to operate while fighting alongside allies.

Mitigating The Challenges: Proposed Solutions

Indian Armed Forces are undergoing major transformation as part of the nation's vision of *Viksit Bharat* (Developed India). The jointness and integration forms the basis of any military discussion to enhance operational efficiency in the multi domain threat environment. Certain solutions, keeping the lessons from Ukraine in mind, may be considered in the overall scheme of transformation.

- **Finalise and Implement Integrated Theatre Commands.** Pushing through the theatre command reform with consensus will create a unified structure for joint operations. This will clarify command and control in war, reduce duplication, and force integration at all levels. Once established, these theatre commands are given the authority and resources to train as joint entities.

- **Common Doctrine and Joint Planning.** The Joint Doctrines need to trickle down to become common knowledge. Regular joint wargames—not just field exercises but also map exercises and simulations—can help planners from different services align their strategies. Initiatives such as creating integrated battle groups or scenario-specific architectures—like an amphibious task force comprising navy and army components, or an air-land task force for mountainous terrain—on a standing basis will enhance operational familiarity.

- **Interoperable Communications and Networking.** Technically, India should invest in a unified communications grid for its military. This could mean ensuring every new platform procured is compatible with a tri-service secure network. Legacy systems can be retrofitted with common radios or encryption. Projects under the 'Network Centric Warfare' umbrella need prioritisation so that information flows freely between services in real time. Establishing a Joint Cyber and Space Command will also help integrate new domains with traditional ones.

- **Expand Joint Logistics.** The armed forces have recently established Joint Logistics Nodes at select locations—such as Port Blair, Guwahati, and Mumbai—to provide common support to all services. This is a good start; however, these establishments should be regularly vetted through joint exercises.

- **Enhance Foreign Military Cooperation Frameworks.** Internationally, India can deepen its participation in multilateral forums and exercises. India could also consider posting liaison officers at key allied commands to increase familiarity and information sharing. On the technology front, fully leveraging the signed agreements is essential.

- **Gradual Standardisation and Co-development**. While India has chosen the path of *Atmanirbharta* (Self-reliance), it has also diversified its arms procurement. In case of external procurements, it should push for co-development projects. Whenever possible, India can choose systems that improve compatibility, even if buying from abroad. Joining international standardisation groups (such as those for logistics units, mapping, etc.) will facilitate joint operations with other forces.

- **Confidence Building and Trust**. To get past hesitancy, India and its partners should practise information sharing in less critical areas to build confidence for more crucial moments. For instance, sharing naval 'White Shipping' data (commercial vessel tracking) is already done with many countries to improve maritime domain awareness. This could be expanded to sharing airspace pictures for civil aircraft or basic radar tracking, which builds habits that can translate to the military domain when needed. Engaging in table-top exercises for intelligence sharing during hypothetical scenarios can iron out protocols and trust issues in advance.

- **Strengthening India's Defence Cooperation with Key Global Allies**. India's strategic outlook has increasingly acknowledged the value of defence cooperation with like-minded countries, not as traditional alliances but as partnerships that enhance India's own security and global stability. Drawing on the lessons from Ukraine, India can identify specific areas like intelligence sharing, defence technology, industrial capacity during conflicts, cyber, and space to strengthen collaboration with its key global allies.

Conclusion

The conflict in Ukraine is separated from India by geography, scale, and context, yet it converges on a central truth of 21st Century warfare, i.e., no military can prevail alone without jointness and cooperation. By systematically addressing internal silos and external collaboration hurdles, India can gradually achieve a level of jointness and interoperability that enables it to act as a cohesive force at home and a reliable partner abroad. The Ukraine conflict highlights the gaps in integration, resulting in missed opportunities and magnified risks. As a professional battle-hardened armed forces, India can rise to the challenge by proactively addressing the issues of concern.

Endnotes

[1] Neelanjana Banerjee, "India's Lessons from the Ukraine War: The Future of Warfare", *BharatShakti*, 02 Mar 2025, accessed 10 Mar 2025 https://bharatshakti.in/indias-lessons-from-the-ukraine-war-the-future-of-warfare/

[2] Ella Sherman, "Ukrainian Artillerymen Running Low on Ammo Say Drones Crucially Make Their Aim 250% Better", *Business Insider*, 02 Feb 2024, accessed 10 Apr 2025 https://www.businessinsider.com/ukraines-military-is-using-drones-to-make-ammunition-more-accurate-2024-2

[3] Rakesh Sharma, "The Ukraine-Russia War: Military Lessons for India", *NatStrat*, 26 Apr 2024, accessed 12 Feb 2025 https://www.natstrat.org/articledetail/publications/ukraine-russia-war-military-lessons-and-legacies-for-india-133.html

[4] Yuri Zoria, "Forbes: Ukraine's Anti-Tank Missiles Still Outshoot Drones in Kursk Combat", *Euromaidan Press*, 13 Dec 2024, accessed 10 Apr 2025 https://euromaidanpress.com/2024/12/13/forbes-ukraines-anti-tank-missiles-still-outshoot-drones-in-kursk-combat/

[5] Banerjee, "India's Lessons"

[6] Center for Strategic and International Studies, "Land Domain Lessons from Russia-Ukraine | Conflict in Focus" *CSIS*, 20 Feb 2025, accessed 15 Mar 2025 https://www.csis.org/analysis/land-domain-lessons-russia-ukraine-conflict-focus

[7] Sharma, "The Ukraine-Russia War"

[8] David Barno and Nora Bensahel, "Learning from Real Wars: Gaza and Ukraine", *War on the Rocks*, 06 Dec 2023, accessed 16 Feb 2025 https://warontherocks.com/2023/12/learning-from-real-wars-gaza-and-ukraine/

[9] BBC, "Moskva Sinking: US Gave Intelligence That Helped Ukraine Sink Russian Cruiser–Reports", *BBC News*, 06 May 2022, accessed 30 Mar 2025 https://www.bbc.com/news/world-us-canada-61343044

[10] Khyati Singh, "Learning from a Distance: Cyber Lessons for India from Russia-Ukraine War", *Centre for Air Power Studies*, 23 Apr 2023, accessed 17 Feb 2025 https://capsindia.org/learning-from-a-distance-cyber-lessons-for-india-from-russia-ukraine-war/#_edn1

[11] Franchois Quiqet, "Viasat Attack: A Space Cyber Attack Post Mortem Investigation", *SpaceSecurity.info*, 12 Dec 2023, accessed 30 Mar 2025 https://www.spacesecurity.info/en/space-cyber-attack-post-mortem-a-viasat-attack-investigation/

[12] Michael Kofman and Rob Lee, "Perseverance and Adaptation: Ukraine's Counteroffensive at Three Months" *War on the Rocks*, 04 Sep 2023, accessed 30 Mar 2025 https://warontherocks.com/2023/09/perseverance-and-adaptation-ukraines-counteroffensive-at-three-months/

[13] Howard Altman, "NATO Operations Chief's Five Lessons Learned from War in Ukraine", *The War Zone*, 06 Mar 2025, accessed 17 Mar 2025 https://www.twz.com/news-features/nato-operations-chiefs-five-lessons-learned-from-war-in-ukraine

[14] Sharah Shamim. "How Will US Pause on Intelligence Sharing Affect Ukraine?" *Al Jazeera*, 06 Mar 2025, accessed 17 Mar 2025 https://www.aljazeera.com/news/2025/3/6/how-will-us-pause-on-intelligence-sharing-affect-ukraine

[15] Vivienne Machi, "Inside the Multinational Logistics Cell Coordinating Military Aid for Ukraine", *Defense News*, 20 Jul 2022, accessed 08 Feb 2025 https://www.defensenews.com/global/europe/2022/07/21/inside-the-multinational-logistics-cell-coordinating-military-aid-for-ukraine/

[16] NATO Strategic Warfare Development Command, "Joint Analysis, Training and Education Centre", *NATO Allied Command Transformation*, accessed 18 Feb 2025 https://www.act.nato.int/activities/jatec/

[17] Singh, "Learning from a Distance"

A Nuanced Look at Indian Strategic Leadership

Colonel Piyush

Abstract

This article examines India's strategic leadership through the lens of its evolving strategic culture, with particular reference to the Kargil War (1999), the Galwan Valley clash (2020), and emerging patterns of strategic assertiveness, including Operation Sindoor (2025). It challenges the simplistic narratives that portray Indian strategic leadership as either reactive or lacking vision. Drawing on historical and contemporary examples, the article underscores India's capacity for adaptation, institutional evolution, and decisive action. It also explores how India's unique strategic culture—rooted in civilisational values yet responsive to geopolitical exigencies—has shaped its strategic posture. The article concludes with recommendations on strengthening strategic leadership through institutional reforms, capacity building, and inter-agency coherence.

Introduction

India's strategic leadership is often viewed through a binary lens—either overly idealistic and reactive, or assertive only in isolated bursts. This article challenges such characterisations by situating Indian strategic leadership within the broader framework of strategic culture. It examines how India's leadership has responded to key crises such as the Kargil War in 1999, the Galwan Valley clash in 2020, and more recently Operation Sindoor in 2025, drawing lessons on adaptation, assertiveness, and institutional evolution. In doing so, the article offers a more nuanced understanding of leadership that goes beyond tactical brilliance or political rhetoric.

This article is structured around four key themes. First, it explores the evolution of Indian strategic culture and leadership. Second, it interrogates common misconceptions surrounding India's strategic assertiveness. Third, it analyses leadership responses to key conflicts.

And finally, it presents a way forward, offering policy-oriented recommendations on strengthening strategic leadership.

Understanding Strategic Culture

Strategic culture refers to the deeply embedded beliefs, assumptions, and behavioural patterns that influence how nations think about the use of force, diplomacy, deterrence, and conflict. These cultural undercurrents shape the strategic choices of leaders and institutions over time. In the Indian context, strategic culture has been the subject of much debate.

George Tanham's influential RAND study argued that India lacked a coherent strategic culture and that its decision-making was ad-hoc, reactive, and dominated by civilian bureaucracy rather than military institutions.[1] However, Indian scholars like Krishnaswamy Subrahmanyam have forcefully refuted this claim, arguing that India possesses a long-standing but uniquely indigenous strategic tradition—one that blends civilisational ideals with pragmatic statecraft.[2]

Unlike the American emphasis on power projection or the Chinese focus on strategic ambiguity and legalism, Indian strategic culture has historically favoured legitimacy, restraint, and calibrated escalation. This orientation, however, has evolved substantially—especially after 1999—into a more assertive, future-facing posture that seeks to balance moral legitimacy with credible deterrence.[3]

This evolution has been catalysed by India's experience in dealing with crises. The failures of 1962, the triumph of 1971, and the lessons of Kargil and Galwan have cumulatively reshaped institutional thinking within the political, military, and bureaucratic spheres. Today, Indian strategic leadership is increasingly characterised by proactiveness, inter-agency cooperation, and a recognition of the multi-domain nature of threats.[4]

Shattering Misconceptions

Strategic Assertiveness and Leadership Vision. Two prevalent misconceptions cloud the perception of Indian strategic leadership. The first asserts that Indian leaders—political, military, and bureaucratic—have lacked vision, long-term planning, and decisive capability. However, such a characterisation fails to acknowledge the structural complexity and progress India has made.

India's Rise: Growth and Modernisation. India's sustained economic rise, for instance, has seen gross domestic product grow at an average of 6–7 per cent over last two decades. According to the World Bank, poverty declined significantly, with those below the USD 1.90 per day line dropping from 42.0 per cent in 2005 to 13.5 per cent in 2019.[5] This growth has been coupled with defence modernisation, reflected in India consistently ranking among the top five military spenders globally, increasing joint exercises, and expanded blue-water naval presence.

Strategic Leadership. Such structural shifts are unlikely to occur without coherent strategic leadership. India's ability to manage economic growth, enhance global partnerships, and maintain strategic stability in a volatile neighbourhood suggests leadership guided by a vision—albeit shaped by competing domestic and institutional pulls.

Debunking the Narrative of Benevolence. The second misconception is more cultural—it frames India as inherently peace-loving, non-expeditionary, and strategically passive. While India draws on a civilisational heritage that values non-violence, this should not be mistaken for strategic timidity. When national interests have been threatened, India has demonstrated calculated resolve.

Calibrated Assertiveness. India's historical interventions reflect the assertiveness as under:

- **Post-Independence Internal Consolidation**. Operation Polo in 1948 (Hyderabad), Operation Vijay in 1961 (Goa), and the air-landed operations in Kashmir during 1947–48.
- **Regional Power Projection**. The 1971 Bangladesh War, the Indian Peace Keeping Force in Sri Lanka in 1987, Operation Cactus in the Maldives in 1988, and India's support to Bhutan during the Doklam standoff in 2017.
- **Post-1990s Global-Strategic Actions**. The Kargil War in 1999, the Surgical Strikes in 2016, the Balakot Air Strikes in 2019, the maritime hostage rescue of MV Ruen in 2024 involving Marine Commandos and the Indian Navy, and Operation Sindoor.

Evolving Strategic Culture. These actions reflect a strategic culture that, while traditionally restrained, has matured into one that embraces calibrated assertiveness.[6] This evolution became especially visible post-2016, marking a shift where the vocabulary of Indian diplomacy began incorporating terms like 'Strategic Autonomy', 'Coercive Diplomacy', and 'Non-contact Warfare'. These are not signs of aggression, but of a leadership posture that is increasingly confident, deliberate, and capable of leveraging multi-domain capabilities.

Moral Legitimacy and Deterrence. It is inaccurate to assume that India's global image rests solely on the principles of *Vasudhaiva Kutumbakam* (The world is one family) or Gandhian non-violence. These values co-exist with decisive national security action when necessary. What is emerging is an India that combines moral legitimacy with a clear capacity for deterrence.

Strategic Leadership Under Pressure: Limitations and Reforms

It is a cliché or norm to blame the leadership for all failures. While criticism exists, strategic leaders have shown decisive responses.

Critiques of Leadership. Strategic leadership—especially in the military domain—is frequently criticised for lapses in preparedness, weak strategic communication, or institutional inertia. However, such blanket assessments overlook the operational constraints, legacy systems, and incremental reforms that shape India's national security apparatus.

Structural Vulnerabilities. There have indeed been moments where inter-agency coordination faltered or procurement processes proved sluggish. Delays in acquiring critical assets such as drones, intelligence, surveillance, and reconnaissance platforms and air defence systems before the Galwan clash in 2020 exposed some of these structural vulnerabilities. Similarly, limitations in jointness across services—long recognised but insufficiently addressed—hampered integrated responses during crises like Kargil and early phases of Galwan.[7]

Reforms and Milestones. Nonetheless, strategic leadership has demonstrated resilience and a capacity to adapt in the face of such challenges. The post-Kargil establishment of the National Security Council Secretariat (NSCS), creation of a Defence Intelligence Agency

(DIA) and post-Galwan acceleration of reforms—such as the establishment of the Chief of Defence Staff (CDS), Department of Military Affairs and renewed integration of HQ Integrated Defence Staff (IDS)—are significant milestones.[8]

Institutionalising Synergy. These reforms reflect an intent to institutionalise joint planning, enhance civil-military synergy, and develop unified threat perceptions. While operational outcomes depend on multiple actors, the direction set by political and military leadership indicates a commitment to building long-term strategic capacity.

Leadership Under Pressure. Leadership under pressure is best judged by its ability to adapt. In both Kargil and Galwan, Indian military and political leaders demonstrated clarity, resolve, and calculated restraint. Moreover, the increasing visibility of top military commanders in public discourse—offering press briefings, strategic messaging, and professional assessments—marks a shift towards transparent and accountable leadership.

Strategic Leadership in Action: Lessons From Kargil, Galwan, and Sindoor

Strategic Responses to Crises. Strategic responses to major security crises provide critical insight into the quality and evolution of leadership. The Kargil Conflict in 1999, the Galwan Valley clash in 2020, and the recent Operation Sindoor in 2025 provide valuable case studies for assessing India's strategic preparedness, civil–military coordination, and leadership under pressure.

Kargil Conflict (1999): Surprise, Recovery, and Institutional Reform. The Kargil War exposed serious vulnerabilities in India's strategic intelligence and operational readiness. Initially, strategic leadership underestimated Pakistan's duplicity—engaging in peace talks even as it infiltrated troops into Indian territory. This was partly due to over-reliance on Track II diplomacy and a benign interpretation of Pakistan's intentions.[9]

Failures and Gaps. Failures were evident in three major areas: intelligence coordination, troop deployment gaps along the Line of Control (LoC), and civil-military communication. The Kargil Review Committee (KRC) Report later confirmed that India lacked integrated threat assessments and early warning mechanisms.[10] Nevertheless, once the intrusion was confirmed, both political and military leadership demonstrated exceptional resolve. The decision to restrict military action to Indian territory—eschewing escalation—won India global diplomatic support.

Catalysing Reforms. The war catalysed reforms such as the establishment of the NSCS, DIA, and the integration of service-specific intelligence under a more unified structure. The military also adopted more robust surveillance measures, expanded winter patrols and enhanced forward deployment of sensors and Unmanned Aerial Vehicles (UAVs).[11]

Lessons from Kargil

- ❑ Strategic surprise is a recurring threat; institutional vigilance must be constant.
- ❑ Civil–military trust, though tested, can be rebuilt through coordinated and transparent decision-making.
- ❑ Leadership maturity lies not just in battlefield victories but in strategic restraint and post-conflict reform.

Galwan Valley Clash (2020): Realignment and Multi-Domain Assertion. The Galwan episode was not just a tactical clash—it was a strategic wake-up call. Despite improved intelligence post-Kargil, India underestimated China's assertiveness under Xi Jinping's regional expansionism. Strategic leaders, buoyed by diplomatic gains post-Doklam in 2017, assumed deterrence was working. Galwan shattered that assumption.[12]

Bold Counterstroke. The immediate response, however, marked a shift from past patterns. India carried out rapid mobilisation, deployed additional divisions to Ladakh, and activated air and surveillance assets under high-altitude constraints. Simultaneously, Indian forces occupied the Kailash range heights, a bold counterstroke that compelled China to negotiate from a position of parity.

Robust Diplomatic Signalling. Political leadership engaged in robust diplomatic signalling, activating the instruments of diplomatic, informational, military, and economic through military strength, economic disengagement (such as app bans and trade scrutiny), and diplomatic alignment with Quadrilateral Security Dialogue (QUAD) partners.

Lessons from Galwan

- ❑ Strategic confidence must not replace tactical preparedness.
- ❑ Multi-domain responses are now central to India's crisis management playbook.
- ❑ Leadership assertiveness—military and political—can redefine deterrence credibility.

Operation Sindoor (2025): Posture, Preparedness, and Precision. Operation Sindoor, launched in response to a terrorist attack in Pahalgam in Apr 2025, showcased India's evolution into a force capable of combining strategic messaging with calibrated escalation.

Precision Strikes with Restraint. The Indian Air Force carried out precision strikes on launchpads across the LoC using indigenously upgraded precision-guided munitions. Simultaneously, disruption was imposed on enemy air defence nodes. Political leadership was assertive but controlled, issuing minimal public statements while allowing the military to operate within clearly defined strategic objectives.

Shaping the Narrative. India also shaped the international narrative through early briefings to global partners, pre-empting adversarial propaganda. Unlike past operations, there was synchronised civil-military-media coordination. The result was a highly successful, high-impact, and diplomatically defensible operation.

Lessons from Sindoor

- ❑ Strategic leadership has matured to boldly strike and manage escalation.
- ❑ Technology, timing, and trust between political and military leadership are now crucial enablers.
- ❑ India is increasingly projecting itself as a credible, restrained, but ready regional power.

India on the Global Stage: Strategic Maturity and Perception Management

Beyond the Battlefield. Strategic leadership is no longer confined to battlefield decisions—it encompasses the management of perceptions, alliances, and narratives in an increasingly interconnected world. India's rise as a global actor is as much about deterrence and defence capability as it is about how it positions itself diplomatically, normatively, and symbolically.

From Balancer to Rule-Shaper. Over the past decade, India has transitioned from a regional balancer to a rule-shaper in the Indo-Pacific. Through initiatives like Security and Growth for All in the Region, hosting the G20 Summit in 2023 and expanding QUAD engagements, India's leadership has demonstrated the capacity to manage diverse theatres of influence.[13]

Proactive Strategic Communication. Strategic communication has become a critical tool. The Ministry of External Affairs (MEA), Indian Armed Forces, and the Prime Minister's office have increasingly employed coordinated messaging during crises—be it post-Balakot in 2019, Galwan in 2020, or Sindoor in 2025. The emphasis has shifted from reactive media handling to proactive narrative building. This includes satellite imagery releases, briefings for foreign missions, and leveraging diaspora communities to shape international opinion.

Perception-Building through Military Diplomacy. Indian military also contributes to perception-building through naval diplomacy, peace keeping, and humanitarian assistance and disaster relief missions. As of 2024, India ranked among the top contributors to United Nations peacekeeping forces and conducted over 40 bilateral and multilateral exercises annually—including Malabar, Yudh Abhyas, and Milan.[14]

Strategic Communities. The strategic community—including think tanks, veterans, and scholars—now plays a more prominent role in articulating India's worldview, bridging public discourse and statecraft. This greater engagement enhances credibility and provides democratic validation for strategic choices.

Indicators of Strategic Maturity

- Assertive yet responsible military conduct, exemplified by the non-escalatory doctrine in Operation Sindoor.
- Global partnerships without bloc dependence, as seen in India's balancing of ties with Russia, the United States, and Association of Southeast Asian Nations.
- Participation in norm-shaping institutions such as the Group of Twenty; Brazil, Russia, India, China, South Africa Plus; and Indo-Pacific Economic Framework.
- Greater reliance on indigenous platforms—such as Tejas, BrahMos, and UAVs—for deterrence signalling.
- Elevated public trust in leadership during crises, reflecting narrative coherence.

Pragmatism with Principle. India's leadership posture today blends pragmatism with principled engagement—seeking strategic autonomy while contributing to regional stability. This evolving image is not merely rhetorical; it is rooted in institutional learning, leadership consistency, and public confidence.

The Path Ahead: Strengthening Indian Strategic Leadership

India's journey from strategic restraint to assertive equilibrium is far from complete. While past crises have catalysed institutional learning, there remains a pressing need to embed strategic leadership principles into India's defence and governance architecture more systematically. The following areas deserve focused attention:

- **Institutional Reforms and Jointness**. Despite progress since the KRC, integration across the three services, defence bureaucracy and intelligence agencies is still suboptimal. True jointness—beyond infrastructure sharing—requires institutional culture shifts, not just structural tinkering. India must fast-track Theatre Command implementation, revise the role and authority of the CDS and ensure seamless integration of HQ IDS with operational commands.[15]

- **Leadership Capacity Building**. Strategic leadership cannot be improvised during crises—it must be cultivated through career-long exposure to complexity. This demands a revamp of military education (e.g., Higher Command and equivalent courses, National Defence College curriculum) to incorporate systems thinking, scenario gaming, geopolitical strategy, and media engagement. Cross-postings with MEA, Ministry of Home Affairs, Defence Research and Development Organisation, and National Institution for Transforming India Aayog could enhance cross-domain learning.[16]
- **Civil-Military Synergy and Strategic Literacy**. Political leaders must be supported by a cadre of trained strategic advisers—military and civilian—who understand the interplay of force, diplomacy, and technology. This requires strategic literacy to be embedded in both Indian Administrative Service and armed forces training. The NSCS must play a bigger role in coordinating this education ecosystem.
- **Fostering a Strategic Culture**. Strategic culture is not just inherited—it is shaped by what a nation chooses to remember, reward, and institutionalise. India must invest in defence think tanks, indigenous strategic scholarship, and open source wargaming tools. Leadership must be comfortable with dissent, red-teaming, and critical feedback—essential traits for navigating a volatile, uncertain world.

Conclusion

The trajectory of Indian strategic leadership—from the reactive posture of early decades to the assertive maturity seen in recent crises—signals a nation that is evolving deliberately and confidently. The Kargil War exposed vulnerabilities, Galwan tested resolve, and Operation Sindoor showcased calibrated capability. In each instance, leadership was not flawless, but it proved adaptive, composed, and increasingly strategic.

Leadership in today's security environment must be anticipatory, integrative, and technologically aware. It must think not only in terms of wars fought but also in terms of narratives won, alliances nurtured, and threats deterred without escalation.

India's strategic leaders—political, military, and institutional—must now consolidate gains made through crisis-driven reform and shift toward long-term strategic planning. The future lies not just in responding to conflict, but in shaping the environment to prevent it. In this lies the essence of 21st Century strategic leadership.

Endnotes

1 George K Tanham, "Indian Strategic Thought: An Interpretive Essay", Santa Monica, *CA: RAND Corporation*, 1992, accessed 13 Jun 2025 https://www.rand.org/pubs/reports/R4207.html

2 K. Subrahmanyam, "Indian Strategic Culture" in *India's Foreign Policy: A Reader,* edited by David M. Malone, C. Raja Mohan, and Srinath Raghavan, New Delhi: Oxford University Press, 2015, accessed 13 Jun 2025 https://global.oup.com/academic/product/indias-foreign-policy-9780199458328

3 Stephen P. Cohen, *India: Emerging Power*, Brookings Institution Press, 2001, accessed 13 Jun 2025 https://www.brookings.edu/books/india-emerging-power/

4 Rajesh M. Basrur, "India's Strategic Culture: The Debate and Its Consequences", *Journal of Strategic Studies*, vol. 36, no. 4 (2013): 487–510, accessed 14 Jun 2025 https://doi.org/10.1080/01402390.2012.743885

5 World Bank, *Poverty & Equity Brief–India*, 2021, accessed 14 Jun 2025 https://databank.worldbank.org/source/poverty-and-equity/brief/India

6 Srinath Raghavan, *India's War: The Making of Modern South Asia, 1939–1945* (New Delhi: Penguin Allen Lane, 2016); Happymon Jacob, "India's Evolving Military Strategy", *The Hindu*, Feb 2020, accessed 10 Jun 2025

7 Lieutenant General DS Hooda (Retd), "Galwan and the Urgency of Defence Reform," *The Hindu*, accessed 18 Jun 2020

8 Kargil Review Committee Report, Government of India, 2000; Arzan Tarapore, "India's New Joint Chiefs", *War on the Rocks*, 14 Jan 2020, accessed 15 Jun 2025 https://warontherocks.com/2020/01/indias-new-joint-chiefs/

9 General VP Malik, *Kargil: From Surprise to Victory*, New Delhi: HarperCollins, 2006

10 Kargil Review Committee Report, Government of India, 2000

11 Arvind Gupta, "Post-Kargil Security Reforms", *IDSA Issue Brief*, Jul 2009, accessed 10 Jun 2025

12 Lieutenant General DS Hooda (Retd), "Galwan and the Future of India-China Engagement", *Observer Research Foundation*, 2021, accessed 14 Jun 2025

[13] Ministry of External Affairs, "Annual Report 2023–24", *MEA*, 2024, accessed 15 Jun 2025 https://www.mea.gov.in/Images/CPV/38005_Final-MEA-AR-2023-English.pdf

[14] UN Peacekeeping Statistics, 2024; "Indian Navy Annual Report", 2023–24, accessed 18 Jun 2025

[15] Lieutenant General Prakash Menon (Retd), "The Challenge of Theatre Commands in India", *The Print*, 2022, accessed 15 Jun 2025 https://theprint.in/opinion/raising-air-power-violation-is-chinas-mind-game-indias-challenge-is-to-call-the-bluff/1083908/

[16] Gurmeet Kanwal, "Military Education for Strategic Leadership", *IDSA* Comment, 2020, accessed 10 Jun 2025